OEDIPUS,
PHILOSOPHER

MERIDIAN

Crossing Aesthetics

Werner Hamacher
& David E. Wellbery
Editors

Translated by
Catherine Porter

Stanford
University
Press

———

Stanford
California

OEDIPUS,
PHILOSOPHER

Jean-Joseph Goux

Stanford University Press
Stanford, California
© 1993 by the Board of Trustees of the
Leland Stanford Junior University
Printed in the United States of America

Original printing 1993
Last figure below indicates year of this printing:
04   03   02   01   00   99   98   97   96   95

CIP data appear at the end of the book

Published with the assistance of Rice University

Stanford University Press publications are distributed exclusively by Stanford University Press within the United States, Canada, and Mexico; they are distributed exclusively by Cambridge University Press throughout the rest of the world.

Contents

OEDIPUS,
PHILOSOPHER

Introduction

What if the logic of the Oedipus myth were subjected to rigorous and thoroughgoing analysis with the tools of anthropology, comparative mythology, and narratology? Might such an analysis modify or even invalidate the approach to the "Oedipus complex" that Freud derived from his psychoanalytic experience? In theory it might seem not only ill-advised but also illegitimate to expect such an outcome. When Freud discovered—first in himself, through self-analysis, and then in the dreams of his male patients—persistent fantasies of patricide and maternal incest, he was promptly reminded of the fate of King Oedipus, on which Sophocles based the most perfect tragedy of Greek theater. But Freud saw the myth and the tragedy as literary expressions of a fantasmatic core; for him, the task of interpretation belonged to psychoanalysis alone. The persistence and universality of the psychological "complex" would account for the myth's existence and the power its theatrical deployment has for us. From Freud's standpoint, then, no increase in our understanding of the logic of the myth could be expected to shed any light at all on the formation of the complex. For Freud, the complex explained the myth; he did not see the myth as a purveyor of knowledge that would be entitled, as such, to interrogate the psychoanalytic experience.

Freud's postulate appears to be corroborated by the gulf that in fact separates mythographic or anthropological approaches to the

Oedipus legend, by and large, from the psychoanalytic approach. Marie Delcourt and Jean-Pierre Vernant have resolutely turned their backs on the Freudian reading more often than they have enriched or subverted it.[1] Driek Van der Sterren, Didier Anzieu, and André Green have discovered little about the myth or the tragedy that might challenge or threaten psychoanalytic knowledge.[2]

The approach I have adopted here runs counter to the epistemological postulate of Freudian theory. Reduced to a provocative antithesis, my own thesis might be expressed as follows: it is the Oedipus myth that explains the complex. In other words, it is within a specific historical institution of subjectivity, within the framework of a particular symbolic mechanism (of which the Oedipus myth is the most powerful manifestation), that something like the "Oedipus complex" has been able to command attention and elicit description. It is because the West is Oedipean that Freud discovered the "Oedipus complex." And in this sense, the logic of the Oedipus myth as myth may clarify—or even subvert—Freud's description of the Oedipus "complex." This analytic reframing may even give Freud's discovery the possibility of speaking to us, perhaps differently, at a time when historical attrition threatens to nullify the concepts on which it was based.

This book is in many respects a perilous enterprise for its author. Readers may approach it from a number of different directions: it interweaves anthropological and mythographical considerations with the most heated issues confronting psychoanalysis today and with arguments of considerable philosophical import. Reduced to its essential thrust, however, what I shall attempt to demonstrate can be formulated in a few fairly brief theses whose interconnections are manifest. Let me state them here and now in their peremptory nudity, while hoping to persuade my reader of their validity further on, through multiple lines of argument.

§ 1 The myth of Oedipus is an anomaly. Matricide, not patricide, is at the heart of the heroic myth in its typical and universal form. The hero who is to become king is the hero who kills the female dragon, the female serpent, the female monstrosity, in bloody combat. By murdering a dangerous, dark, feminine force, the hero liberates the bride. Compared to this widely attested prototype, which I shall call the "monomyth," the Oedipus story is an aberrant myth, obtained by a disruption of the initial narrative form.

§ 2 This disruption explains not only the mechanism of the myth's generation as narrative but also the feature that best defines it differentially: the Oedipus myth is a myth of failed royal investiture, or of avoided masculine initiation. The failure (or the avoidance) is systematically and rigorously linked to the mythic anomaly of patricide and incest.

§ 3 What is more, the mechanism by which the trial of initiatory investiture is disrupted can be fully explained only within the framework of the archaic functional tripartition (the sacred, war, fertility) brought to light by Georges Dumézil in the Indo-European sphere. The Oedipus myth is a transformation of the monomythic plot via a systematic disruption of the canonical schema of the triple ordeal that is correlated with the hero's three sins.

§ 4 This mythic subversion of the functional tripartition is what "founds" Greek reason. In spite of (or because of) the misidentification of the radical essence of masculine desire to which the Oedipus myth leads, this myth expresses the truth (or the characteristic error) of the West, its metaphysical and anthropological distinctiveness. Implicitly for Sophocles and explicitly for Hegel, Oedipus is the prototypical figure of the philosopher, the one who challenges sacred enigmas in order to establish the perspective of man and self. This Oedipean configuration impresses upon all of philosophy, from its origins to the various overturnings of idealism, the filiarchal demand that has continuously been carving out a place for itself in that philosophy. This is how we can account for Freud's "error." The Oedipean imaginary haunts the democratic subject and its characteristic rationality. And the separation between consciousness and the unconscious is itself Oedipean.

§ 1 Standard and Nonstandard Myths

The striking resemblance among all the myths of the male hero figure in diverse cultures has given rise in our century to a number of attempts to unearth a "monomyth," a prototypical plot common to all such myths. Whatever variants may arise as the prototype legend is established (owing to the selection of myths for the reference group, but also to the way the chosen myths are segmented, the pertinent features retained, or the condensations to which the material is subjected), the existence of a series of identical motifs subtending each of the individual heroic myths seems beyond question. The resemblances among the principal motifs of these stories and the similarities in their general articulation, from the conditions of the hero's birth to his conquest of power, his marriage, and his death, allow us to posit the existence of a monomyth of the male hero, a prototype myth of royal investiture.[1]

However, questions arise at once. What is the relationship between the monomyth and the myth of Oedipus? Is the monomyth Oedipean or not? Can the monomyth be derived from a constitutive Oedipal deep structure? Or, on the contrary (to consider an eventuality that would decisively undermine the Freudian conviction), isn't the myth of King Oedipus rather a deviation, an exception with respect to a more regular and more fundamental narrative structure?

In order to avoid both the narratological and the anthropological problems posed by the identification of a monomyth of the masculine hero with some claim to universality, I shall limit my investigation to Greek myths. I do not propose to use detailed comparisons of a very large number of myths in order to determine once and for all the monomyth that would be on the soundest footing in formal terms. I shall proceed rather by limiting the number of reference myths, choosing, from the Greek sphere alone, the ones that offer the greatest regularity (taking into account structures already established by previous research) and that manifest at the same time an unquestionable formal and cultural kinship with the Oedipus myth.

Reduced to its minimum narrative core, as determined by a rigorous point-for-point comparison of three Greek myths of royal investiture—the myths of Perseus, Bellerophon, and Jason—and by a systematic disclosure of their common motifs, the structure of what I shall call the Greek monomyth can be articulated quite simply.

This procedure yields the following sequence of episodes. (1) A king fears that a younger man, or one not yet born, will take his place, as an oracle has predicted. He then uses all available means to try to prevent the child's birth, or to get rid of the presumed intruder. (2) The future hero escapes from the king's murderous intentions. Nevertheless, much later he finds himself in a situation in which a different king again attempts to do away with him. But this second king cannot bring himself to commit the crime with his own hands, so he assigns a perilous task in which the future hero is expected to lose his life. (3) The trial takes the form of a fight with a monster. The hero succeeds in defeating the monster, not on his own but with the help of a god, a wise man, or a future bride. (4) Finally, the hero's triumph over the monster allows him to marry the daughter of a king.

The identification and juxtaposition of these common motifs thus lead to the formulation of a highly condensed prototype plot that is richly invested with meaning. It is worth noting that the paradigmatic Greek hero has successive relationships with three different kings. First he is confronted by a persecutor king; then, after being sent away, forcibly distanced, he encounters a dispatcher king who assigns a difficult, dangerous trial in which the hero's success always depends upon a helper. Finally, through his victory in the trial, the hero acquires a bride from the hands of a donor king.

An analysis of the Oedipus plot cannot fail to take into account this monomyth of royal investiture, if only because every Greek who ever heard or told the Oedipus adventure tale was familiar with the other three myths and thus understood or presented the story differentially on the basis of the motifs and the general plot structure they exemplify.

In what respects does the Oedipus myth resemble the prototype plot, and on what crucial points does it differ? How can the differences be explained? Can the mechanism that generates them be reconstituted? And what conclusions do they allow us to draw?

The motif of the male child whose existence is a threat to the king's life is very widespread. In the Perseus and Jason stories, an oracle warns the threatened king before the future hero is born; a very close parallel is offered by the oracle announcing the threat that Oedipus's birth represents for Laïus.

As a result of the oracular warning, the hero is sent off to grow up far from the first, threatened, persecutor king. Perseus is brought up by Polydectes, Jason by the centaur Cheiron, and Oedipus is taken in by the king of Corinth. Between Oedipus and Perseus there is one particularly noteworthy resemblance: each of them (according to one version of the Oedipus myth) is said to have been placed inside a chest and cast adrift on a body of water before being taken in by foster parents.

Similarly, each of the four heroes (Jason, Bellerophon, Perseus, and Oedipus) later confronts a dangerous monster, and each emerges triumphant. This is one of the most striking aspects of the heroic narratives: the protagonist earns the title of hero only by winning a victory over a monstrous creature, a victory distinguishing the hero from the unfortunate multitudes who fail in the trial and perish. Perseus bests the Gorgon, Bellerophon defeats the Chimaera, Jason vanquishes the immortal monster who guards the Golden Fleece, and Oedipus triumphs over the Sphinx.

Except in the case of Jason and the Colchis dragon, whose sex is not clearly defined, each of the monsters the heroes confront is feminine (*la Gorgone, la Chimère, la Sphinge*). Not only do these terrifying beings have similar roles to play, but they are also related in terms of mythic genealogy, making it possible to establish even closer affinities. The Chimaera, the Sphinx, and the Colchis dragon are all children of the snake-woman Echidna. In some versions, the Sphinx is not the daughter of Echidna and the dog Orthus but of Orthus and the Chimaera. Such variants attest to the extremely close kinship among all these creatures. All of them, including the Gorgons, are descendants of Phorcys and Ceto: these sea gods are the ancestors of all the monsters (Cerberus, Hydra, the Nemean lion, and so on) that the Greek heroes endlessly confront and combat. The monsters often result from incestuous pairings, interbreedings of earth and sea. This genealogy has to be taken into account, as we shall see.

~

Finally (and here we touch on a resemblance that alerts us to the principal difference), each of the victories achieved over a monster leads the hero to marriage. Perseus marries Andromeda, Bellerophon marries Philonoë, Jason marries Medea—and Oedipus marries Jocasta. Similar instances of nuptial conclusions to heroic trials could be cited more or less ad infinitum. It is a law of the myth of royal investiture that victory over the monster allows the hero to marry a king's daughter and, sooner or later, to take possession of the kingdom.

The resemblance on this point between the myth of Oedipus and all the other heroic myths has allowed such scholars as J. G. von Hahn, Otto Rank, and Lord Raglan to establish formal parallels without difficulty and to recognize the Oedipus myth as having the same overall structure as the others. Yet it becomes clear that the resemblance poses a major problem if, instead of contenting ourselves with the general form "the hero marries a king's daughter," we examine the content of this motif more closely. It is strange that none of the analysts just cited, including Rank (and moreover in Rank's case there are fundamental reasons for the oversight that have implications for psychoanalysis as a whole), is concerned with this difference; none of them investigates the irregularity of the Oedipus myth.

As is all too well known, in the case of Oedipus the hero is united not with a king's daughter but with a king's wife—who is also his own mother. This crucial deviation in the marriage motif ought to keep Oedipus from being fully identified with the other mythical kings, especially since this difference is not the only one. We are entitled to suspect that a certain mythic logic accounts for these anomalies, for the nuptial outcome is merely one element in a coherent distortion that affects the narrative articulation as a whole.

We are thus led to look not for the aspects of the Oedipus myth that conform to the prototype we have identified, but for those points at which the myth deforms the prototype, and to examine each anomaly attentively and systematically. These anomalies are perhaps more numerous and less obvious than a hasty reading, or a reading oriented in advance by the Freudian code, might lead us to suspect. I am confident enough of the internal rigor of mythic logic to be convinced that the difference in a single motif, especially an important concluding motif like the one we are considering, has repercussions for the entire set of motifs within a myth, and that there can be no variant on a major point that is not accompanied by a systematic distortion. Our approach thus begins to place this myth in a new light. We need not see it, as Freud did, as in a class by itself, absolutely distinct from all other myths (and capable of explaining the others, as if it summed up their truth); nor should we simply identify it with the standard formula of the heroic myth of royal investiture as von Hahn or Raglan did. We need to discover the mythic logic of its structural deformity, the ordered relationship between its anomalies and the standard form, as if it was a systematically distorted (and thereby particularly interesting) variant of the canonical form of the Greek hero myth.

Now, a major motif that is systematically repeated in the three reference myths but absent from the Oedipus story is the motif of the trial imposed by a king. The king Polydectes enjoins Perseus to come back with the Gorgon's head. Iobates, king of Lycia, orders Bellerophon to kill the Chimaera. Pelias, the usurper-uncle, demands that Jason, returning to claim power, go get the Golden Fleece guarded by the Colchis dragon. The circumstances that lead a king to order the future hero off on a perilous mission may vary in their details, but the motif of an imposed trial is constant; moreover, the young hero accepts the trial.

This major motif has not been singled out by any of the scholars who have tried to work out the monomyth. The one case in which we find a possible vestige of this mythical motif is the identification of the dispatcher function in Propp's work. In fact, the motif is fully visible only if the choice of reference myths is limited to Greek sources. In this case, it can no longer be viewed as accidental; it has to be seen as an integral part of the structure of the heroic myth of royal investiture. It sheds decisive light on the significance of the trial, including its role as an initiatory passage.

It is as if a king, instead of personally killing the young hero judged dangerous to himself, was sending the young hero off to a trial regarded as lethal; thus the king substitutes a trial for a murder he is loath to commit himself. The trial is murder in disguise, a device imagined by the king to get rid of his young rival. But the young man rises to the challenge set before him. At the risk of his life he has to prove the king's calculation wrong by his strength and his intelligence, by all the abilities he can mobilize for the occasion. If he is victorious (as is the case, needless to say, in the hero myths), it is in spite of the king's wishes, against the king's expectations, in opposition to the king himself.

The threat of murder, by a royal figure, of someone who may be, or might become, a dangerous rival, is thus expressed in two stages. In the first stage, the king's fear and his murderous project intervene even before the future hero's birth (Acrisius tries to prevent Perseus's birth, Pelias tries to prevent Jason's) or when the future hero is in the king's house (Proëtus sends Bellerophon away so he will be killed). There are variations in the way the second stage of the murder plan comes into play: (a) shortly afterward but instigated by a different royal figure (Iobates for Bellerophon); (b) instigated by the same king, but much later (Pelias for Jason); (c) both much later and instigated by a different royal figure (Polydectes for

Perseus). In all three cases, however, the two phases are quite distinct, and in the second phase the murder plan is converted into the assignment of a trial so difficult and so dangerous as to be deemed mortal. In the three myths under consideration, the trial is presumed to be the means by which the king can kill the future hero.

The difference between this pattern and the Oedipus plot is obvious—so much so that we are obliged to see the difference as a major anomaly capable of shedding light on the myth's other irregularities. In the Oedipus myth, the motif of the trial assigned by a king is simply lacking. The encounter with the Sphinx is never explained as the effect of a categorical and imperious command issued by a hostile king. Oedipus braves the encounter of his own free will, or else he is constrained, at a turning point in the road, by the Sphinx herself.

Now if we look more closely (and it is precisely at this point that another of the myth's anomalies can be clarified), we do find an event that occupies the same structural position in the Oedipus myth as the typical sequence of the assignment of a trial by a hostile king: namely, Oedipus's encounter with Laïus. If we consider the major articulations of the reference myths, and if we take the structural economy of the successive motifs into account, it is fairly clear that the second phase of a king's plan to murder a hero, missing in the Oedipus myth, is replaced by the encounter with Laïus and *his* murder, an event that precedes the confrontation with the Sphinx.

At issue is the moment when the young man, having survived the threat that preceded his birth, has reached the age when he becomes capable of actually taking power and thus of being a real threat to the reigning figure. And we see that if this agonistic moment is resolved, in the prototype structure, by the trial imposed by the king, it leads in Oedipus's case to the king's murder. The dramatic encounter with a king who has sought or is seeking the young hero's death does occur, as it does in the reference myths, along with the phase of aggression, challenge, and boasting that characterizes this motif. But here the king, instead of imposing the risk of a presumably fatal trial on the young man, dies on the spot himself at the young man's hands, as if his royal authority is unrecognized. According to the standard myth, on the narrow road where his chariot blocks the presumptuous young man's way, Laïus should have put a stop to the latter's importunate insistence by challenging him to show his ability to confront some dangerous trial, using language like the following: "Well then! If you are so proud and so sure of your youthful strength, go off and test yourself against an enemy worthy of you, the unvanquished monster, the Sphinx, that haunts the mountains," and so on. Meeting such a challenge would have been authentic proof of manhood for the proud, exuberant young hero, and it would have been a point of honor with him to accept this "impossible" trial and not to kill the old man without glory (by beating him with a stick). But one does not rewrite a myth. With respect to the reference myths, the Oedipean outcome is a patent structural anomaly.

Oedipus does not let himself be "imposed upon" by the king he encounters. It is not for a king, not so as to prove his youthful merit in royal eyes, that he stands up to the dangerous monster. Oedipus does not set out under orders. And when he kills Laïus, the event occurs precisely in the place of a virile and violent trial imposed by a king and requiring the protagonist to summon up all the strengths of body and soul alike. It is as if Oedipus's youthful violence, ripe for the most perilous challenges, violence required for the heroic victory against the female monster, is unleashed on Laïus instead of being directed by Laïus toward the object of their joint rivalry: the horrible, monstrous thing that has frightened everyone else, that spreads terror everywhere, and that only the powerful hero destined for sovereignty can hope to vanquish.

In the Jason and Perseus stories, a supplementary narrative detail comes into play. The trial that is imposed takes an imprudent reply the protagonist himself had made to a question asked by the king and turns it back on the hero. Pelias, seeing Jason approach wearing only one sandal, asks him what punishment he would impose on someone who had conspired against his king. Jason (inspired by Hera) replies that he would send him off to conquer the Golden

Fleece. And that is what Pelias then orders Jason to do. The situation is similar in Perseus's case. At dinner, Polydectes asks what gift his friends will offer him. They all reply that a horse is the most appropriate gift to offer a king. Only Perseus, in an outburst of pride, responds that he would bring Medusa's head, if necessary; Polydectes promptly enjoins him to accomplish that reputedly impossible task. It is significant that the young hero himself, indirectly and unwittingly, sets the task that will be imposed on him, as if it corresponded—although without his knowledge (and initially displaced onto someone else)—to his innermost desire.

The hero's departure resolves the agonistic crisis between the king and the young man. The clash between the young man's impudent braggadocio and the king's authority ultimately leads to the assignment of the task. Given this convergence of motifs, we can only conclude that some sort of dramatic moment comprising aggressiveness and defiance, a moment essential to the passage from one generation to another, found narrative expression in this scenario, a mythical manifestation that must have had its ritual counterpart.

The lack of such a moment in the Oedipus plot has innumerable consequences; a more painstaking study of the deficiency might spare analyses of the "Oedipus complex" from going astray or getting bogged down in various ways. As of now, we are entitled to suspect that in the abnormal but coherent economy of the Oedipus myth, the two major deviations—murder of the second king instead of the imposition of a dangerous trial by him, and the hero's marriage to his own mother instead of marriage to a king's daughter—are interrelated in ways that the conventional interpretation of the plot cannot grasp. However, before noting the mythic mechanisms involved in such a correlation (a correlation referring to a more powerful structure than that of the "Oedipus complex"), we need to exhaust the resources of our differential analysis and make the most of all the deviations we can identify.

The hero cannot emerge victorious from the trial that has been imposed on him without the help of one or more gods. Perseus is assisted by Athena, who teaches him how to tell Medusa from the other two Gorgon sisters. The goddess with blue-green eyes also gives him a polished shield, instructing him never to look directly at Medusa but only at her reflection. Hermes, for his part, arms Perseus with a sharp steel sickle. Similarly, when Bellerophon is preparing to capture Pegasus for his attack on the Chimaera, Athena brings him the golden bridle that will allow him to control the winged horse. Jason, too, is aided by Athena at the start of his long journey (she fits an oracular beam into the prow of the ship *Argos*), and his expedition benefits from Hera's patronage throughout. In each case, with significant constancy, the hero is assisted by the power of the gods. The persistence of this motif calls for thoughtful examination.

For the Greeks, to triumph without help from the gods—and this point must not be overlooked, because it turns out to be singularly clarifying for Oedipus's adventure—is an act of arrogance and madness. Sophocles attests unambiguously to this in *Ajax*:

> "Seek victory, my son" (so warned the sire).
> "But seek it ever with the help of heaven."
> He in his wilful ignorance replied,
> "Father, with gods to aid, a man of naught
> Might well prevail, but I without their help."[2]

This pride (*hubris*) infuriated the goddess Athena, and her resentment caused Ajax's tragic madness. Oedipus too triumphs over the Sphinx without help from the gods, without the virgin Athena, friend of heroes, who helps Perseus, Bellerophon, Jason. Thus, there is no reason to be astonished, as some readers have been, by the well-known passage in *Oedipus the King* in which the chorus stigmatizes the *hubris* characteristic of a tyrant along with the effrontery of those lacking in reverence for sanctuaries. There has been much speculation as to how the chorus's words could apply to Oedipus—even though the latter has just boasted to Teiresias that he vanquished the monster without any revelation from gods or anyone else—by "the flight of [his] own intelligence."[3] What does not seem reprehensible to us (have we not learned to "think for ourselves"?) is, however, mythically speak-ing—and Sophocles knows this—a serious anomaly, a fundamental error tantamount to desecration. To succeed "all alone," "by one-self," implies an effrontery that excludes not just other human beings but also and especially the gods. It is a way of denying divinity, of dismissing the gods in an act of punishable presumptu-ousness. Our differential analysis is conclusive: no hero can claim to have succeeded without the help of a god. And all the heroes of our reference myths (not to mention Odysseus or Heracles) have benefited from having "the good counselor" Athena, the armed virgin, daughter of Zeus and Metis, on their side.

But the gods are not alone in assisting heroes. Before he attacks the Chimaera, Bellerophon consults the seer Polyeidus, who ad-vises him to catch Pegasus while the horse is drinking at the Peirene spring. Jason is helped by the blind seer Phineus, who tells him what road to take and what he has to do to get past the Clash-ing Rocks (Symplegades). Then, it is with Medea's collaboration (Medea herself being inspired by Aphrodite) that he succeeds in taking possession of the Golden Fleece.

This motif of divine and human aid to the hero (a motif we can recognize in weaker form in the helper function in the tales Propp analyzed) is completely absent from Oedipus's story. He succeeds without help from anyone at all: no god, no wise old man, no bride intervenes. This absence has to be viewed as significant, given the constancy of the helper motif in the parallel myths.

~

One other point needs to be taken into account here. Oedipus's victory, which is unassisted, is also not divided into stages. This too is an anomaly. No other hero—not Jason, not Perseus, not Bellero-phon—succeeds in one fell swoop. The other heroes never begin by tackling a single, decisive task. Each of their adventures includes more or less lengthy preparatory stages without which victory could not be achieved and during which some divine or mortal assistance is required. Leaving Jason aside for the moment, and the immense journey he has to undertake in order to conquer the Golden Fleece, we note that neither Perseus nor Bellerophon can proceed directly to the climax of the major trial. When Perseus sets off to find the land of the Gorgons, he first arrives among the Graeae and tricks them into showing him the way; they direct him to the nymphs, who give him a pair of winged sandals, a pouch, and a "cap of darkness" to make him invisible. And even the killing of Medusa is not his final trial: the struggle with the sea dragon to deliver Andromeda still lies ahead.

The difference between these stories and the Oedipus myth is striking. Oedipus achieves victory all at once, without help, without preparatory steps; furthermore, and perhaps even more importantly, he triumphs with a single word. Whereas all the heroes of our reference myths win victory only (at some point or another) in bloody battle, by the power of the sword or spear, Oedipus alone triumphs through sheer intelligence, with his explanation of the famous riddle that is itself a trial by language. His is not a martial victory. The myth is clear on this point, at least in the version Sophocles adopted—which was the prevailing version in his day, if the iconographic evidence can be believed. Oedipus does not kill the Sphinx in an act of warrior's daring. The Sphinx kills herself: she commits suicide by flinging herself into the abyss as soon as the riddle is solved.

In the famous circular representation painted on the bottom of a bowl, we see Oedipus in a seated position, unarmed. A simple traveler's staff leans against his leg. His chin rests on his left hand in the manner of someone who is thinking. The Sphinx is perched on top of a column, her wings raised, like a great bird with a lion's body, and her head, crowned with a sort of diadem, is positioned above Oedipus's head.

This situation could hardly contrast more clearly with Bellerophon's encounter with the Chimaera, or Perseus's with Medusa, confrontations that correspond in mythic logic to Oedipus's meeting with the Sphinx. Thus, in one archaic representation we see Bellerophon mounted on Pegasus, who is flying above the Chimaera. In his hand he holds a long spear, pointing down in the direction of the lion's chest. Killing the Chimaera can only be an act of violence, an act mobilizing the hero's boldness and physical energy, although tactics are also involved, since Bellerophon gets the better of the Chimaera with lead that melts in her throat.

In the Perseus story as well, the heroic exploit entails violence and gore: Medusa's decapitation with a sickle was repeatedly represented in vase paintings. As in Bellerophon's case, the killing of the monster results from an offensive action, an attack with a sharp or pointed instrument, an act that mobilizes a warrior's rage. In Perseus's case, clearly, the bold act of killing includes cutting off and exhibiting the female monster's bloody head—replete with serpents for hair—like a trophy charged with power (it petrifies enemies), a trophy ultimately offered to Athena, who places it on her shield. Nothing of the sort happens with Oedipus. If the Sphinx disappears, it is because she does away with herself. Hers is not a physical defeat. Her self-destruction is an act of spite committed by a dishonored creature whose secret has been exposed. The Sphinx is not killed, she is offended by Oedipus's answer. Here a parallel with the Sirens is compelling. These bird-women first lose their wings to the Muses in a singing competition. Later on they commit suicide because their songs, drowned out by the music Orpheus makes on his lyre, have failed to attract the returning Argonauts. This act of spite is called for by the Sirens' bitter, insurmountable defeat in a nonmartial contest carried out by means of the singing voice. The parallel is all the more inevitable in that the Muses themselves are credited with having taught the Sphinx the riddle she proposes, and the Sphinx is sometimes described as a "singer who chants her riddles," or as a virgin or bitch who inflicts mortal wounds with her "lyreless song." Not to mention the fact that one of the words for riddle (*grīphoi*) also designates a certain kind of fisherman's net,[4] reinforcing the connection with the marine world of the Sirens.

Oedipus's victory over the Sphinx, which establishes his reputation, bears witness above all to his reason. Sophocles does not fail to stress this trait, while perhaps hinting discreetly at what is at stake. In the words of the chorus: "We saw him then, when the she-hawk swept against him, saw with our own eyes his skill [*sophos*], his brilliant triumph—there was the test—he was the joy of Thebes!" Oedipus is not a courageous warrior who has fought in hand-to-hand combat against the adversary; he is an intelligent man, a *sophos* who has solved a riddle. He knew the correct answer to a trial by language. He shed light on the logogryph. He did not become the victor, and then king, by brute force; he earned his victory by solving a problem of the mind. Oedipus's power in the city-state is the power of intelligence. Oedipus is the *sophos*-king. As he himself says of his exploit: "The flight of my own intelligence [*gnōmēi kyrēsas*] hit the mark."[5]

Oedipus's is the intelligence of an autodidact. Oedipus has received no instruction; he has not been initiated in advance into any sacred science. The priest recognizes that Oedipus has succeeded, shortly after arriving before the city, without having been given any information, any lesson (*oud' ekdidachtheis*). But the priest attributes this success to the help of a god. "A god was with you, so they say, and we believe it—you lifted up our lives" (*prosthēkē theou*). *Prosthēkē* means addition, supplement, something added, aid, assistance. However, a little later, in an angry response to Teiresias, Oedipus depicts his own success quite differently, as contrary to the methods of the priests of Apollo whom he mocks almost openly. "When the Sphinx, that chanting Fury, kept her deathwatch here, why silent then, not a word to set our people free? There was a riddle, not for some passerby to solve—it cried out for a prophet. Where were you? Did you rise to the crisis? Not a word, you and your birds, your gods—nothing. No, but I came by, Oedipus the ignorant, I stopped the Sphinx! With no help from the birds, the flight of my own intelligence (*gnōmei kyēsas*) hit the mark."[6] The autodidactic intelligence of young Oedipus achieves victory where the sacred knowledge of old Teiresias failed. Oedipus does not consult the birds, those signs from heaven, that language sent by the gods to reveal their will; he relies only on his own reflection. The power of his young intelligence wins out over the ancestral knowledge of the deciphering of signs. Neither human initiation nor divine assistance has been necessary. Oedipus has succeeded all by himself.

~

Let us recapitulate the main results of our comparative analysis. If the structure of the Oedipus myth is indeed closely parallel to that of the regular heroic myth, which it seems to parody, the following anomalies—some of which are subtle enough to be easily missed while others stand out—are to be noted:

§ A The motif of the trial imposed by a king is absent; in its stead is found the killing of a king, who is the hero's father.

§ B The dangerous confrontation with a female monster presents the following irregularities:

1. no assistance from the gods (neither Athena nor Hermes is present to help the hero);
2. no assistance from mortals (neither advice from a seer-sage nor help from a future bride);
3. no phasing of the trials that lead to the decisive victory;
4. no mobilization of physical force, but the uttering of a single word (hence the corollary of the monster's suicide, in place of her killing as such).

§ C The hero marries not the daughter of a king but his own mother.

～

Thus, in contrast with the prototype hero whose features we have described, Oedipus's victory over the Sphinx is a mythic anomaly. Not only is the confrontation not imposed by an authority (the dispatcher king), but the victor is an autodidact, an atheist, and an intellectual. We shall need to come back to these characteristics. They have an import for the relationship with others (gods or humans) and with oneself, and for the qualities displayed during the trial, that is already evident. We may suspect that there is a link of mythic causality between this distortion of the heroic profile and the other features that constitute the striking anomaly of Oedipus's adventure (patricide and incest), and that articulating this link thoroughly will enable us to go beyond previous analyses and understand more deeply the inner meaning of the Oedipus myth.

To these various anomalies must be added an ordered confusion that involves and traverses them all. The three kings—persecutor (K_1), dispatcher (K_2), and donor (K_3)—among whom the regular myth distinguishes, are reduced, in a complete merging of their differentiated functions, to a single king, Laïus, who is the hero's own father (F). If in all the reference myths we have $K_1 \neq K_2 \neq K_3$

$\neq$ F, the Oedipus myth presents the extraordinary peculiarity of making these three actors identical (while "crossing out," as it were, the usual dispatcher king) and equating them with the hero's own father. Hence the formula $K_1 = K_2 = K_3 = F$.

This reduction of the other to one's own sphere, of differences to sameness, is a feature that provides food for thought about the logic of this myth, as well as, following another path, about the structural stakes of the Oedipus myth. How is such a reduction possible, such a flattening of alterity and difference concerning the king and the father? What fundamental mechanism of the regular myth must be inoperative, or excluded, or eluded, for Oedipus to remain confined within the selfsame sphere of his own identity, instead of working out his destiny through the confrontation of alterities? These questions cannot be avoided.

Such is the picture of the anomalies. Convinced of the extreme rigor of mythic logic, we have to entertain the strong suspicion that these anomalies are not independent of one another, but that they are inscribed within an ordered disordering that is distributed over the myth as a whole and that governs the system of deviations from the prototype myth. However, it is important to stress that the nature of mythic rigor and logic has implications for the truth of the myth. In order to disclose all that the myth has to teach us, it will not suffice to discover the inversions, symmetries, reversals, displacements, and so forth that make it possible to relate the structural anomaly of the Oedipus myth to the general schema of the regular myth in formal terms. Not that there is no way to imagine such an operation, and even the algorithms that would provide a formula for it; but it would be futile to attempt to find the explanation of the deviations, and thus the profound meaning of the myth, solely in a formal rule accounting for the transformations. The rationale underlying these displacements, deviations, and distortions is not that of a systemic transformation; rather, they result, on the level of the narration, from a cognitive activity, from an extensive and coherent application of knowledge about the constraints on human destiny that no transformational algebra could possibly predict.

Lévi-Strauss is sometimes criticized, and rightly so, for conceiving of the myth only as a system of logical combinations and failing to take into account the affects that are invested and channeled in the plurivocal images and symbols, and that the motivational power of the rite, in its mobilizing function, does not allow us to forget.[7] Contrary to the affirmations of structural anthropology, the constraints of mythic thought are not at all those of "a play of transformations in which . . . the same concepts, rearranged, exchange, contradict, or invert their values and their functions, until the resources of this new combinatorial are dissipated or simply exhausted."[8] The constraint of mythic narrative carries much more weight and is much more significant. It rules out any talk of "play," in the logical sense of a permutational operation tending toward formal exhaustivity. It does not reside in the possible outcomes of a pure combinatorial. It refers to affective constraints, to polarizations of desire, to a dramaturgy of passions, to dispositions of the human soul that are at once internal and "objective" in typical existential situations such as birth, death, marriage, or battle. These constraints trace frameworks of meaning that reveal, in language that has a formidable power of condensation, the most tenacious truths, those that are most deeply rooted in symbolic life, that is, life pure and simple in its properly human aspects. Myth can only be considered as manifesting "an autonomous activity of the mind"[9] because it has been in the first place detached, abstracted, dis-affected by a "view from afar," a "disinterested view," as if a grammarian analyzing a batch of military reports exchanged in the course of a long and bloody trench war were to declare that what is at stake in these well-formed sentences, whose formal properties can be described, is an autonomous activity of the mind.

Moreover Lévi-Strauss himself, without noticing that he was contradicting one of his own basic principles, was obliged to recognize in myths, and this contortion is not insignificant, a certain knowledge about madness. Myths contain a rigorous knowledge of the ills of the human soul: knowledge about, and not simply an immediate expression of, these maladies. Far from belonging to the order of symptoms or deliriums, far from translating a psychic disorder, the myth is a form of knowledge about deliriums and symptoms: "it produces, in its own fashion, a theory, and thus places itself on the side of the clinician, not the patient."[10] Contrary to what Lévi-Strauss maintains elsewhere and repeatedly as an inviolable structuralist postulate, there would thus be truth in myths. Through its knowledgeability [*sapience*] the myth rivals "psychiatric" knowledge. Lévi-Strauss goes so far as to say, with reference to mental disorders, that myths "describe them and diagnose them as such, while relating those incidents in a character's life which triggered the disorder in the first place."[11] It is hard to see how myths could possess knowledge concerning the profound disorders of the soul and the constraints of human desires if they were only a logical combinatorial manifesting an autonomous and formal mental activity. One cannot simultaneously claim that myths tell us nothing that can teach us about the order of the world, the nature of reality, or human destiny (in conformity with the methodological postulate that Lévi-Strauss opposes to any temptation to a "gnostic" reading of myths), and also claim that a given myth is organized as knowledge about a given disequilibrium in the human soul, a given derailing of a destiny, as the description and even the precise diagnosis of a case of madness. The lesson of a myth, its ethics, its teaching, are situated precisely here, in this "dia-gnosis." This does not mean that a myth and its transformations do not have rigorous narrative coherence; but if they do, it is because beneath the apparent irrationality of destiny and the symbolic truths that govern these disruptions, there is a deeper rationality, a kind of imaginal logic.

Contrastive analysis leads to the following proposition: the one who does not kill the female monster in a bloody battle is the one whose destiny is to marry his own mother. It is as if the violent and victorious confrontation with the Medusa or the Chimaera is an obligatory struggle without which access to a nuptial union acceptable to the gods cannot be achieved. The killing of the female monster—and not merely her elimination by intelligence—would be the condition of nonincestuous marriage. That is what our differential reading would teach us. Oedipus is the one who, despite all the appearances of success in his encounter with the Sphinx, does not achieve complete and normal success in the decisive phase of the killing of the female monster. It is as if explaining the riddle was not a complete and adequate trial, not sufficient to endow the hero with the full capacity to marry the princess. The hero has to fight, has to shed blood, in a struggle that mobilizes the energy of his entire being. He has to pierce with his sword or decapitate the horrible, dangerous, monstrous female who is herself the offspring of the serpent-woman, the immortal Echidna. Oedipus's adventure lacks this lethal act.

Freud completely fails to see this structure in the Oedipal myth, this differential kernel that gives it its full meaning. He knows nothing, and for fundamental reasons, about the fight with Echidna's children. Why would the killing of the female monster be the condition of nonincestuous marriage? The Freudian interpretation leaves us unarmed in the face of such a question. When Freud or Rank maintain that the killing of the Sphinx is a substitute for the murder of the father, they are abusing our patience while confronting us with the display of their own obsessions. For on the one hand (like the Chimaera, the Gorgon, Crommyon's sow, or the Hydra of Lerna) the Sphinx is a female creature (the term is feminine in Greek and also in German, which ought to have put Freud on notice), but in Oedipus's case the father has already been murdered, and this doubling is hard to understand. Why a symbolic substitute (and thus a disguise) for the murder of the father if the father's murder has already taken place, in the open? Moreover, the Sphinx is not killed, but commits suicide.

We must simply recognize that the Sphinx, like Echidna, the mother of the monsters, remains uninterpretable in the Freudian code. The Sphinx is the unthought element of Freudian psychoanalysis, a riddle unresolved by the Freudian movement. And one that for structural reasons cannot be resolved, for its solution would threaten the entire Freudian edifice, based as it is on a certain

fundamentally erroneous interpretation of the Oedipus myth—
and, more seriously still, of the Oedipus complex.

The riddle of the Sphinx? An expression to be taken in two
senses: the riddle that the Sphinx proposes, and the one that the
Sphinx herself constitutes. Oedipus thought he had resolved the
first and Freud the second. But what if neither had found the
answer?

§ 2 Psychoanalysis and Murder

"Monstricide" is the great unthought element of Freudian doctrine. The schism that shook psychoanalysis at the very outset, Freud's break with the heretic Jung, is not unrelated to this issue. Jung did not put Oedipal rivalry with the father at the heart of his interpretation of neuroses. For him, patricide was not the central event; the Oedipus myth was not his myth of reference. What Jung perceived, in his own way—which is sometimes obscure and disconcerting, but which points to a real problem—was the extraordinary consistency and centrality of a motif that Freud was nevertheless unable to explain: the hero's struggle with the monster. In the heroic mythologies of all cultures, this "mythologeme" stands out. Despite the efforts of Freud and his disciples to the contrary, it is virtually impossible to interpret this heroic killing (which coincides with a sacrifice on the hero's part) as a substitute for the killing of the father. Nothing justifies such an interpretation. To see an image of the father, even disguised and displaced, in the multiple forms of (female) dragons that populate the daring hero's nightmares is to take rather too lightly what the myth itself stipulates: the monster's female sex, its cavernous dwelling-place, and so forth.

On this point, Jung was not mistaken to remain intransigent in his quarrel with Freud. No concept in Freudian doctrine can come to terms with this monster. And Jung, seeking the meaning of this dangerous creature, was right to look to the mother, to the dark, enveloping, stifling mother who binds and captivates her son, holds him back, traps him in the numberless coils of her reptilian attachment. Indeed, it is only at the end of a bloody battle against this oppressive and devouring female monster, only when the son has mobilized all his manly energies to kill her, to free himself from her, that he can marry the princess, the girl he has been promised, who is *not* his mother, and whom the dragon was holding prisoner or to whom she was blocking access. To kill the monster after making the hazardous trip back to the dark lair where she lives is thus for the hero to sever a bond, to make a vital sacrifice, to inflict a bloody cut that allows the protagonist to become the spouse of the girl who had been the monster's prisoner.

The victory over the monster, a typical, universal exploit of countless mythological heroes, thus has the deep meaning of matricide. It is matricide and not, as Freud thought, patricide, that is universally held to be the most difficult task, the central exploit that constitutes the hero as "man" (*vir*), authorizing him to marry and qualifying him for royal status. The great initiatory trial, the trial in which the postulant risks death in order to emerge from childhood and become a man, is this struggle that takes place in dark and cavernous depths, and not a killing of the father carried out in the broad daylight of tribal polemics.

To be sure, what is killed so perilously and obscurely in this matricide is not the mother "in person" (or even an imaginary representation of her person)—and that is why Freud, who tended to personalize the unconscious conflict excessively in order to present it as a family drama, was never able to recognize the central, nuclear position of matricide. What is confronted and consumed is a negative dimension (accessible only through metaphors that are always inadequate): a shadowy, dark, devouring reptile, a monster inhabiting cavernous, watery depths, a dimension that myth alone can conceptualize—let us not shy away from this paradoxical word. When Hesiod speaks of Echidna, the (immortal) mother of (mortal) monsters, with the upper body of a woman and the lower body of a snake, a denizen of deep sea caves, he touches on an imaginal concept that is potentially more powerful, through the complex of meanings it organizes, than any concepts derived from Freudian psychoanalysis. Let us consider the term "phallic mother," for example: this concept is poorer and more limited than the knowledge that the myth preserves and structures.

Matricide is thus the great unthought element of Freudian doctrine. What Freud did not perceive, and what is nevertheless signified in the myths of the prototype hero, is that the nuptial outcome is possible only by way of such a violent combat. The desire for the mother is a deadly desire. The return to the cavern, to the uterus, to hell, requires that the hero engage in a confrontation in which his own life is at stake. He can emerge triumphant only if he breaks the powerful bond, delivers himself from the lethal attachment through an act of bloody violence directed against the monster-mother, an act that is also a sacrifice of his own attachment. This matricide alone constitutes the liberation of woman—it gives access to the bride, once the dark maternal element has been separated from the bright nuptial feminine element.

Now, what is striking in this operation is that the father appears to have no part in it. Access to the feminine is not achieved by obedience to a paternal law that would make the mother taboo and would oblige the hero to seek his bride elsewhere; the matricidal victory is what yields the reward of nuptial access, what provides the gift of the nonmaternal feminine. If a father figure (but one who, in the standard myth, is not the hero's own father) has a part in this confrontation, he is not the agent of prohibition, but plays the role we have identified as that of the dispatcher king. This king imposes a trial by virtue of an authority whose source is royal prestige rather than law. He stimulates the young hero's sense of honor, his love of competition, by challenging him to succeed in a trial deemed perilous and virtually impossible. Emulation rather than coercion impels the young man to rush headlong into battle.

The plot of the monomyth is thus very different from the Oedipal conflict. Neither the paternal dimension nor the maternal one plays the same role. The Oedipus myth is organized around the causal sequence patricide→incest, while the monomyth is resolved in the sequence matricide→engagement. With Oedipus, the killing of the father leads to the tragedy of incest, whereas with the prototype hero the triggering injunction of the dispatcher king leads to the victory over the monster-mother that opens the way to the nuptial bond.

It is understandable, then, that Freud, haunted by the Oedipus complex and failing to perceive how what we have called the monomyth could function as a constitutive structure, should have had so much trouble conceptualizing "the dissolution of the Oedipus complex," the stage beyond the conflict established by the Oedipal structure. He was unable to envision this follow-up stage except as an attenuation of the tensions instituted by the Oedipus complex, or as an aftereffect of that complex (with the constitution of a superego that internalizes the taboo, the barrier), but never really as another, a different structure.

Yet the monomyth is that other structure. Making matricide (which opens onto the nonmaternal feminine) rather than patricide (which opens onto maternal incest) the central obstacle, and without resorting to a taboo, the monomyth accounts for the masculine subject's access to his fundamental desire. From this perspective, the quest as presented by the monomyth corresponds rigorously to the constitutive axis of masculine desire, whereas the Oedipus myth gives a distorted, skewed version of this desire. For beneath the impulse to avoid initiation, there is a still more fundamental desire to be initiated, to accept the task imposed, to confront severance (death, the trial of the cutting blade that kills the monster-mother but also, painfully, frees the hero from her) in order to be reborn, delivered.

This Freudian failure to understand what is nevertheless a persistent, standard myth thus amply justifies what certain heretical theoreticians of the unconscious have suspected. Nothing in Freudian doctrine allows us to understand what is truly at stake in the universally attested great bloody battle between the hero and the monster, a battle of which the Oedipus myth presents only a caricature, or at best, as we have shown, an aberrant and partial version, since it is based solely on the solution of the riddle. It is legitimate that the Oedipal son should be considered as a possibility that not only does not cover the entire typology of masculine desire, but one that presents only a superficial and distorted version of that desire. The fact that this critique has been developed and strengthened by Jung's intellectual heirs makes perfect sense.[1] But the serious inadequacies of Freud's conceptualization of the Oedipus complex have also had to be acknowledged in a much less likely place.

Under the cover of an intransigent and ostentatious fidelity to Freud, Jacques Lacan worked tirelessly at a convoluted revision of psychoanalysis. Protected by reiterated declarations of orthodoxy, Lacan overturned several of Freud's postulates, but it is hardly surprising that his most radical reconsideration should have centered on the notion of the Oedipus complex. Very early and very quickly, Lacan ran up against the inadequacy of the Freudian theoretical construction in this area, so much so that a critique of the Oedipus complex became an indispensable requirement of his program. What Lacan saw himself facing in "the vital situation of the neuroses" constituted "a rather different structure from the one that is given traditionally—the incestuous desire for the mother, the interdiction by the father, its effects of blocking and, in the vicinity, the more or less luxuriant proliferation of symptoms." Hence the portentous suspicion that made it possible to anticipate a veritable schism: "I think that this difference ought to lead us to discuss the general anthropology that emerges from the analytic doctrine as it is currently being taught. In a word, the entire schema of the Oedipus complex is subject to criticism."[2]

However, this critique of the Oedipus complex, for a variety of reasons both strategic and theoretical, has always remained suspended, reserved, withheld. Lacan announced it in clear and unambiguous terms, but he himself only hinted at its outlines here and there, never systematizing its argument and its import. Radical criticism of the Oedipus complex remained as a subterranean guiding thread that no doubt oriented the most innovative intuitions and the most fertile of Lacan's gropings, but it remained a thread that he was never able or willing to articulate fully and systematically in a challenge to Freudian dogma.

We can nevertheless reconstruct the principal considerations involved in the Lacanian critique of the Oedipus complex.[3] They have to do, essentially, with the place of castration and the status of prohibition. According to Freud, in the Oedipus complex the father, by brandishing the threat of castration, becomes the one who prohibits access to the desired mother. However, Lacan is determined to show that that desire for the mother is not the most radical form of desire, nor is the threatened paternal castration the most radical form of castration. Rather than revealing the true nature of desire (the object of true desire is impossible and not simply forbidden) and reaching the most decisive form of castration (a confrontation with the lack of the Thing, more terrible than the paternal threat), the Oedipus complex constitutes a veil that dissimulates the overwhelming radicality of that desire and that castration. The Oedipus complex has the function of repressing castration. Faced with the absence of the Thing (the primordial object of desire that the mother situates but with which she cannot be identified), the Oedipus complex positions paternal conflict as a veil. The Oedipal subject is protected by the paternal threat (which makes him believe that the object of his desire for absolute jouissance is simply forbidden) from the radical confrontation with castration and death. To desire according to the Oedipus complex is to elude the fundamental desire of the masculine subject, which requires passing through castration.

In other words, caught up in the Oedipal configuration, the masculine subject entertains the fantasy that the father's killing would open the way to the desired union with the mother. The father appears as the major obstacle that it would suffice to overturn, as the interdiction that it would suffice to abolish, in order to make possible what is fantasized as absolute jouissance. The Oedipal subject imagines that the interposition of the father is what forbids access to the mother. And he constantly entertains the fantasy of killing, convinced that he will find absolute jouissance afterward. To be sure, the Oedipal subject is not Oedipus (who commits these two crimes unwittingly); the Oedipal subject is the one who entertains the unconscious imagination of the causal sequence patricide→incest, a sequence whose narrative consistency appears to be ensured by the myth. For Lacan, and for good reasons, this Oedipal fantasy does not account for masculine desire in its most radical form.

From our point of view, the decisive element is the fact that this revision of Freudian analysis, initiated but never pursued to its ultimate consequences by Lacan, points in precisely the same direction as the timeless lesson of the heroic plot we have been able to discern through differential myth analysis. By extirpating himself from the Freudian limitation, Lacan simply rediscovered, and with difficulty, a truth that was known by the tradition that has been sedimented, for example, in the Greek myths of royal investiture—that is, of successful initiation. Lacan's correction of Freud necessarily restores the myth of King Oedipus to the irregular, aberrant place it was assigned by the mythic mechanism, a place it should never have lost. What Lacan discovers and presents in contorted language can be predicted directly once we have identified the monomyth: it is this monomyth (in its amply attested universality) and not the singular history of Oedipus that contains the truth of masculine destiny and desire.

Just as, with respect to the standard myth of royal initiation, the Oedipus myth is an anomaly that can be explained only by the disruption of the conventional plot, with respect to the fundamental and constitutive desire of the masculine subject, the Oedipus complex is a deceptive fantasy that troubles and disrupts masculine desire instead of revealing it. In the differential relationship between the monomyth and the Oedipus myth, mythic knowledge has already set up the opposition between authentic desire and the desire gone astray. Although seductive and powerful, the destiny of Oedipus is, in terms of traditional truth, an aberration (a tragedy) that corresponds to an ethical deviation and not to a basic structure of masculine desire. In narrative terms, the Oedipus myth is derivative, secondary. It could not possibly provide a foundation for the true desire that is repeated and stressed in the monomyth.

The relation (discernible owing to differential myth analysis) between the monomyth and the Oedipus myth is thus the same as the relation between the radical axis of masculine desire and the Oedipus complex. Just as Lacan could call the Oedipus complex a "myth" in the pejorative sense of the term, the Oedipus myth may be said to be a myth within a myth, a secondary plot resulting from the transformation and disruption of a more fundamental and constitutive prototype plot.

Once we enter into this double juxtaposition, the parallels become exceptionally enlightening. Just as the avoidance of initiation (and thus of symbolic death) makes the Oedipus myth aberrant with respect to the monomyth, which is for its part a myth of initiation confronted and achieved, so it is the avoidance of castration that makes the Oedipus complex a fantasy, a neurosis, a myth in the pejorative sense, with respect to the truth of masculine desire, which is to confront symbolic castration as lack. What Freud and the Freudians have laboriously attempted to conceptualize under the label of castration (which is not, as they have finally had to acknowledge, a severing of the penis, an operation that the initial choice of the word castration inevitably evoked) is nothing other than initiation, and more precisely the phase of "death" and sacrifice that is the condition of a second birth. The metabiological necessity that requires the male human being to be born a second time in order to become a man is what destines him to undergo the severing that psychoanalysis attempts to locate in the unconscious under the label of castration. But it is not certain that this term, one symbol among others (and more reductive than some), is more instructive than the system of multiple symbols that the initiatory situation puts into play. Everything Lacan conceives in terms of castration (including the strange "desire for castration" that remains, in this context, enigmatic) is conveyed by mythicoritual knowledge in terms of a trial, with all the rhizomes of fundamental symbolizations that a trial governs: the meeting with the monster (in which the terrible aspect of the Thing is revealed beyond the mother, and linked with death), the discovery of what has to be traversed (bloody sacrifice) in order for the imaginary object of masculine rivalry (the Golden Fleece, Medusa's head) to be transmuted into a symbolic trophy, and so forth.

The Oedipus plot, considered in isolation, as it was by Freud, shows only a fatal chain of events leading from patricide to incest. The juxtaposition of this plot with that of the monomyth makes it possible to perceive much deeper correlations richly endowed with a wisdom that cannot be reduced to the Freudian knowledge it challenges. These correlations can be put into relief if, for example, we first distinguish the hero's relation to the feminine element, then analyze his relation to the masculine element, and finally weave these two types of correlations together.

On the level of the hero's relation to the feminine, our differential myth analysis of the Oedipus plot allows us to spell out the following lesson: it is the protagonist who does *not* kill the female monster in a bloody struggle who marries his own mother. On the level of the hero's relation to the masculine, we can say that the protagonist on whom the trial had *not* been imposed (by a dispatcher king) is the one who kills his own father. Incest and patricide thus appear as perverse and distorted but perfectly rule-governed results of two deficiencies, or lacunae, concerning the relation to the feminine and the masculine elements respectively. Only the juxtaposition we have undertaken can reveal these gaps in the Oedipus story. They are gaps with respect to a more powerful standard structure, with respect to a wrinkle in the symbolic that the monomyth exposes. These two gaps or deficiencies intersect correlatively in turn: the protagonist upon whom the trial has *not* been imposed by a king is the protagonist who does *not* kill the monster-female.

The structure outlined by this set of mythic correlations tells us more about the Oedipean configuration than Freudian theorizing does. In narrative terms, patricide occupies the place of the royal mandate, as if the king killed had not been capable of imposing the difficult trial, of deflecting the young man's aggressiveness away from the king's own person toward a dangerous enterprise. Moreover, the bloody murder that should have been accomplished in the feminine sphere (the hazardous victory over the female monster) takes place in the masculine sphere instead (the killing of the old man, Laïus). When Oedipus encounters the Sphinx, he has already lived through the moment of murder, but in a displaced and perverse way, for the outburst of aggressiveness was directed toward his own father rather than the female monster. Thus the anomaly of a confrontation with a king that fails to produce an imposed trial (and a manly decision to accept the challenge) reverberates in the anomaly of a victory over the monster in which the warrior's physical strength plays no role, and then in the incestuous outcome of the marriage. Avoidance of initiation has already begun in Oedipus's encounter with Laïus.

The opposition between paternal authority and desire is nowhere to be found in the monomyth. The dispatcher king imposes a perilous trial. This imposition may have the function of diverting the protagonist from incest, but its scope and significance are very different from an interdiction. The idea of interdiction suggests an obedience that destroys desire. Yet the young hero of the monomyth, far from evading the order that sends him off to probable death, accepts the mandate as a challenge. The honor of being a man (*vir, anēr*) prevails. In the hero's powerful and intimate desire to become a man by assuming the risk of the trial, obedience to the dispatcher king's commandment is explicitly conjugated with the achievement, through a perilous quest, of a nonincestuous nuptial destiny that requires precisely such a proof of valor. In the monomyth, authority of the paternal type (the royal mandate) is thus not opposed to the masculine subject's radical desire, but instead allows its realization. What the regular myth exposes that psychoanalysis misses is the function of sacrifice. Sacrifice allows the protagonist simultaneously to accept the task designated by royal authority and to pledge his manhood to the deadly struggle that is the bloody initiatory separation from the monster-mother. Thus, where certain of Freud's commentators attempt to locate a "desire for castration" (a term that cannot avoid an oddly perverse accent), the regular myth situates a desire for heroism, risk, and sacrifice, a desire whose instituting resonance has an ethical sense that conforms better to the fundamental desire. The quest for a trial, the daring risk of one's life (and such a quest is indeed at issue in Perseus's boasting, or Bellerophon's) is more constitutive than interdiction. And it is by defiantly seeking the trial that the young hero meets the initiatory death (or symbolic castration) that allows him to be reborn, animated by a new, nonincestuous desire directed toward the bride.

Not only does the Freudian reading fail to recognize the monomyth, it misconstrues the understanding articulated in the Oedipus myth itself; it simply misses the point. For at the heart of the Oedipus drama—and this point cannot be stressed enough—there is an absence: no authority offers a cause to the young protagonist's desire for heroism and sacrifice. The myth of Oedipus is not a myth of paternal interdiction, but a myth of the absence of the trial-imposing king. The logic of the myth is extraordinarily rigorous: in structural and narrative terms, Oedipus encounters King Laïus in the place of the encounter with a dispatcher king. And instead of being sent off to kill a dangerous monster, instead of directing his powers of aggression and defiance toward a task unanimously judged dangerous and worthy, Oedipus remains mired in the stage of mortal rivalry with his own father. The killing of the father is thus, in terms of mythic knowledge, an aberration that takes the place of a conventional act: a challenge tendered by a royal figure, and accepted by the young hero, to go off and conquer the "impossible" (the Golden Fleece, Medusa's head)—a challenge through which the hero would encounter anguish and confront death. In place of such noble deeds, in place of a perilous quest for unanimously coveted objects, royal talismans that the hero can conquer only after traversing death and mutilation, Oedipus is condemned to a sordid and dishonoring combat in which he beats an old man to death with a stick.

This contrast can be formulated differently. The protagonist's mortal rivalry with his real father shields him from a much more difficult and risky outcome: castration in its most radical aspect. As we have seen, the myth already "knows" what Lacan ventured to suggest only with difficulty and restraint, for fear of upsetting the entire Freudian edifice. Whereas Freud depicts the father as the agent of the threat of castration, Lacan began to suspect that paternal castration (thus, castration with a human face) dispenses the young hero from a much more radical form in which the profound truth of masculine desire is played out: the agonizing face-to-face confrontation with the Thing. Now, as the relation between the monomyth and the Oedipus myth clearly shows, his lethal rivalry with his own father dispenses Oedipus from the imposition of a perilous trial. Although he still goes to meet the Sphinx (where the face-to-face confrontation with the Thing ought to be played out), he has already been exempted from the bloody ordeal; his intelligent answer to the riddle suffices to take him across the threshold and make the monster disappear.

By attributing the threat of castration to a strong, angry father who wants to prevent or avenge his son's incestuous desire for his (the father's) own wife, Freud unduly humanizes the cause of the break; he deprives it of its prehuman, superhuman, inhuman necessity. In this sense, although on a different level, he is behaving like Oedipus, who answers the riddle of the Sphinx with the word "man." The initiatory adventure frees the young man from his agonizing and abyssal attraction to the maternal dimension. But the hero's painful and bloody liberation (the severing of the living link with the monster-mother, which can only be experienced as a mutilation), does not result from his father's vengeful rage. Incestuous desire is intrinsically agonizing; no conventional interdiction makes it so. It is the young man's desire itself that creates, out of its own inclinations, a horrible, anguish-generating monster.

Notwithstanding the absence of a father whose thundering voice might reinforce this vital obstacle by giving it the articulated force of an edict, the obstacle remains fully present, experienced in absolute anguish. It is the scene in which Freud himself is caught up that doubtless leaves him in his ignorance. He sees the father as the muscular bearer of the law, forbidding the cult of maternal idols and of any incestuous imagination,[4] and he thinks that the cause of the obstacle lies there. He does not know that an apparently paternal interdiction may hide another that is not paternal, and not maternal either; rather, like the gods of Egypt, it does not even have a human face.

The symbolism of the Sphinx, for example, a seductive woman

and a devouring dog, indicates this as clearly as possible. In the Sphinx, who is a guardian, there is room for no law of a paternal cast. It is a matter of a vital defense and not of a commanding edict issued by an angry father. The Sphinx still plunges into animality, even if, in her very morphology, the creature realizes the articulation between humanity and animality. According to a general theme, divine teramorphic or teranthropomorphic beings are the ones who perform the tortures of initiation. They are always superhuman beings carrying out a sacred act in the name of the gods. The Sphinx, and not a father, is the being to whom is imputed the torture and death of the son—because of the desire she arouses. It is significant that in certain versions, the Sphinx is held to be an animal that makes young people uneasy because of the sexual relations she would seek to have with them.[5] Here can be read the young man's dangerous desire for a negative, dark, animal femininity, for a horrifying union in which he risks being completely annihilated. There, again, the episode of the Sphinx is the meeting with the mystery of sexuality and of death, in which the young man has to run the risk of disappearing. He has to experience the fact that his own desire for the dark mother is lethal. It is this confrontation alone that allows, after a symbolic death, the hero's rebirth with a new identity.

In the struggle against the frightful beast, dragon, or Medusa, the hero develops his masculinity; he mobilizes inner forces that transform his infantile dependence into a concentrated and combative manhood. That is why, in the paradigmatic myth of the hero, it is the force of arms and not merely shrewdness that determines the victory over the female monster. In the case of Oedipus, it appears clearly that his full manhood has not been mobilized, that it is the intelligence of the head and not the courage of the chest (to go back to Plato's distinction) that made success possible. To fill out this distinction, we might add that his erotic drives have not been tested or surmounted either, since Oedipus was not seduced by the "lyreless songs" of the winged virgin; he short-circuited her disturbing charms with a well-chosen word. Thus, it is against a false power that the myth warns: the power that does not result from a genuine combat, the power that is not the achievement of mon-stricide but the intellectual avoidance of seduction by the monster, and the philosopher's dispensation from the task of murdering her.

The myth of Oedipus the king is a myth of avoidance of initia-tion. To put the point in more Freudian terms, but terms that Freud himself was unable to develop, it presents the complete critical tableau of the fantasmatic orientation that is founded on the avoidance of symbolic castration. The avoidance of castration is the Oedipal neurosis.

The myth teaches what can happen when the telestic process is arrested by the reflective intellect. Oedipus, placed in the position of a postulant at the threshold of a sanctuary guarded by the Sphinx, ought to have died in his capacity as son of his own mother. That is how he would have found the bride. But to say that Oedipus, by avoiding the trial of true matricide, was unable to succeed in liberating the bride, is also to say that he is fated to remain entirely the prisoner of his own mother. Whereas through his intelligent response he appears to escape the clutches of the singing temptress forever, his destiny remains tightly controlled by his mother in the most realistic and most profane way possible. The tragedy of Oedipus is the vengeance of the desire for the mother when this desire has not been burned away, transfigured in depth by the trial, but only set aside by the reflective response, by monocentered self-consciousness. The Sphinx avenges herself for *not* having been killed. Deaf to the seductive voices of the enchant-resses that draw young men into a mortal embrace, Oedipus has called a halt to all fascination in responding with a pure, cold concept. That is what leads the Sphinx to kill herself. The fate that pursues Oedipus is not vengeance for a murder accomplished, but spite for a deadly but also regenerative act that has not been carried out. The nuptial feminine that is the beast's prisoner (or as certain myths state clearly, that lies within the monster) has not been separated, disengaged, brought to autonomous existence. It is this absence of the monster-mother's murder, this nonmatricide, that pursues Oedipus.

The liberation of the feminine thus remains unaccomplished in

Oedipus's destiny. He is the one who does not liberate the bride. The suicide of the Sphinx is a spiteful lover's anger, turned inward, the anger of the black monster that will now never be enacted by a metamorphosis capable of liberating the nuptial truth of the feminine.

Thus, it is natural for the modern Oedipal world—which draws its sustenance from the permanent suicide of the Sphinx, constituted as the inaugural and continuing victory of philosophical reason and self-consciousness—to maintain an incomplete and, as it were, involuted and atrophied sensitivity to the feminine. Unlike the true hero, who went down into the depths, into the abyss, where he killed the reptilian monster and found the genuine treasure, Oedipus remains incredulous and detached in the face of the seductions and terrors of the return: he avoids descent and matricide, instead of accomplishing them victoriously. Oedipus, who believed that the anthropological perspective (the human face) could forever close the anguishing opening, is pursued by the spite of the Sphinx, and not by her desire for justice. Nevertheless, this spite is as terrible as vengeance.

Thus, the mystery of the Sphinx, which remains intact for Freud, is cleared up only when it is brought into relation with the trial, the risk of death, conditions of the crossing of a threshold. How can the Sphinx of the Greeks be recognized in this place? And how can the precise unveiling of her function overturn our entire approach to the myth as the genealogy of the Oedipus complex?

§ 3 The Rite of the Sphinx

In every premodern society, one encounters some more or less complex ritualization through which, when young people reach a certain age, they cease to be regarded as children, are promoted to full-fledged membership in the adult world, and viewed as capable of procreating in their turn, via marriage. But if this adolescent initiation is particularly important by virtue of the ideas and images it puts into play, the rites and myths it enacts, it is also important because it constitutes the model for all initiations, even those that no longer involve the passage from puberty to adulthood, strictly speaking. Scholars have shown that there are no major differences, in terms of the fundamental symbolics involved, between the initiation rite of puberty, heroic or royal initiation rites, and initiation into sacred mysteries. Whether what is at stake is the passage from childhood to adult membership in the community, admission into a secret brotherhood (of warriors or shamans, for example), royal investiture, or entry into the arcane secrets of a religion based on mystery, the various modes of initiation are closely related, whatever differences may be manifested—and these may be considerable—in the degree of symbolic elaboration and in the details of the ritual scenarios. It is noteworthy that the general principle of initiation remains constant even when different "entrances" or "sacralizations" and very diverse religious traditions are involved. In varied forms, the themes of separation, descent into the world of the dead or regression back to the womb, bloody trial, provisional death, reception of a secret teaching, renaissance, and resurrection, can always be found.[1]

The central phase, the deepest core of every initiation is constituted by the rite that provides a pathetic symbolization of the neophyte's death (a return to chaos or hell, to the bowels of the earth, the primordial womb, and so on), followed, after a period of uncertainty and mourning, by the initiate's return among the living, as in a "second birth." The initiate is someone who is born a second time. The death traversed by the postulant corresponds to a phase of disaggregation, dismembering, and fragmentation without which the recomposition of identity on a new basis cannot occur. The novice is supposed to be swallowed by a monster, cut into pieces, burned, and so forth. He undergoes an ordeal that is supposed to leave an indelible trace, or some substitute for bodily mutilation, such as circumcision, the extraction of a tooth, scarification, the tearing out of hair.

But the descent into the world of the dead is also what permits contact with the ancestors. No resurrection takes place without some revelation of knowledge. The young man's assimilation into a community of adult men coincides with the acquisition of a new identity (by way of a name, a form of dress, special obligations and duties) that is made possible by his reception of a sacred teaching. The community's most venerable traditions, its mystic relations with divine beings from the beginning of time, are transmitted to the new initiate. Gradually, the most secret core of the world view of the group to which he belongs is revealed to him: the founding myths of the tribe, the history of the great ancestor whose existence and timeless adventures are at the origin of the line to which his initiation connects him. This traditional knowledge is acquired in the course of ceremonies and trials that use various techniques (fasts, drugs, isolation) to bring about an emotionally intense encounter with the things held to be sacred, and in which fear (before the mystery) plays an important role.

Metaphors of gestation, regeneration, and the birth process make the initiation a form of birth: not the first, physical birth by extraction from the mother's body, but a second birth, by way of the spirits, the ancestors, the fathers. This latter aspect of initiation reveals one of its essential dimensions: becoming a "man" (*anēr, vir*) in a sense means ceasing to be one's mother's child so as to become one's father's son—not so much the son of one's own real father as of the dead fathers, the ancestors. It means becoming a descendant of the founding male line, heir to the eponymous founding hero. Only the son of the fathers can become a father in his turn. Thus, at bottom the ritual passage at puberty is a violent uprooting from the world of mothers, and a symbolic incorporation into the company of fathers and the chain of ancestors. Only this regendering through the fathers and inscription into their genealogy allows access to manhood and makes marriage and procreation possible.

The simply parental or familial description of the puberty rite, matrix of all initiations, is thus straightforward: violent separation from the mother, and incorporation into the fathers' world, with the acquisition of the status of "manhood" that makes marriage and procreation possible. Initiation is a passage and a break: from a close relation with the mother's world to a nonincestuous (exogamous) liaison with a woman, the ancestors serving as intermediaries. Shattering the mother-child symbiosis, the father introduces himself as a third party into this more or less murky two-way relationship; he cuts their union to the quick (wounding both mother and child, for both experience the separation as a loss) in order to bring the son to birth in a new kinship, defined now by symbolic paternity.

This process, which is at the heart of initiation, accounts at multiple levels for the violence that necessarily presides over an initiation, whether that violence is visibly manifested in a rite (by the extraction of teeth, a bodily incision, torture of any sort) or in more spiritualized forms (fear, the dark night of the soul). Something must be cut: a powerful vital link, an umbilical cord, must be painfully and irreversibly severed. A way of being has to die, has to be killed, so a new way of life can appear. What is severed is a certain relationship of fusion with the maternal dimension. What is at stake is not of course merely the external and visible bond, but something more powerful and more deeply rooted, with respect to which the person of the real mother is almost unimportant. In fact, the central initiatory trial makes the postulant both a victim and an assassin. On the one hand, something has to be cut, painfully severed. And at the same time, this ordeal (which will allow another birth) is also, mythically, the active killing of the enveloping, clawing, stifling, all-encompassing part of the "mother," that part that prevents the young man's growth, keeps him focused on the past, retards his vital development in a dangerous and deadly fashion. In a word, the postulant suffers mortally as he kills what binds him. The killing of the mother (or rather of the devouring, all-encompassing, suffocating maternal dimension) is the torment of the killer. One of the two complementary aspects of the ordeal (passive suffering or active heroism) can be stressed in a given initiatory or mythic episode, but these apparently contrary aspects are at bottom one and the same. Each takes its place only at the heart of the other.

Let us be careful to avoid one of the shoals on which psychoanalysis has foundered. It is not appropriate to use the single term "castration" to interpret all the operations of severing encompassed by initiation, as if the term could account for them all and reduce them to a sexual signification. Circumcision, subincision, scarification, the pulling of teeth or hair, all these refer to a sacrificial cutting of which the image of castration is only one possible symbolization. In a chain of equivalences whose ultimate meaning remains necessarily an unknown quantity, a meaning that transcends all figurations and that the notion of "sacrificial severing" approaches only in a very abstract way, the bloody image of the severing of genital organs is in turn only one of the possible valences. Like the others, it signifies that the postulant is mutilated in his innermost being, at the very source of his power to exist and his capacity for jouissance—but the foreshortened sex organ itself is merely a metaphor for such mutilation, even if we are prepared to view it, within a certain fantasmatic context, as the most evocative image, the one with the most powerful resonances.

The most powerful, but not necessarily the most complete. Gouging out an eye, for example, does not symbolize castration; it is a different way of symbolizing the sacrificial severing that emphasizes not its sexual meaning but its relation to knowledge, to "light." The assertion of an unknown signification of which castration is only one possible image is important if we are to avoid disqualifying, a priori, all the nuanced wealth of meanings (physical, mental, spiritual, and so on) that are attached, each in its own way, to the metaphorization of that unknown. The play of equivalences is what allows us to intuit what that sacrificial severing means, and not the forced reduction of everything that symbolizes the severing to a single, explicit signified. The sacrificial severing is not merely an operation that can be summed up by a mutilation of the sexualized body; it involves a trial that is experienced by the entire being. We have to map out the full spectrum of all these significations, intuitions, and images.

"Killing of the dark mother" and "sacrifice of the son" are two symbolic expressions for a single event. It is a question of a tortuous tearing in which the maternal root is cut off: the mother-monster dies of it, as does the son-of-the-mother who lived only through that bond. The severing of the snake-mother is both the assassination of a terrible dragon and the bloody sacrifice of the son-of-the-mother. The hero who carries out this act, sword in hand—mobilizing all his aggressive powers, and not simply the shrewdness of pure intelligence—is at once murderer and victim. He will have to die for his murder. But the double death will nevertheless constitute his victory, his renaissance as a son of his ancestors.

Thus, both the heroic victory over the monster and the "defeat" that leads to death and fragmentation are placed, according to the mythicoritual variants, at precisely the same moment of the hero's adventure, and they present an identical meaning: at issue in each case is a murder that coincides with the confrontation of destructive forces in terror, dismemberment, and separation. The one who dies and the one who kills are the same. The hero's killing of the dragon is the killing of a part of himself, an event that also signifies his own death, his own mortal, fragmenting, agonizing loss.

The connections between rite and myth are not completely straightforward, however, insofar as the hero's fight with the (female) dragon is concerned. The struggle typically allows the hero to liberate a young woman and to acquire a kingdom; this makes its initiatory significance all the clearer. Yet myths and rites are not easy to articulate in detail, in this regard. The chief difficulty arises from the existence of two seemingly incompatible motifs. On the one hand (and this motif is unanimously expressed in particular by the rites), the dragon is supposed to swallow, devour, and digest the neophyte who will undergo a temporary death, but who will be regurgitated and spit out again in the end as a new man. On the other hand (and this motif is expressed in particular by the myths), the dragon is killed by a hero as part of the victorious outcome of a difficult and bloody armed combat.

These two episodes may appear hard to reconcile. Their incompatibility is nevertheless attenuated by the great number of narratives that describe the murder of the dragon from within, from inside the belly of the beast. The hero is swallowed up, ingurgitated; he passes some time in the monster's burning bowels, but there too he attacks victoriously. He tears out the monster's heart, cuts her belly open so he can get away, and so on. The hero is thus not only the one who is swallowed and who dies, he is also the one who kills the swallower. What is more, the myth seems to stipulate, as Propp puts it concisely, that "one can only kill the swallower by being swallowed."[2] The hero has to hurl himself inside the beast, has to penetrate it, let himself be ingurgitated so he can proceed to kill the monster and come back to the light of day. Thus, the ritual and archaic signification of the myth is presumably better preserved in the narratives in which the hero penetrates into the bowels of the monster than in those where he kills her from outside.

With the disappearance of the rite, the significance of the acts of swallowing and regurgitation is blurred. The monster remains a devouring creature (this is true of both the Chimaera and the Sphinx, "eaters of raw flesh"), but the young men devoured are not the same as the stronger or cleverer young man who kills the monster. Hero myths retain only the aspect of victory, forgetting the more ambiguous element of swallowing-up and "death," or rather attributing that element to the unhappy hero in a schism unknown in initiatory rites. The struggle no longer takes place inside the dragon, in the depths of her belly, but outside. According to Propp, the many tales in which the hero throws heated stones or magic objects to provoke the swallower's death from the inside, rather than penetrating the dragon's body directly himself, are later versions recalling, by substitution, an initial situation in which the heroic neophyte is swallowed up himself. The story of Bellerophon offers another instance of this motif in which a burning object penetrates the monster's body: the lead at the tip of Bellerophon's lance melts on contact with the flames coming out of the Chimaera's mouth and kills her from within.

The Greek material, however, preserves the memory of the hero's entry into the dragon's innermost depths. According to one version of the myth, in order to save Hesione, Heracles leaped into the maw of the sea dragon and stayed there three days, during which he lost all his hair because of the raging heat inside the monster; he emerged victorious after cutting up the beast's stomach.[3] But Heracles' descent into Hades to capture Cerberus (the last and most difficult of his tasks) can also be understood as signifying a gigantic swallowing-up. In initiation rites, the monster's belly is constantly identified with the other world, or the world of the dead. Descents *in inferno* or *in utero* (or under the earth, generally through a cave) have identical meanings. Any descent into Hades (including Aeneas's) has the same initiatory meaning as ingurgitation by a monster.

Another testimony to the rite of swallowing followed by regurgitation is the astonishing Attic vase picture showing Jason being regurgitated in front of Athena by the dragon guarding the Golden Fleece. This representation corresponds to no known literary version of the myth, but its archaic ritual meaning is hardly open to doubt.

The motifs of the hero being swallowed up by a monster and then killing the monster from within have all but disappeared from most mythic versions for reasons that are not entirely clear: perhaps because, as the associated rites were forgotten, the motifs became incomprehensible and implausible, or perhaps because they were replaced by more elaborate versions like the descent into hell. In any event, these motifs have to be understood in connection with the active murder of the monster. In a first, passive phase, the initiate is swallowed up into the world of the dead, the bowels of Mother Earth, the cosmic matrix—all these meanings are homogeneous with "the dragon's belly." But at the darkest point in this sojourn he survives death and wages active battle. He uses force to destroy the vital principle of the monstrous animal; he appropriates that principle (or the treasure the animal was guarding) for himself, and his victory signifies a new birth. Although Greek heroic myths emphasize the active exploit, and tend to suppress or consign to a lower level the phase of devouring by the monster, or else to consider it as a stage from which the hero escapes by his own strength and with the help of the gods, the fact remains that both of these phases, passive and active, must be taken into account if we are to grasp the full import of the mythicoritual images of initiation.

In any case, the killing of the dragon is the decisive phase of the heroic or initiatory work, the phase that makes the liberation of the young woman possible. Here again, no matter what variants we may find (the young woman may be incarcerated by, or imprisoned inside, the monster; she may be handed over for the monster to devour, or offered up as the stakes of a battle, and so on), in the standard myth, at the moment of victory over the monster and thus at the moment of initiatory renaissance, the young woman is always liberated and obtained in marriage.

~

In light of the ethnological evidence, it is virtually certain that the Sphinx belongs to the category of teranthropomorphic beings that regularly come forward in liminal ritual situations—on the threshold of the trial. Scholars have occasionally insisted on the pedagogical function of these monsters: to shatter the initiate's conformist and secular world view, free him from the trivialities of daily life, and also frighten and disorient him, so as to manifest the anguishing power of the sacred.[4] These divinities, masters of initiation, are the ones who mutilate, devour, kill the novice. The dismemberment of the boy's body, which is supposed to be eaten raw (*ōmophagia*), following the model of the death of the young Dionysus dismembered by the Titans, is part of the Dionysian rites. The fact that some have understood the killing of the initiate as an actual occurrence is due of course to a concretizing and literalizing misinterpretation. The description of the initiation rites of other cultures gives us a better perspective on the rites of ancient Greece.[5]

The Sphinx, "eater of raw flesh,"[6] is unquestionably one of the mythicoritual representations of the monster who presides over initiations. She simultaneously protects the mysteries and offers access to them. This ambivalence recalls the destiny of the initiate as he confronts the teranthropomorphic initiator: the novice is at once the initiator's victim and its killer. The novice is killed, swallowed up by the primordial animal, but at the same time he kills the animal heroically; he ends up by putting on the animal's skin, appropriating its strength and all the qualities it symbolizes. The irreducible complexity that we find again and again in the oldest mythicoritual situations and that is glossed over in the heroic myths (in which the hero seems to survive by killing but without experiencing his own death) refers to a double movement inherent in the initiatory passage. The myth attempts to make this apparent contradiction logical by introducing a temporal opposition: the Sphinx (or the Chimaera) kills travelers, but a hero finally kills her and gains access to what she was protecting.

At the moment of initiatory passage, the women in many cases are convinced that their sons are about to be killed and devoured by a hostile divinity whose true name they may not know but whose muted, thunderous rumblings they have heard.[7] The mothers weep for the novices as people weep for the dead. If we compare this ritual to the passage in Euripides' *Phoenician Women* where the chorus describes the ravages of the Sphinx, we cannot help but be struck by the analogy. The Sphinx, "the wingèd maid, the mountain portent of grief . . . whose music was no music at all," came to carry off the young men on behalf of a bloodthirsty god, while the women, mothers and virgins, grieved over the young men's disappearance. Euripides expresses the laments of these women in a few syncopated phrases:

> You came, you came,
> you wingèd thing, earth's offspring, monster's child,
> to seize the sons of Cadmus.
> Half a maiden, a fearful beast,
> with roving wings and claws that fed on blood.
> You who snatched the youths from Dirce's plain,
> crying your Fury's shriek,
> the song that knows no music,
> you brought, you brought sorrows upon our land,
> bloody ones—and bloody was the god
> who brought these things about.
> Mournings of the mothers,
> mournings of the maidens,
> filled our homes with grief.
> Groan and cry ran back and forth
> from one to another through the town,
> and thunder groaned as they did
> each time the wingèd bird seized one of the city's men.[8]

Nothing is missing from the evocation, in Euripides' text, of a ritual kidnapping of novices by a monstrous being accompanied by the laments of grieving women: "Mournings of the mothers, mournings of the maidens, filled our homes with grief." The expression of grief is clearly not an isolated incident but an authentic ritual in which an entire group of mothers and virgins participates. "Groan and cry ran back and forth from one to another through the town." Significantly, there is no mention of grieving fathers. The young men have been forcibly removed from their mothers, and the "bloody god" in whose name the young men disappear from the sight of their devastated mothers is the god who demands that they become warriors and thus men.

Euripides' text also indicates that the Sphinx, the terrible monster with roving wings, "snatched the youths from Dirce's plain," that is, from a cave that was the source of the river Dirce, and also the lair of "bloody Ares," the dragon guarding the spring whom Cadmus killed and whose teeth Cadmus planted, giving birth to an entire army ("the race that grew from the teeth of the crimson-crested monster"). But the source of the river Dirce is also the birthplace of Dionysus, or rather of the "second birth" of the god who had been snatched away by his father, Zeus, in his sixth month of gestation, from the womb of his thunderstruck mother Semele; Zeus sewed him up in his own thigh and brought him forth at term, fully developed and alive.

> —O Dirce, holy river,
> child of Achelöus' water,
> yours the springs that welcomed once
> divinity, the son of Zeus!
> For Zeus the father snatched his son
> from deathless flame, crying:
> *Dithyrambus, come!*
> *Enter my male womb.*[9]

Now, the initiatory significance of this second birth is beyond all doubt: the novice adolescent has to die as son-of-his-mother and he has to be engendered anew by the fathers. The obstetrical symbolism of this reengenderment is one of the best-verified constants of the metaphors of initiation. And every initiate repeats the story of this "twice-born" god.

It may seem surprising that the weeping and wailing of the mothers and virgins are said to be like "thunder [that] groaned . . . each time the wingèd bird seized one of the city's men." As it happens, in ancient Greece the *rhombos*, an instrument used during initiations (identical to the "bull-roarer" described by ethnologists), produced a low rumbling sound that was quite specifically identified with the sound of thunder, "the thunder of Zagreus." In the ancient rites, the women who heard the *rhombos* believed that they were hearing the ancestors coming to carry their sons off to the world of the dead. The only anomaly is that Euripides seems to attribute the thundering noise to the cries and sobs of the women themselves (the comparison is not self-evident, moreover), whereas in initiations the sound is perceived as the voice of the dead and the ancestors. The fact remains, nevertheless, that this association of the Sphinx's kidnapping of young men, the mourning cries of their mothers, and the rumbling of thunder seems to echo ancient puberty rites of passage.

The Greeks were inclined to attribute an Egyptian origin, often erroneously, to whatever struck them as archaic and mysterious. Thus, legend frequently credits ancient Egypt, land of tombs and Sphinxes, with the earliest initiations. According to one legend, it was Cadmus who brought the initiatory practices from Egypt; Cadmus was simultaneously viewed as the mythic inventor of the alphabet.[10] Consequently, we may be entitled to suspect that the legend according to which the Greek Sphinx is of Egyptian origin (although distinguishable from the Egyptian Sphinx by virtue of its wings and its female gender)[11] is somehow related to the legend according to which the initiations Cadmus brought to Thebes were of Egyptian origin. Now, Cadmus is Oedipus' great-great-grandfather. In this light, Sophocles' emphasis on the founding ancestor of Thebes, from the very first words spoken in *Oedipus the King* ("My children, generations of the living in the line of Kadmos"), may well have an oblique significance, as may the discourse of the priest who addresses Oedipus shortly afterward. Referring to Thebes as the devastated "house of Cadmus," the priest goes on to say: "You freed us from the Sphinx, you came to Thebes and cut us loose from the bloody tribute we had paid that harsh, brutal singer."[12] If it is Cadmus himself, Oedipus's great-great-grandfather, who is credited with instituting initiatory practices, and thus with introducing the sacrificial ordeal of the Sphinx, the signifying link between the "house of Cadmus" and "the bloody tribute . . . paid that harsh, brutal singer" may be closer than an unprepared reading might suggest.

But another approach may clarify the Sphinx's place in initiation. It is generally recognized that tragic theater originated in Dionysiac ritual, even though later tragedy came to include many non-Dionysiac elements drawn from epics, hero cults, and ceremonies that lacked any direct connection with Dionysus. Nevertheless, the very forms of tragedy retain clear traces of the primitive Dionysiac drama and of the initiations that replay its scenario of death and rebirth.

We know that in the earliest stage, theatrical spectacles consisted of a tetralogy that included three tragedies and a satyric drama. This arrangement faithfully repeated the unfolding of a myth-icoritual scenario of Dionysiac initiation. Whereas the three tragedies dealt in succession with (1) the struggles and sufferings of the god, (2) his bodily dismemberment, and (3) the mourning laments that accompany his death, the satyr play corresponded to the joy and hilarity that greeted his rebirth.

This ultimate phase, brazen and explosive, also corresponded to the final phase of initiation, namely, marriage. Here we find the well-attested connection between the intervention of the Dionysiac troop of Satyrs and the emergence of the young girl, the ascent (*anodos*) of Kore. The young girl leaves the infernal regions to emerge from the earth, which can then recover its springtime vegetation, its fertility.

We also know that in the historical development of tragedy an important differentiation evolved: the satyr play became more and more distinct from the three tragedies that preceded it. It lost its archaic significance as the final phase of the Dionysiac initiatory drama. Tragedy became independent and distinct as a genre in itself; it became the essence of the drama, apart from the theophanic episode (the appearance of the god), which is sometimes retained at the end.[13]

Aeschylus's tragedies seem to have preserved their trilogical and even tetralogical structure. Aeschylus was the author of a Theban trilogy that included *Laïus*, *Oedipus*, and *The Seven Against Thebes*; of these only the third tragedy remains. A satyric piece, completing the cycle, was entitled *The Sphinx*. Taken together, these texts would undoubtedly have shed a crucial light on our approach to the Oedipus myth. As Gilbert Murray remarks, "it would be interesting to know how Dionysus and his train were brought into connection with the Sphinx and Oedipus and whether there was any appearance of the God as deliverer or bringer of new life."[14]

However, regarding the relations between Dionysus and the Sphinx, certain iconographic documents are extremely informative. The Vagnonville bowl is noteworthy in this respect. It provides the missing link in our effort to establish the ritual and mythic connection between the "dog who speaks in riddles" and the young god of resurrecting drunkenness. A Sphinx is seated atop a tumulus that is being attacked with picks by two Satyrs. The sepulchral character of the mound is beyond question. As in similar cases, here a stone base pierced with holes supports a mound of earth.[15] This bowl, mentioned by Jane Harrison, is not the only one of its type. A black, red-figured bowl painted by Myson also shows two Satyrs destroying a tomb with picks. A Sphinx is seated atop the tumulus.[16] Similar representations of horse-tailed Satyrs working to break open a tomb by force are found in numerous other instances, without the Sphinx but with an additional element that provides the key to the meaning of the scene: from the earth, through the tomb, the head and shoulders of a young girl arise. What we see in these virtually canonical images is the ascension (*anodos*) of Kore. A number of vases represent this *anodos*, the mythic moment when a young girl, still enclosed within the rounded contours of a tumulus, reaches upward, her body half free from the earth, her hands or arms raised. Her emergence is greeted by the ecstatic dance of goat-footed Pans and horse-tailed Satyrs. Dionysus himself, with his thyrsus, awaits the moment of breakthrough. A winged Eros is sometimes represented. In certain cases there seems to be some contamination between Kore's ascent within the sepulchral mound and Pandora's emergence from the vase that contained her; this would explain why the Satyrs or Pans use either a pick or a hammer similar to the one used by Hephaestus. But this contamination only strengthens the meaning attached to the image of the young girl. Pandora is a virgin in the process of being born; what is more, her emergence from the vase is the birth of the first woman.[17]

See note 15

See note 16

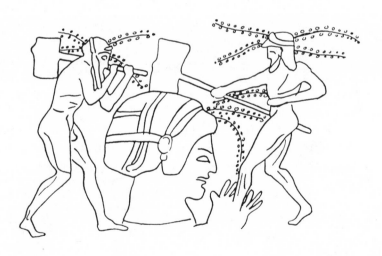

See note 17

We may deduce then that the Sphinx represented on the Vagnonville bowl or the one painted by Myson is not simply a disquieting monster, a *Kēr* haunting a tomb. The presence of two
Satyrs who are making the same gestures and who possess the same
attributes as the ones breaking open the mound from which a Kore
will emerge attests to a more specific function. By juxtaposing these
images, we can reconstitute a crucial fragment of a ritual and
mythic drama that resituates the Oedipus story within a broader
complex that has not been analyzed as such up to now. As we have
surmised, the Sphinx and the young girl are closely connected. The
Sphinx guards a tumulus in which the young girl is held prisoner
(contained). The neophyte finds himself confronting this guardian
during the course of his telestic itinerary. But only the final intervention of Dionysus's Satyrs to break open the mound with picks
or hammers can make Kore's *anodos* possible, can allow the young
girl to emerge from the chtonian depths in which she had been
enveloped. Here we have both the satyric phase of the Dionysian
drama and the final phase of the young man's initiation: the
deliverance of the girl who is to be his bride. But a purely intellectual confrontation with the Sphinx does not suffice to achieve this
end. There is no doubt about it: the neophyte has to be "killed" by
the Sphinx, has to suffer difficult and painful trials that amount to a
form of death, a descent into Hades—even if that "descent" begins
with the protagonist being wafted aloft in the claws of the winged
guardian.

In the Oedipus story, the protagonist uses unconventional means
to triumph over the Sphinx (he succeeds without the help of the
gods, through reflective intelligence alone), and he does not make it
to the final phase of the telestic itinerary. He does not liberate the
young girl who is kept inside the tomb by the monster. For the
Sphinx to be truly vanquished, the intervention of Dionysus is
required; the *hubris* of an autonomous Apollonian reflection does
not suffice: this observation more than confirms our interpretation
of the Oedipus myth as a tragedy of failed initiation.

We should also recall that the famous circular representation of
Oedipus seated in front of the Sphinx, who is perched on a sort of

column, comes from the inside of a bowl[18] whose exterior represents a series of horse-tailed (nonithyphallic) Satyrs. In this scene, which is not easy to interpret, one of the Satyrs seems to be attempting to strike a young boy, while another bears an amphora. Here again the association—to my knowledge neglected up to now—on a single bowl between the Sphinx (in a central and interior position) and a family of Satyrs (around the external wall of the bowl) would be hard to pass off as an effect of pure chance. It offers an astonishing corroboration of a situation we have previously encountered: a monument with the Sphinx perched on top and a joyous band of Satyrs frolicking around the base. There is even a curious vase painting in which a seated Satyr replaces the Sphinx on her pedestal in front of Oedipus. It is as if the triggering of the satyric phase had to coincide with the moment of response.[19] There is thus a close connection between the Sphinx and the Dionysian Satyrs in their function as markers of the final phase of initiation.

If the Sphinx was originally intended to be positioned on top of a tumulus (the tomb of a Kore to be delivered from the power of Hades), we can understand why representations of "Oedipus before the Sphinx" constantly depict her seated on an artificial support, a sort of pedestal or column, rather than a rock. In certain representations, the column is particularly large, evoking a burial monument. It may be that the Sphinx is a guardian of tombs in some general way, and that she is used in this sense as a figure of sepulchral ornamentation. But when the tomb in question is one that Satyrs are about to break open, we can only conclude that the motif of rebirth is involved. And the resemblance with Kore's reascension is so striking that we need hardly hesitate to see these representations as depicting the emergence into daylight of the girl delivered from the kingdom of the dead and promised to a fruitful coupling by the joyous announcers of spring's renewal and the return of sexual fervor. This implication of renaissance doubtless even accounts for the use of the Sphinx in sepulchral ornamentation. In this view, the winged virgin with predator's claws is not merely the guardian of a tomb, like the griffins or snakes that protect a treasure from desecration by looters; she is the symbol of the resurrection of the soul (which is also a winged virgin) after death. Real death and initiatory death: the two are indistinguishable if real death is, like the other, also a passage, the ultimate passage.

The fact that the Sphinx is so frequently depicted in Greek funerary iconography[20] is significant in this respect. The role of the Sphinx appears quite different here from what we might be led to expect from the evidence of texts or of many more recent monuments in which the monster is specifically linked with the Oedipus legend. In statuary and funerary bas-relief, the Sphinx is often shown with a paw posed on the severed head of the deceased: she is the animal that seizes the dead person's soul to drag it off to Hades. By decapitation and the imposition of the clawed foot, the Sphinx offers the deceased the promise of immortality; she guarantees his survival in the next world. The Sphinx is depicted in a highly convincing fashion as—simultaneously—the monster that kills and the monster that ensures rebirth in the other world. For one must die in order to be reborn. The symbol of the Sphinx refers to a notion whose power and persistence are very familiar, the notion that death is rebirth, and thus the supreme rite of passage. "To die is to be initiated," according to the Greek adage.[21] To conceive of dying as the crossing of an initiatory threshold, that is, as a violent separation from the secular world followed by a rebirth on another ontological level, is to express confidence in the soul's survival. The theme is such a recurrent one that we seem to be touching here on a genuine anthropological invariant. Initiation is a symbolic death, and real death is an initiation, the most solemn of the rites of passage, the most important of thresholds.

It is impossible to understand anything at all about the Oedipus story without taking into account the meaning attributed to the Sphinx as a psychopompos or guide of souls, a meaning amply attested by her insistent presence on tombs, and one that uncovers an ambivalence at the symbolic level neglected by conventional interpretations. It is remarkable that the later fascination exercised by the Oedipus legend should have tended to cover over (while never completely effacing) the Sphinx's original funerary and initiatory role, whereas this role and this role alone holds the key to the meaning of the Oedipean trial.

The Sphinx is a severer of heads. This phenomenon deserves to be pondered. It is by decapitating that she kills, so as to drag the soul into the other world. She tears off the head, the locus of human reason. Confronted with the divine Sphinx, man is obliged to renounce what has been his source of pride. She assures passage into an elsewhere that human intelligence cannot comprehend. She allows man to cross the great threshold that separates life from death and that surpasses his comprehension. Hence the riddle, which is a trial that involves the head and that requires its sacrifice. But the sacrifice of the head is precisely the sacrifice that Oedipus is unwilling to make. He reasons; he reflects; he refuses to allow himself to be robbed of his thinking ability, refuses to give up his power to reason. Oedipus philosophizes. Oedipus does not want to lose his head. Weak-footed, Oedipus is strong-minded; he is not intimidated by the Sphinx's insidious question, for to him her enigmatic profundity, the secret hiding places of meaning, the rich obscurity of hidden revelations of the initiatory arcanum (the cryptophoric symbol, in a word) is all superstition. No dimension of meaning can resist clarification, no riddle can be divine, no enigma can transcend the reflection of which a human head is capable. Keeping his wits about him, holding his head up, trusting in his own intelligence, denying the unknown, Oedipus affirms the autonomy and self-sufficiency of his own human reason. As for the head severed by the Sphinx, it is the sacrifice made by the secular ego in order to gain access by death, and after resurrection, to a higher identity.

~

It is difficult, at this point, to entertain any further doubt: the terrifying confrontation with the "winged virgin" is the mythicoritual emblem of an initiatory trial. In addition to the elements and connections that we have already adduced, we can call upon further iconographic evidence to enrich and strengthen our interpretation. This evidence has remained an almost untapped re-

See note 22

See note 23

source up to now, because without our hypothesis it is unintelligible, whereas with our hypothesis it takes on a decisive meaning. A fifth-century Attic vase[22] shows a Sphinx with unfolded wings standing on a column. Two beardless young men are seated on chairs, one on either side of the column. What is remarkable is that both young men are enveloped in cloaks pulled up over the tops of their heads. One of them appears to be holding a long knotted stick. On the other side of the vase can be seen two Satyrs (whose constant association with the Sphinx we have already noted and analyzed).

In comparison, let us look at another vase (from the fifth century B.C.) that represents a Sphinx seated on a column.[23] A bearded man is sitting on a chair in front of her. Around the man several figures are kneeling on the ground; these figures are completely enveloped in cloaks pulled up over their heads, as in the preceding representation. Only their eyes and noses can be seen.

In these two vases, what do the postures and the cloaks signify? Why are these seated characters wrapped in cloaks that cover the tops of their heads?

These representations faithfully recall, although in a strongly urbanized fashion, a ritual situation connected with the initiatory trial centered on the Sphinx. First of all, the seated posture is characteristic of mourning and initiation rites.[24] It is attested as signifying the ritual death of the neophyte, while the new birth is linked to the idea of getting up, resuming a standing position (which also signifies resurrection, *anastasis*). Furthermore, the cloaks in which the young men are completely enveloped, heads and all, are also frequently represented in scenes of mourning, especially for women. And we find this same enveloping (which may have a relationship with the shroud) elsewhere, for example in a scene representing the arrival of a newcomer in the world of Hades, led by Hermes.[25] Here we should recall that on the occasion of the Apatouriae, the Attic festival of the passage from puberty to adulthood, the shaven-headed participants wear black masks, as if in mourning; they are "on the side of the dead," dressed in the costume of ritual reclusion.[26] This black chlamys of initiatory death is probably what the neophytes are wearing as they sit before the Sphinx who is kneeling on her pillar on the two vases we are considering. The young men are the "dead," awaiting the moment, after their trial, when they will be reborn under the impulse of Dionysus.

Thus, if our reading is correct, these representations recall the ritual meaning of the Sphinx in a very specific way. It is noteworthy that this iconographic evidence offers not just a chance encounter in the mountains, but an authentic formal disposition, a ritualized staging: the Sphinx on the column with the seated, cloaked young men, terrorized, arrayed beside or around her. Compared to this situation, the presence of Oedipus offers an exceptional element, as if amid a group of eight horrified neophytes whose eyes alone are visible through the folds of their black chlamydes, the bearded Oedipus was bringing this ritual confrontation with the monster to an end. We are already far removed from the archaic "eater of raw flesh." Is it not Oedipus who, prefiguring and typifying Greek destiny, rationalized the terrible and agonizing encounter to such an extent that the riddle, a trial by language, became the sole and sufficient moment of initiatory passage?

§ 4 The Triple Trial

The prototype hero can achieve the goals of marriage and sovereignty, in the end, only if he has successfully confronted a series of trials. Whether we consider these trials as they are exposed in mythic form or in the ritual form that must have been closely tied to the myths, the presumption that the heroic trials signified preparation for marriage and kingship does not leave much room for doubt. The anomalies of Oedipus's marriage and his accession to power can only suggest a flaw in the trial as such. It is as if (to take into account a type of transverse causality that myth and ritual constantly exemplify) there were some deficiency, some deviation with respect to the conventional progression of the investiture trials, some flaw that has specific repercussions in the anomalies of Oedipus's destiny. Confident that mythic displacements and distortions obey a rigorous logic, we may even surmise that each of the two criminal deviations that constitute the tragedy of Oedipus's fate corresponds to a specific lack or defect. For the confrontation of the trials obeys a rule; it is inscribed within a sacred tradition. Any distortion necessarily entails serious consequences, which are not just random but are strictly tied, by symbolic causality, to the nature of the distortion. The preparation for kingship, as an initiatory ritual (and no doubt as the quintessential example of any initiation allowing access to manhood in the passage at puberty), would not be valid without scrupulous respect for the sacred requirements.

But can the standard mythic or ritual trials be clearly delineated, so as to mark more precisely those that, in contrast, are missing in Oedipus's case? Oedipus's major exploit, the one that rendered him worthy of marriage and the kingdom, is that he freed Thebes from the crafty virgin, the "eater of raw flesh," by solving her riddle. In our initial analysis we were struck by the exclusively intellectual character of this trial, in contrast with the typical trial, which always presents at least one bloody episode. These distinctions need further exploration, however. Our analysis has to be extended to a new level of interpretation at this point, a level quite distinct from the conclusions reached so far.

Our narrative and comparative exegesis of the Oedipus myth has demonstrated the myth's structural anomaly, and has allowed its characterization as a myth of failed or avoided initiation (or of irregular royal investiture). This initial conclusion, reached by a methodology relying principally upon the differential analysis of narrative motifs, seems likely to withstand even hostile suspicions and well-documented critiques. Now it is a question of going one step further on the basis of a more specific interpretation. If this new interpretation—which provides increased coherence and greater amplitude to the results already achieved—should be deemed in the long run overly hypothetical or excessively adventurous, those earlier results would not be threatened; indeed, even if the new interpretation had to be abandoned entirely for some unforeseeable reason (historical, mythographical, etc.), such a move would not invalidate what has gone before. Part of the mythicoritual rationality of the Oedipean narrative would be lost, along with the theoretical or even philosophical advantage of its insertion within a broader ideological framework; but this loss, however disappointing to our desire for maximum intelligibility, would not undermine the basis of the foregoing exegesis. Thus, I shall venture to proceed with this supplementary interpretation, whose explanatory power will become increasingly evident.

In his work on the "crushing demons" with which he identified the Sphinx, the mythologist Ludwig Laistner pointed out a century ago that these mythical or legendary demons impose three types of trials on their victims: caresses, blows, and questions.[1] As for the Sphinx, it is striking that she is known not only as a monster who proposes a difficult or insoluble riddle, but also as a brutal killer (severer of heads, eater of raw flesh), and furthermore, as Marie Delcourt has astutely noted, as a dangerous sexual seductress who threatens to carry young men off in a lethal erotic abduction.

If, instead of seeking to distinguish among these trials as so many disparate versions of an ill-established mythic figure, we consider them in their totality, it is eminently clear that they correspond quite precisely to the three functional domains (the sacred, war, agricultural and sexual fertility) that Georges Dumézil repeatedly designated in his pathbreaking studies that seek to demonstrate the recurrence and the fundamental structuring role of these domains in the Indo-European cultural arena.[2] Caresses, blows, and questions: the first trial concerns sexual desire, the second, physical strength, and the third, intelligence. The three functional domains described by Dumézil are all here, in inverse order. The meaning of the trials is becoming clear: they appeal, in a graduated and systematic way, to the three virtues that characterize Dumézil's three functions. By resisting the seductress's caresses, the hero must demonstrate the virtue of temperance, must surmount his lustful tendencies. By standing up to blows, the hero must prove his courage and physical strength. Finally, by answering questions, the hero must deploy all the resources of his knowledge and intelligence.

It is not hard to pinpoint a very resistant structure here that must have belonged to the mythicoritual mechanisms of initiation in the cultural arenas Dumézil analyzed. As he indicated, and as his followers demonstrated in greater detail, the Indo-European king is situated above the tripartite functionality, as it were: the king accomplishes the synthesis of the three functions in his own person. Neither priest nor warrior nor farmer, he belongs to each of these groups simultaneously, even as he is situated above all of them.[3]

As Dumézil showed, one of the salient features of the exploit in almost all Indo-European myths is the tripartite nature of the adversary. The three-headed demon of Indo-Iranian legend kills the god Indra; the stone giant with the three-cornered heart slays the god Thôrr; the three snakes of the three hearts of Mech appear in Irish myth; Heracles kills the three-headed Geryon; finally, in what is no doubt a later formula, the Celtic hero Cúchulainn kills three superhuman brothers in succession, as one of the Horaces kills the three Curiatii in the Roman legend. Dumézil even adds the *tarvos trigaranos*, "bull with three cranes," of Gallic imagery.

Although in *Horace et les Curiaces*, published in 1942, Dumézil showed the stability of the motif of the adversary's tripartite nature in the heroic exploit, at that stage in his research he did not yet connect this triplicity to the functional tripartition.[4] Little by little, however, it became clearer that initiation must have involved qualities and perils corresponding to the three functions.

The king is generally credited with good deeds and positive qualities, or on the contrary with calamities and defects, that are clearly distributed within the trifunctional framework. Talismans corresponding to these three functions, bringing together their virtues and powers, are also attributed to the king. Thus, in Dumézil's perspective, the operation of acquiring these virtues is ritualized by a triple initiatory trial. Three levels of initiation correspond to the three types of functional trials (the sacred, war, fertility) that the postulant must traverse in order to become a king, or more broadly speaking, an accomplished man. An increasing number of indications prove that not only royal investiture but very probably also to a great extent rites of passage marking the entry of young men into adult life were originally conceived within a trifunctional perspective.[5] In the Cretan system, for example, at the point where the young man passes into adult society he ritually receives three objects—a steer, battle garb, and a bowl—each of which has a place in the functional framework. In this view, then, the goal of the initiatory rite of passage at puberty or upon royal investiture was the production of accomplished men, men who symbolically united the qualities corresponding to the three functions: the sacred, war, and agrarian productivity.

Our reckoning with the tripartite division of the initiatory trials, a division that is not immediately apparent in the foregoing narratological analysis (but that will become apparent in the course of the more thorough exegesis to follow) unquestionably constitutes a crucially important resource for our approach. For if the regular trial (at least in the cultural arena to which the myths in question belong) implies a triplicity that corresponds to the Dumézilean functional domains, then what is lacking in an irregular initiatory trial can be designated with unexpected precision, and it can be inscribed within an extremely powerful symbolic mechanism, a mechanism that weaves inextricably together the timeless imperatives of a social imaginary and the constraints inherent in the constitution of the subject—here in the exemplary form of the hero.

Now, this trifunctional approach to the interpretation of myths is corroborated in a striking way if one considers (and to my knowledge this has not been done to date) the morphology that the Greek myths attribute to the monsters we know as the Sphinx and the Chimaera.

The Sphinx, as the myth tells us, consists of three components: the head of a woman, the body of a lion, the wings of an eagle. It is clear that, without pushing the mythological data too far, we can connect each of these parts with one of Dumézil's three functions. The woman is the seductive component corresponding to the sexual trial that is characteristic of the third function. The lion's body is related to the values of warriorlike strength proper to the second function. As for the eagle's wings, through their affinity with the heavens and with the animal associated with Zeus, they constitute a no less clear symbol of the first function.

The Sphinx thus has the manifest significance of "triple adversary," much more strikingly even than does the three-headed Geryon. The latter is only triple in a global sense, through a multiplication that is perhaps only a way of emphasizing his strength, since the myth makes no distinctions among the three heads. The imaginary morphology of the Sphinx, on the other hand, retains the functional differentiation of the probative exploits. To undergo the trial of the Sphinx, to vanquish this monster authentically, is to demonstrate possession of the three major qualities that correspond to the functional tripartition. First, temperance, which allows the protagonist to avoid giving in to the sensual provocation of a woman.[6] Second, courage, the ability to mobilize the warrior's fury, the power to fight against a lion and like a lion. Finally, intelligence, understanding of higher and divine matters, knowledge of the sacred dimension with which the riddle is most directly concerned. Only victory over this adversary who is at once single and triple allows the neophyte to become an initiate, a complete man (*teleios anthrōpos*) who integrates within himself the qualities corresponding to the three functional levels.

It is noteworthy that this tripartite morphology of the monster is also present in the case of the Chimaera. Most versions of the myth agree in attributing three parts to the composite body of Bellerophon's adversary: the body of a goat, the head of a lion, the hindquarters of a snake. This is how Hesiod presents the Chimaera, "who had three heads, one of a grim-eyed lion, another of a goat, and another of a snake, a fierce dragon."[7] Here again, each separate part can easily and confidently be correlated with one of the functional levels. The goat, an agricultural asset, is a source of milk and, in Greek myth, a wetnurse par excellence. The goat Amaltheia fed Zeus in infancy; her horn became the horn of plenty and provided a mythic designation for other symbols of agrarian wealth.[8] Furthermore, the couplings of goats with shepherds were reputed to result in the birth of Satyrs. These two aspects, nutritive and sexual, both refer to the third function. The lion corresponds no less clearly to the warrior function, as it does in the case of the Sphinx. As for the snake, its meaning may be varied and ambivalent, not easily reduced to a single formula that would apply in every case. We can nevertheless acknowledge that in contrastive terms, and to the extent that the attribution of the two other components leaves no room for doubt, the serpent is related here to the first function, especially in its magical and mysterious form. In the myths of Teiresias, Cassandra, and Melampus, contact with snakes purifies and gives the gift of prophecy, which is a first-function quality.

The importance of the triplicity of the monstrous body appears in a striking way in certain three-dimensional representations of the Chimaera, in which three heads—lion, goat, and snake—emerge from a single, rather undifferentiated body as if lined up one behind the other. Beyond the fact that the Chimaera is attested among the Hittites, whose fidelity to Indo-European tradition has been demonstrated, the trifunctional interpretation is all the more plausible in that the composition of the Chimaera stands out by a kind of obvious arbitrariness. Why a lion, a goat, and a snake? Is the goat such a threatening animal that it must be included among the components of a tripartite monster?

Thus, the Chimaera, like the Sphinx, can be viewed as a triple adversary that the hero must conquer by demonstrating his possession of the three types of virtue characteristic of each of the functional levels. In the Chimaera, however, the component of female seduction seems less transparent than in the Sphinx. The Chimaera's head is not the head of a virgin with the power to enchant, but the head of a lion with fiery breath. In the Bellerophon story, two episodes concern the hero's resistance to feminine seduction, which might account for the limited presence of this motif in his confrontation with the Chimaera. A queen, the wife of Bellerophon's host, attempts to seduce the protagonist, but he declines her advances. Later, in the war against the king of Lycia, he goes to battle supported by the advancing wave of the sea; his men plead with him in vain, but the women, by taking off their clothes, succeed in getting him to withdraw. Not that he yields to a repulsive force, but he responds rather, according to Plutarch, out of modesty. Dumézil, relating this episode to other mythic narratives, underlines the initiatory significance of this motif of the "shameless women."[9]

In other respects, the ongoing controversy over the historical origins of the Sphinx may not be resolved, but it can be circumvented by the tripartite interpretation of the composite mythic monsters. Without claiming that the winged Sphinx is a Hellenic creation or even of Indo-European origin (although it is also attested, like the Chimaera, among the Hittites)—indeed, whatever its earliest origins and whatever the conditions of its eventual borrowing may have been (and as to those conditions, nothing certain has yet been established)—we may venture to suppose that a tripartite interpretation has adapted its symbolic configuration, adjusting it to the conditions of a structure of thought that is known to have been extraordinarily resilient in the course of multiple transpositions and displacements. This would not be the first case in which such an appropriation has been detected; it could be compared to the reclassification within the tripartite theological vision of divinities who were not originally of Indo-European formation—Hera, Athena, Aphrodite in the judgment of Paris. The interpretation of the tripartite structure of the initiatory monster that is proposed here, while it may appear slightly venture-some, or even somewhat forced for the purposes of the argument, will be corroborated in a startling manner, as I shall show further on, by Plato himself, for in one passage in the *Republic*, Plato reconstitutes a monstrous initiatory being according to the very same principle of the functional tripartition.[10]

If the vigilant dragon who guards the Golden Fleece does not present the appearance of a triple monster, like the Sphinx and the Chimaera, does this mean we should abandon the attempt to locate some traces, even vestigial ones, of the triplicity of the heroic trial in Jason's case? An attentive analysis of the successive trials Jason undergoes before achieving his ultimate victory (his conquest of the Fleece and his simultaneous departure with Medea, who helped him and whom he is to marry) offers, on the contrary, a remarkable surprise.

To be convinced of this, it suffices to reread the magnificent passage in the *Argonautica* in which Jason tries to explain to the king of Colchis the noble purpose of his voyage, and tries to persuade him to turn over the Fleece.[11] Jason explains that he has been sent by a god, and by the terrifying order of a king of Hellas. At this point Aeëtes loses his temper, becomes insulting, and refuses to hand over the Golden Fleece to an unknown foreigner. But he is soon mollified by Jason's words, for Jason indicates his willingness to enter the king's service. Aeëtes finally agrees to give him the Fleece, but only after a trial. What is the task (*aethlos*) destined to prove the young man's ardent strength (*menos*) and valor (*alkē*)? It is a prodigious and authentically royal task, since the king himself claims to be the only one capable of carrying it out. On the plain of Ares there are two brazen-footed, fire-breathing bulls. Jason's task is to yoke them and use them to plow up a four-acre fallow field. Next, he must plant the furrows, not with grains of wheat but with the teeth of a serpent, a "dragon of Ares"; as they grow, these teeth will turn into a troop of warriors, "earthborn men."[12] Jason then has to fight them, strike them down with his sword, kill them on the spot. He has to accomplish this task in a single day, between dawn and dusk, in order to be worthy of the Golden Fleece.

Accepting the challenge, he harnesses the bulls to the plow, works the soils, sows the teeth, and rests. Once the "earthborn men" have come up from the furrows, he returns to the field and (after causing confusion by hurling a boulder into their midst) kills them all before nightfall. Jason has succeeded in the trials, and within the allotted time. But Aeëtes does not keep his promises. So, during the night, with the help of Medea, who puts the dragon to sleep with drugs, the young hero approaches the oak tree onto which the coveted Fleece has been nailed, seizes the Fleece, and flees toward the ship with the girl who is to be his bride.

Now, it is worth noting, as we retrace this sequence of events, that Jason has faced three different types of trial in succession:

§ 1 He has harnessed the bulls to the brass plow, plowed a huge field, and seeded it.

§ 2 Sword in hand, he has fought the "earthborn men" and killed them.

§ 3 He has succeeded in getting the best of the watchful dragon (whom Apollonios Rhodius always calls "the serpent," *ophis*), and in seizing the Golden Fleece.

Here we are obliged to acknowledge—even if the conclusion is almost embarrassing by virtue of the perfect logic it reveals—that we have encountered a graduated series of trials, each belonging to a different functional level of the tripartite hierarchy, presented in inverse order.

The trial of the yoke, the plowing and sowing of seeds, belongs uncontestably to the realm of agricultural tasks, that is, to the third function.[13] The sword fight unmistakably belongs to the warrior function. Finally, the Golden Fleece stolen from the snake clearly appears to be a trial that directly involves the sacred (the well-guarded magic object), and thus that belongs to the first function.

The distribution of the trials among the phases of a single day is doubtless no accident. In the morning, Jason harnesses the bulls and plows the field. From afternoon to evening he fights the warriors. And during the night, he makes off with the Fleece. Thus, the triplicity of the trial is not located in the ellipsis of a composite monster who condenses into a single being the three initiatory encounters, like the Chimaera; rather, it is developed in the narrative succession of three quite distinct trials.

It is significant that Jason does not use his sword to fight the snake, who is reputedly immortal, but instead resorts to the ruse of a drug and magic formulas (administered by Medea). Here we have a pacific victory that contrasts with the preceding trial of violent struggle, a sword fight, against the "deadly harvest." The magic potion (and of course everything having to do with sorcery) is attested elsewhere as a first-function power.[14]

The Golden Fleece is easy to recognize as a "royal talisman,"[15] and thus the trials leading to its conquest also clearly have the meaning of royal investiture. But if it is quite clear in the narrative articulation that the Golden Fleece is positioned as a first-function talisman, can we find some connection that offers (apart from its substance, gold, and the fact that it comes from a miraculous flying ram sacrificed to Zeus) even more specific confirmation of this role on the basis of its very nature as fleece? Fleece, like all skin, is quite obviously related to clothing. When Jason brings the Fleece back from the wood where it was attached to an oak tree, he strides on "with the fleece covering his left shoulder from the height of his neck to his feet."[16] Jason thus cloaks himself in the Fleece as he would in a coat, the very Fleece that he has just captured (and that gleams, we are told, "like the lightning of Zeus"), before hiding it from the sight and touch of others with "a mantle newly-woven." The coat is attested in several convergent cases as one of the three functional objects that constitute part of the ritual equipment of the occasion of royal investiture, and precisely as an object pertaining to the first function.[17]

The Golden Fleece, a precious and coveted object, a royal talisman, recalls the untranslatable notion of *agalma*. Value, wealth, offering, glory, joy, honor, sign: none of these words taken separately will do. And yet "the idea of *agalma* is associated with . . . the most remote aspect of the conception of the golden fleece."[18] What is at stake is not wealth in the economic sense, of course, but power of sacred origin. It is worth noting that the acquisition of this coveted object marks the culminating phase (if not the final phase, in narrative terms) of the drama of preparation or probation Jason undergoes. It is precisely when he conquers this *agalma* by carrying out the perilous trial ordered by Pelias that he also wins Medea's heart: he steals the girl away from her father to take her off with him and make her his wife. As in every initiation, the victorious completion of the trials makes marriage possible. The Golden Fleece, we are told, serves as cover on the wedding bed.

In the case of Perseus, such a clear organization would be hard to find. There is no doubt, however, that Perseus faces a series of trials, and that he triumphs only with the help of the gods. His adventure presents the same overall movement: an initial impulse to face trials under orders from a king, and then near the final phase of the trials a confrontation with a different king, whose daughter will become the hero's wife despite obstacles put in the way of the marriage. The distinctions among the persecutor king, the dispatcher king, and the donor king are perfectly clear. We may also note that amorous desire plays a determining role in the success of the final trial. Perseus falls in love with Andromeda, whom he sees bound naked to a rock, about to be devoured by a female sea monster, and his love is what drives him into battle. In the story of Jason, it is Medea who falls in love with the young hero and provides critical help for his conquest of the coveted Fleece. Thus, Athena is not the only one who favors these heroes; in the final phase of the struggle (and only in the final phase), they also have Aphrodite's aid: we are told that she inspired Medea. The desired or desiring future bride is an essential element in the victorious outcome of the trial. The heroic adventure presents a curious tripartite chronology: Hera sends the monsters; Athena provides the courage and the means to confront them; Aphrodite supplies the desire and the opportunity for victory. The three functional goddesses thus play their roles within the strict order of the tripartition.

Now, it is significant that the ultimate amorous attraction (which can doubtless be adopted as an element of our prototype legend) is completely absent from the Oedipus myth. Oedipus is not assisted by Athena in his confrontation, nor is he helped or spurred on in his victory over the Sphinx by amorous desire for a bride he has already encountered. He succeeds all by himself, and for himself alone. Neither a king imposing a trial (at the beginning) nor a desired or desiring bride (at the end) contributes any justification or momentum to the confrontation. Oedipus's victory is pure: it is not inscribed within the traditional imaginary of qualification, that is, within the regular constraints of the initiatory situation; instead, on this point too, it proves aberrant. To be sure, in Euripides' version, Creon promises the queen's bed to the one who can explain the enigma of the crafty virgin. But Oedipus is never inspired by the desire to win a princess he loves, like Perseus, or helped by a princess who loves him, like Jason. Aphrodite is absent. She does not endorse or facilitate Oedipus's victory in any way, and this fact alerts us to the aberration of its stakes. It is as if pure will to power leads Oedipus to confront the Sphinx. Here again, only contrastive analysis allows us to bring this aspect into relief.

The regular heroic myths, those we have compared so as to discern their characteristic structure, are myths of successful royal initiation. The structural anomaly of the Oedipus myth can be accounted for in detail if we see it as a myth of failed or eluded royal initiation.

A complete royal investiture requires success in a series of three trials, each of which corresponds to one of the hierarchical levels of the functional tripartition: the sacred, war, and fertility. We can even assume that the trials present themselves to the hero in the inverse order of their hierarchical succession, for this inverse order is also the order of increasing difficulty: first a trial involving the virtues connected with sexuality or agrarian fertility, then a trial involving the warrior's virtues, and lastly the highest-level trial, involving a certain knowledge of the sacred.

While this triple initiation must have structured the rites of passage at puberty even for young men who were not called to a royal function,[19] the triplicity of the trials is particularly necessary for the hero with a royal calling. Indeed, the king is expected to realize the synthesis of the three functions in his own person. As Plato will remind us, the king is a complete man; he is supposed to exemplify and harmonize in himself the conjoined characteristic virtues of each of the functional levels.

The difference between Oedipus and a regularly qualified king is now clearly apparent: it brings the swollen-footed hero into focus in all his disquieting singularity. Oedipus, too, becomes king. Or, to be more precise, he becomes a tyrant, that is, not a more authoritarian and despotic sovereign than any other, but a sovereign whose legitimacy is open to question. This difference sums up Oedipus's imposture. Unlike the typical king, he has not undergone the traditional investiture. He has not been consecrated according to legitimate practices. He has not undergone the complete, tripartite initiatory trial, but only the trial of the riddle. Thus, he cannot fully achieve the balanced synthesis of the three functions that is a sign and a factor of royal justice. His virtues are not in equilibrium. Something is limping.

Now, if we look for what is out of kilter in the light of trifunctional justice, shall we not find it precisely in the zone of the two remaining functions, those that Oedipus has not faced in an initiatory confrontation? Isn't the incest with Jocasta, as a transgression of a sexual taboo, and even the principal sexual taboo, unmistakably a perversion involving the third function? Similarly, the patricidal violence, the beating of an old man with a stick at a crossroads, the presumptuous anger, would be a distortion of the agonal courage that presumes a righteous anger and a just use of strength. Wouldn't the murder of the aging father by the more vigorous son be the most impious misuse of physical force possible?

Thus, by an implacable mythic logic, the two manifest crimes of Oedipus, patricide and incest, belong to the two realms in which he has not undergone the trials of the initiatory passage. His royal investiture, based solely on his answer to the riddle, is irregular. Oedipus is not a complete king. He has conquered the monster by the sole power, the consummate power, of his reflection, but this very virtue of intelligence, in its disproportion, has unbalanced him. His power is based exclusively on an exorbitant first-function virtue; as for the other two functions, Oedipus has taken them to the extreme, basing his power in these areas not on the two corresponding virtues but on two crimes.

Incest and patricide, beyond all strictly narrative connections, but by a transverse and synthetic symbolic causality, are thus the shadow, the disastrous negative, of the flaw in the probative experience. Oedipus has not manifested and tested the virtues of the second and third functions. If he has demonstrated his intelligence through his response to the Sphinx's riddle (and this apparent victory itself turns out to be suspect), he has not gone through the sacred ordeal to confront his own aggressive, warlike power or the dangerous powers of sexuality. The two crimes that he will later discover he has unwittingly committed are the correlatives of his defective initiation, which is to say, also, of the avoidance of matricide.

We must linger, however, over one suspicion. Does Oedipus genuinely succeed in the first-function trial, and only that one, dispensing himself from the other two (by an evasion with grave consequences), or is there not even in his apparent intellectual victory over the Sphinx something dubious, irregular, even profanatory, in mythic terms? If this is the case, the foregoing interpretation, even while remaining valid in its overall structural mechanism, would have to be somewhat refined. Oedipus would be the protagonist whose one and only probative success apparently (in the eyes of all) lies in his reckoning with the riddle (thus already exposing himself, according to mythic logic, to two functional crimes); but he succeeds in this test only by an impious and, as it were, sacrilegious stratagem. Isn't Oedipus's reply a challenge to the

Sphinx, a disavowal of initiation through intellectual presumptuousness, rather than a genuine success in the supreme trial?

What invites this suspicion is the myth itself, in the details of its irregularities. For finally, in the standard myth, the trials are graduated, the protagonist has to begin by succeeding in the first two trials, those involving temperance and courage, before he faces the third. And even more importantly, he always needs the help of gods or wise men in order to succeed. To be precise, in the typical mythicoritual configuration, the neophyte always has to learn the response from a wiser initiator and remember it until the moment comes when he needs it in the trial. He never invents it himself. This detail points to the context of transmission that the initiatory passage constitutes. For the traditional mind, to know is to inherit knowledge, to receive it respectfully from the divine masters, and not to produce it oneself. That Oedipus found the solution to the enigma all by himself, without being instructed by gods or men, may appear to our modern minds as an eminent proof of his high intelligence. To the traditional mind, this can only be the gravest sign of a sacrilegious rupture in the initiatory transmission, the very proof of the irregularity of the passage, a scandalous feature of Oedipus's presumptuousness and intellectual self-satisfaction.

This sacrilegious posture thus at bottom amounts to nothing less than a denial of the lofty mysteries shielded by the Sphinx. Oedipus offends the Sphinx and leaves her destitute; this is much more significant than the fact that he solves the riddle she poses. He does not kill the Sphinx; he dismisses in a word everything she stands for, namely, the initiatory passage itself. But we must not overlook the meaning of the reply, "Man": man and not the divine, whether celestial or monstrous. Thus, what Oedipus disavows is the sacred itself, an element that belongs initially to the first function but that concerns them all, and an element without which the initiation itself loses its meaning.

Nietzsche understood that the actions that define the figure of the Theban hero must not be considered in isolation but rather must be regarded as a threefold unity. "Oedipus, his father's murderer, his mother's lover, solver of the Sphinx's riddle! What is the meaning of this triple fate?"[20] The "triple fate" is a mysterious trinity whose coherence we are beginning to perceive. Nietzsche is not mistaken when he infers that, inscribed within what he calls "the terrible triad of Oedipean fates," there are three ways to "break the consecrated tables of the natural order."[21] Two of these are patricide and incest; that much is self-evident. But Nietzsche was able to see that solving the riddle is no less grave a transgression. He discerns an "unnatural wisdom" in Oedipus's response. For its part, the differential logic of the myth has also revealed an anomaly in Oedipus's victory. He has triumphed in a single word, without the help of the gods; his action has resulted in the Sphinx's suicide, not her bloody murder. Profanation, sacrilege: here is the real meaning of Oedipus's attitude toward the creature that presides over initiation. There is some indication that Sophocles may be suggesting such a crime, indirectly, when at the end of the second episode (before we know what Oedipus is guilty of) the chorus condemns the "pride" [*hubris*] that "breeds the tyrant" and insists: "But if any man comes striding, high and mighty in all he says and does, no fear of justice, no reverence for the temples of the gods—let a rough doom tear him down, repay his pride, breakneck, ruinous pride!"[22] The victory over the Sphinx would reveal that lack of reverence.

From this point on, according to this reading, the "terrible triad" of Oedipus's fate will designate three crimes rigorously linked with the three functional levels. The episode of the Sphinx, despite its appearance of legitimate victory, is a perversion of a first-function virtue. Oedipus "climbed the height of wisdom"; he was "the man who unraveled the beast-woman's dark riddle";[23] but the entire differential economy of the myth that we have uncovered, as well as the immediate outcome of the victory over the Sphinx, bears witness to the deceptive and perverted nature of Oedipus's success. The two other components of his fate, murderous violence against the father and incest with the mother, correspond unambiguously to the perversion of the two other functional virtues.

To be sure, the deepest motifs of the myth cannot be reduced to the play of a simple tripartite form. Such a move would amount to an undue weakening of its import. However, in the concert of multiple meanings that a great myth realizes, the role of the trifunctional schema seems undeniable. This is all the more true in that the tripartition itself can hardly be regarded as a mere formal constraint. The tripartition orients and organizes characteristic meanings. The meaning of the Oedipus myth is that of a deviant initiation. The disruption of the standard mythic plot affects each of the registers involved in the probative experience: knowledge, strength, and sexuality.

If initiation is intended to establish harmony within the individual and justice within the royal spirit through the hierarchized equilibrium of the three virtues that correspond to the three functions, a deficiency in the initiation will result in an imbalance and a fall. It is consistent that the tragedy was able to appropriate a myth in which an avoided—though apparently successful—initiation leads to a chain of catastrophes. Oedipus is the perverted figure of the legitimate archaic king. He brings the three powers together in criminal form. The discovery of his imposture is the mainspring of the tragic reversal.

Oedipus's fate has to be deciphered, then, as a "terrible triad" of functional calamities. For at the end of his adventure there are in fact three disasters, each one corresponding to one of the three evaded realms of initiation that traverse Oedipus's life: not only patricide and incest, whose significance we have already seen, but also blindness, which is quite clearly the most suitable punishment for a first-function crime, especially if this crime consists in the presumption of exposing the sacred itself to the full light of day.

As we know, Dumézil was able to demonstrate, using a very large number of examples (from the adventures of Heracles to the judgment of Paris), that the arrangement of the narrative logic of a myth or epic could be rigorously explained as a succession of actions belonging to the various functional levels.

A major part of the structure of the myth of Heracles can be accounted for within the general framework of the "three sins of the hero." Heracles commits (and eventually expiates) three successive errors that mark three phases of his life. The first, which amounts to hesitation in the face of an order from Zeus, is punished by madness. The second consists in the treacherous murder of an enemy, with physical illness as its penalty. The third, finally, involves a scandalous adultery and leads to an incurable burn and voluntary death.[24] The same triple character of sins can be identified in the case of other, less important heroes, for example in the *hubris* of King Laomedon.[25]

Comparison of the Heracles myth with the Oedipus story casts a telling light on the latter that makes this myth's structural affinity with the ideology of the functional tripartition more and more visible. What is more, not only do Oedipus's three sins correspond strictly to functional crimes, but they are crimes pushed to their extreme limit. Thus, to take them up in inverse order with respect to their functional level, Oedipus is not content, like Heracles, to commit a scandalous adultery: he sleeps with his own mother, which certainly constitutes a third-function crime, but one that is taken, as it were, to the absolute limit. Similarly, Oedipus is not content merely to kill an enemy under treacherous conditions: he kills his own father, which again constitutes not a killing like any other but the most terrible of murders. Finally—and this is the least noticed of Oedipus's three sins, the one that, for extremely powerful historical reasons, has prevented us up to now from discerning the implacable logic of fates that weighs upon him—Oedipus is not content to violate the sacred status of heralds as Laomedon did, or to hesitate before the order of Zeus, as Heracles did: Oedipus defeats the Sphinx without the help of gods or wise men, with a single word. Or rather, he offends the Sphinx instead of fighting her. Here is the most enigmatic aspect of Oedipus's sin, and for good reason—but there is no doubt that what is involved is a first-function crime, and here again, most serious of all, we find something resembling atheism on Oedipus's part in his profanation of the initiatory tradition. In a rigorous but singular and hyperbolic form we thus rediscover in the Oedipus story, as a pervasive structuring mechanism, the "three sins of the hero" that Dumézil identified in other myths.

This tendency of Oedipus's manifest sins (patricide and incest) to be excessive, extreme, or hyperbolic has a logic of its own that haunts his other, more hidden crime. This other crime is invisible in the eyes of the people who have taken him as their king; indeed, they regard it as his greatest success. The singularity of the first-function crime in Oedipus's case is that it involves the initiatory moment itself, that is, the relation to the Sphinx. This is why it is necessarily accompanied by extreme consequences. In the story of Heracles, the struggle against the monsters is never completely avoided: on the contrary, the hero descends into Hades to take Cerberus back, he fights the Hydra of Lerna and the Lion of Nemea, he cleans out the Augeian stables, and so on. None of the twelve trials ordered by King Eurystheus is avoided; each one is carried out with a maximum of effort, and the fault committed against the sacred thus does not bear upon the profoundest, most decisive formative moment of the initiatory experience.

For Oedipus, on the contrary, it is the initiatory trial itself that is skewed. The patricidal act and its incestuous outcome have to be understood, in their excess, as the inevitable corollary of this deviation of the initiation. If Oedipus's two visible crimes are extreme cases of second- and third-function crimes, this is because a crime that is invisible to the uninitiated, but nevertheless a hyperbolic crime that only initiates like Teiresias can fully understand, orients the entire destiny of the Theban hero. Even though it may appear to be a glorious victory in the eyes of the stupefied people, Oedipus's triumph over the Sphinx, for reasons that we have gradually exposed, nevertheless has the significance of a sacrilegious anomaly that can only lead to crime and perversion and cannot help but arouse the anger of the gods—or rather of the god who presides with Dionysus over initiations, Apollo.

Here, then, is the locus of the singularity of the Oedipus myth. If in it finally we rediscover "the three sins of the hero," the discovery does not thereby reduce the myth to a conventional schema; on the contrary, it brings to light the rigorous mechanism of its singularity—what we have called its regulated irregularity. If the trifunctional meaning of Oedipus's crimes can be identified unambiguously, the ingenious and profoundly meaningful way their occurrences are organized nevertheless gives this myth an original import and endows it with a unique lesson. Continually and consistently, the Oedipus myth deals with the exorbitant—and in some measure involuntary—crimes of the hero as a myth of eluded initiation.

Moreover, a profound necessity connects the Oedipus myth with "the three sins of the hero." Initiation is the sacred trial that sends the neophyte forth to confront the risk of committing faults corresponding to each of the three functional fields, and allows him to acquire the virtues of each of these fields while rejecting their illegitimate aspects. Thus, the failed or eluded initiation is bound to produce ethically dramatic results. It destines the protagonist to commit three functional crimes, and in their most excessive form, moreover, since the sacrifice of the dangerous and negative element of each of these kernels of desire will not have been accomplished. From this point on in our analysis, if the theme of the hero's three crimes can perfectly well appear at a turning point of a myth whose principal meaning is not initiatory failure (for there are other paths that can lead to this series of illegitimate acts), on the other hand, a myth of initiatory failure—and the Oedipus story is such a myth par excellence—cannot fail to bring out in a particularly clear, compelling, and extreme way, three paradigmatic crimes.

However, if the Oedipus myth does present the triple trespass, and even in a limit-stretching, hyperbolic form, it does so with one important singularity: Oedipus is not aware of his crimes as such. Thus, this myth, in a way that gives it its full tragic force, allies extreme forms of transgression with the perfection of ignorance, tied nevertheless to consummate knowledge (the "knowledge" Oedipus manifests before the Sphinx). This feature, proper to the Oedipus myth, thus requires a special interpretation that gives it a status apart. It includes a lesson about the relation between ethics and knowledge that is not conveyed, for example, by the myth of Heracles. This singularity accounts for the role that the myth was able to play at a certain point in the evolution of philosophy. In it could be typified a cluster of problems and horizons of incomparable richness, a cluster that has not ceased to yield probing questions for us even today.

In fact, the meaning of the Oedipus myth lies in the disruption that draws the actions of the unwitting hero away from the standard heroic plot toward the schema of the three crimes. Within the same sphere of collective memory at least two different, if not opposing, narrative schemas appear to present, inconspicuously, the unstated conditions of the Oedipus myth, the background against which this singular figure arises. The meaning of the myth, the thought it articulates, arises from the strange difference, and from the strange resemblance, between these two narrative systems, even if the relationship remains implicit or latent. It constitutes more than a combination of the two: its power and its ruse is that it leads to error by a sort of travesty. On the surface, it evokes the regular myth of royal investiture. In depth, it is a myth of the three functional sins. From this effect it draws its tragic potential. From this ambiguous position between two great narrative sequences, playing on both at once, it draws all of its instructive potential. It is not enough to say that the myth stands at the intersection of these two series, for they are contradictory and mutually exclusive. Through a kind of narrative sleight of hand, the myth takes on the appearances of the one while being structured at the deepest level by the other.[26]

Such an interpretation of the Oedipus plot, which inscribes it within a mythicoritual mechanism that is much more rigorous and also much more ancient than had been suspected up to now, cannot fail to upset all the readings that have been proposed in modern times, resituating them in a radically new light.

Into what dimension does this decoding carry the Hegelian interpretation of Oedipus as the inaugural philosopher? Is it not at once more deeply justified than might have been imagined, but also richer in historical consequences and backgrounds that still remain to be elucidated? And what about the famous "Oedipus complex" that is at the base of the whole Freudian edifice? What becomes of this, if the Oedipus plot can be rigorously construed as a myth of failed, or rather eluded, masculine initiation? Will not psychoanalysis itself, and the whole theory and practice of the unconscious, have to be at the very least revised in the light of this discovery of the deviant meaning of the Oedipus myth, and in light of the mechanism (much more complex than the action of two infantile fantasies) that generated the mythic intrigue?

And what can be said at present about the possible conjunction of these modern uses of the myth? If the Oedipus plot is that of the avoidance of initiation, the same illumination may allow us to understand better how Oedipus can have been convoked as the emblematic figure of philosophy, the eponymous hero of the nuclear Freudian complex, and also the paradigm of the *pharmakos*, the scapegoat. And this understanding in turn may well open the way to new thinking about the constitution of the subject in Western history.

But if the interpretation of Oedipus through initiatory failure cannot help but bring about profound modifications in our understanding of the modern reworkings of the myth, if this interpretation can account better than any other for the myth's persistence in the imaginary of Western man, it also allows us to see its inscription within Greek culture, both in detail and in general, in a different light. Isn't it the religious and political background of Sophoclean tragedy (and of tragedy in general) that is suddenly spread out before our eyes?

And isn't it the incomparable privilege of Oedipus before the Sphinx, as the ambiguous and sublime emblem of Hellenic reason, that little by little breaks into the edifice of our knowledge and unveils its most deeply buried mystery?

§ 5 Greek Subversion

The avoidance of initiation is also a liberation. It opens up a new horizon. It defines a subject who, in his disruption and his disproportionality, can live out other possibilities. The adventure of Oedipus inaugurates the era of the hero whose identity is not defined by a tradition and a transmission, a hero with whom a new mode of subjectivity emerges.

The modern subject, the subject whose designs evolve gradually from Protagoras to Descartes and Nietzsche, is initially determined by the posture of Oedipus. The metamythical transposition of incestuous desire and patricide clearly results in the two complementary tendencies that pervade the philosophical impulse in its most modern form: to constitute itself as a subject who possesses nature, matter, the Earth; and to do so through an autonomous will to power that owes nothing to the directives of any authority. The two tyrannical tendencies that the initiatory crisis was supposed to destroy, the dream of patricide and the dream of incest, turn out to be surreptitiously maintained in their full vigor and virulence. Instead of being seared away and deactivated, these tendencies survive, deferred and transposed. They are at the origin of an insatiable curiosity, a desire to see, to reveal, to profane the deepest mysteries, to raise the veil, to see the naked truth, to penetrate the secrets of nature or matter, in order to become master and owner. And all this by oneself, by an autodidactic reflection that excludes all traditions and revelations. The radical and insistent tendency of philosophizing thus emerges from the beginning in a cryptic form, through the passion of Oedipus. And it is remarkable that the philosophy of the Moderns, that of Descartes and Nietzsche, carries this dual tendency to extremes, to its very limit, and thus makes it possible to disclose, after the fact, the Oedipean core of this insistence, whereas the Ancients, with Plato and Aristotle, still fell short of what was programmed by the posture of Oedipus.

When Plato describes the tyrant as a disordered being who dreams of being united with his mother and who kills his father, he contrasts this figure with that of the true philosopher-king, a man formed by a fitting education, a man who respects his father and submits to reason, a man in whom the three functional virtues corresponding to the three parts of his soul are arrayed hierarchically in a harmony and equilibrium known as justice. The philosopher-king, unlike the tyrant, whose power has no legitimacy, has actually undergone the qualifying trials of sovereign investiture. Behind this Platonic image of the initiate of royal rank we can easily see its archaic origin, its ritual and mythic extraction. Plato is transposing the tripartite economy of the initiatory trial and the status of the sovereign as the synthesis of the three functions. Plato has recuperated the philosophical impulse in order to reinvest it at once in a traditional schema, creating the figure of the philosopher-king.

But according to the same tripartite economy, Oedipus as seen by Sophocles is precisely the philosopher-tyrant, the noninitiate who usurps the royal function and who, through the rigorous mechanism of disruption of the hierarchical virtues, cannot help but fall into the abyss of patricide and incest. For Sophocles, who remains faithful to the sacerdotal vision of truth (in the tragedy, it is Teiresias whose position proves to be right in the end), the philosopher can be only such a disordered tyrant, since through intellectual presumptuousness he has avoided authentic initiation. The philosopher has no way of reinscribing himself, as Plato would have it, within the framework of the functional tripartition. He is the one who dangerously subverts the tripartition, and he cannot help but come to a tragic end. Oedipus, the *sophos*, cannot long remain in the king's place; he has not undergone the trials of the triple initiation that would have made him a living synthesis of the three functions. Having profaned the trial by a sacrilegious response, having overvalued shrewdness, having evaded the challenge of brute force and the challenge of sexual seduction, he can only succumb to the forces that he has ignored. By means of this tragic representation, Sophocles exposes the traditionalist and ritualist view that regards any challenge to the tripartite hierarchy as a danger. Reworking the plot of the myth, making it more pointed, perhaps, here and there, he adopts the lesson inscribed in its internal structure: Oedipus is the false king, the tyrant who has committed two inexpiable crimes that are themselves linked to a third, and each of the three corresponds systematically to one of the three functional levels.

But it is Oedipus, still, whose posture delineates the symbolic conditions of exit from this archaic regime. Hence the historical power of the Oedipus myth: in him a new subjectivity takes shape, a subjectivity that breaks free from the conditions of the trifunctional hierarchy to invent a new form of being and thinking. This is why the Oedipus myth played such a decisive role in Greece. This is why Oedipus is the paradigmatic hero of Hellenic reason. Greece marks the passage from a traditional mode of symbolizing, dominated by the tripartite ideology (thus corresponding to a military-sacerdotal type of power) to a new mode that distorts that archaic framework in order to invent philosophy, politics, the individual, the juridical subject, and the democratic debate among free and equal citizens. This historic passage is not simple. It is hazardous. And it is experienced by many as a sacrilege that will be punished, sooner or later, by the gods. The tragedy of Oedipus lies at this turning point. Oedipus typifies the new subject, the one who subverts the tripartition and owes his power to a source other than that of the traditional investiture. Although Sophocles, in his "reactionary" fear, predicts that only unhappiness and perdition can be the outcome of such presumptuousness in conformity with the myth, Oedipus is the symbolic precursor of the philosophical posture that will persist into our day, giving Western culture its historical uniqueness. Sophocles himself, toward the end of his long life, may have perceived the grandeur of Oedipus's position, and with *Oedipus at Colonus*, despite tragedy and death, he finally made Oedipus a figure of the future.

Greece is the European society in which it is most difficult to relocate the principles of the tripartite ideology characteristic of the Indo-European arena. The "Greek miracle" is the abandonment of that rigid framework, a development that leads to an exit from that ideology into an extraordinary drift. But it has also been supposed that this change of direction corresponds to a specific internal evolution, and not to the massive intrusion of external elements that would have completely dislocated these frameworks.[1] The Oedipus plot, as we have analyzed it, provides astonishing corroboration of this point of view. Occupying a pivotal place in this break, it reveals both the archaic, tripartite Indo-European framework and the Greek inflection of the exit from that framework. The Oedipus myth is the myth of the Greek exit from the ideology of the functional tripartition. It reveals by what stance, at what risks, with what tensions and contradictions the subversion of that hierarchical system can come about. And it is of course of the highest significance that this exit was inscribed symbolically, that it could be expressed in an imaginal configuration, could be presented in the precise and rigorous mechanisms of a plot.

We shall not attempt to reestablish here all the historical conditions that may have contributed to such a change. Among the factors that played a determining role, the disappearance of the priestly class is doubtless crucial.[2] If this view is correct, the disappearance of the priestly class led in turn to the plurifunctionality of the second function and then of the third. The traditional conception of sovereignty was then modified in the direction of secularization. The Greeks maintained the tripartite and hierarchical division of the ideals and virtues (as Plato attests, and also Plutarch), but the highest ideal (wisdom) was detached from its ancestral bond with priestly sovereignty. It was at this point that philosophy could be born. On the one hand, this reading of history implies that the acquisition of wisdom was no longer subordinated to the long chain of a tradition faithfully transmitted by specialists of the sacred, but it also implies, conversely, that this shift led the Greeks to accord the highest place to reason, since philosophical reflection retained the preeminent place that had been outlined by its sacerdotal antecedent.

The "Greek miracle" or "mutation" resides, then, in this double movement (which implies a certain internalization of the tripartition that we shall examine more closely later on). It is noteworthy that the interpretation of the Oedipus myth that we have undertaken (and this is still more clearly true for the tragedy that Sophocles drew from the myth) makes this myth appear quite precisely as a myth of the eviction of sacerdotal power. Oedipus is an "everyman" who becomes the sovereign ruler through his intelligence alone; not having been initiated, he stands apart from any knowledge transmitted by the sacerdotal institution, and apart from any investiture. Oedipus is a king who is not consecrated, who has not undergone the trials of the sacred. He reigns in opposition to Teiresias and not with him or under his spiritual jurisdiction. Teiresias here is indeed the mythical representative of a sacerdotal function that in actual fact has long since disappeared. Hence the unparalleled historical and ideological privilege of the Oedipus myth as a tool for getting at the deep significance of the Greek transformation, or better still, for grasping the originality of the Greek response in its reworking of the Indo-European tripartition Greece had inherited. The myth, and then the tragedy, initiate an anxious interrogation of which certain questions can be rendered as follows: "What happens when the sovereign is no longer an initiated, consecrated king?" Or, in different but related terms: "What happens when the philosopher, newly arrived on the scene, claims to replace the priest of Apollo?" These are the uncertainties that are put into play, explored, problematized, in the story of Oedipus. But it is not only the disappearance of the sacerdotal caste and of the sovereign's initiatory investiture that can be recognized in the profound contemporaneity with which the Oedipus myth is invested. In parallel to the dissolution of the archaic way of life, the dissolution of the institution of the *genos* is precipitated. The *genos* included all those who maintained the cult of a common ancestor; the *genos* had its leader, its patrimony, its rites, its justice. Starting with the Draconian code, the state took the place of the *genos* in judging individual responsibility, and this brought about equality among individuals belonging to different generations. Some schol- ⟍ ars have regarded the freeing of sons with respect to their fathers as an essential factor in the Greek mutation.[3]

The autodidactic and individualistic tendency that characterizes philosophical thought in its very essence is clearly inscribed in this liberation of the sons from the authority of the father and the fathers. First with Protagoras or Socrates, and then in its later phases (Descartes, Nietzsche), philosophy can be viewed as a thought of the son. What is more, its destiny as filiarchal thought is inscribed in its program from the beginning, but remains muted by the properly tragic enormity of the task. This destiny becomes explicit only gradually, in the course of a history in which Descartes exposes the Oedipean strategy of the philosophic enterprise more fully than it had ever been done before, and in which Nietzsche would push this strategy to its limit, encountering its tragic outcome in the process.

This interpretation sheds decisive light on the face-to-face confrontation between Teiresias and Oedipus that enlivens the first episode of Sophocles' play. The opposition between the two characters is given a prominence that no other reading can match.

Teiresias, the old priest of Apollo, is the initiate par excellence.[4] He is a repository of ancestral wisdom, possessor of a gift of supernatural clairvoyance conferred on him not by men but by the gods. He knows how to decipher the meaning of prophecies, premonitions, and presumably dreams as well. In short, he is a master in the interpretation of the signs sent by the gods. Teiresias is the highest incarnation of the virtues and powers belonging to the first function: his domain is that of truth, his authority entirely spiritual. This old man, blind, but gifted with clairvoyance, full of high priestly wisdom that gives him a place apart, comes into conflict with the pretensions of young Oedipus, the stranger who became sovereign by following extraordinary and suspect paths lacking in ritual regularity. Oedipus was not consecrated king according to the procedure hallowed by tradition, the only procedure recognized by the gods. The trials of qualification that would have made him the living synthesis of the three functions, that would have united in his person the virtues and powers of intelligence, strength, and fertility, did not take place. Oedipus upset the Sphinx instead of vanquishing her. He offended the lofty mysteries of royal initiation instead of receiving their secret illumination. With him, despite the appearances to which the Theban people succumbed, the sacred transmission was broken. According to the divine and priestly requirements, Oedipus is a usurper. If he has triumphed against the disquieting obstacle that the Sphinx set up against him, it is by virtue of a profanatory shrewdness, that of a young autodidact betraying excessive confidence in the resources of his own reason, and not by virtue of a privileged acquaintance with the gods. Oedipus succeeded all by himself, without soliciting either sacred teachings or divine help, thereby claiming he could obtain on his own what was supposed to be conferred on him only by initiatory transmission. This is why Oedipus is not a king (*anax*) but, in the Greek sense, a tyrant (*tyrannos*).

The traditional qualifying trial, like any other ritual exercise, loses its transforming power as soon as it ceases to mobilize sacred forces and becomes subject to reflective reasoning alone. Teiresias undoubtedly regarded Oedipus as approaching a terrifying trial—one that ought to have marked him irreversibly—with incredulous detachment tantamount to a disavowal of the divine. In comparison with the decisive encounter in which Teiresias lost his sight, the word Oedipus produces is an imposture. Teiresias is in the best position to comprehend this secret usurpation and to be troubled by it. The distance between Teiresias and Oedipus is the distance between two forms of knowledge, two ways of reasoning, two irreconcilable modes of sovereignty. The one is the wise old man, priest of Apollo, knower of destinies and interpreter of divine signs, custodian and transmitter of a timeless wisdom; the other is the brash young philosopher who believes only in his own reflection, who believes only in man, and who takes as certainties only facts that methodical investigation has provided him. It is this profound opposition that Sophocles allows us to perceive in the stormy encounter between the two irreconcilable figures. The old man is the initiate; the young man claims to have transcended the initiatory mode of knowledge through autonomous reflection.

Everything in Sophocles' text is ordered so as to make this clear. The very first word King Oedipus utters when Teiresias approaches him is not without a certain irony. It concerns precisely the type of knowledge with which the leader of the chorus has just credited this divine interpreter: "Lord Tiresias sees with the eyes of Lord Apollo. Anyone searching for the truth, my king, might learn it from the prophet, clear as day." "O Tiresias, master of all the mysteries of our life, all you teach [*didakta*, what can be taught] and all you dare not tell [*arrēta*, what must not be divulged], signs in the heavens, signs that walk the earth! Blind as you are, you can feel all the more what sickness haunts our city." Oedipus depicts Teiresias as learned in exoteric knowledge, knowledge that can be divulged, communicated to all, but also as a possessor of esoteric truths, about which silence must be kept, sacred truths and mysteries that can only be the object of an initiatory transmission. And it is significant that immediately afterward, Teiresias refuses to reveal to Oedipus what he knows, arousing in Oedipus an impatient ire: "What? You know and you won't tell?" It is Teiresias's refusal to disclose what he knows, this mutism, that leaves Oedipus furious and threatening. In his rising anger, his private contempt for Teiresias surfaces, belying the flattering welcome with which he had greeted the old man's arrival. Not only does Oedipus now accuse the soothsayer of having plotted the crime, but he insults the old man's blindness and the sublime protestation by which the latter declares that he is the bearer of the living truth: "Who primed you for this? Not your prophet's trade." Here Oedipus gives himself away. He admits that he does not believe in Teiresias's divinatory powers—or in divination (*manteia*) in general. He had thus been mocking the old man earlier when he asked him to decipher the flight of birds. Now he admits that he is all skepticism where the interpretation of divine signs is concerned. Moreover, isn't his incredulity reinforced by his very success with the Sphinx? He reminds Teiresias succinctly of this success, emphasizing that when "not a word, you and your birds, your gods—nothing" had been able to help the greatest of soothsayers, he himself, by his intelligence (*gnōmēi*) alone, was able to do away with the monster.[5]

It is his own rejection of mantic knowledge and of all mystical truth that Oedipus is expressing in this dialogue, and expressing against Teiresias, who embodies that knowledge. Oedipus takes advantage of his exploit and his status as a noninitiate formed by no master and inspired by no god. And he derides the blind soothsayer who claims to have access, beyond the eyes of the flesh, to second sight. The clash between these two figures of knowledge is extremely violent, summing up two moments in the conception of knowledge, one prephilosophic and based on received wisdom, the other philosophic.

What is striking about this confrontation is that in it we find a specific expression of the conflict between priestly authority and royal power, an expression that is very enlightening when it is interpreted in terms of the functional partition. Teiresias, who incontestably embodies the virtues and powers of the first function, those of the priesthood, continually lays claim to his own preeminence, or at least to his equality with respect to the king. Sure of the grandeur of his function, he always addresses Oedipus from the position of someone endowed with a moral superiority that protects him from any pressure and exempts him from any subjection. When Oedipus threatens to punish him for words he deems overbold, Teiresias's haughty reply is sublime. Oedipus: "You think you can get away with this?" Teiresias: "I have already. The truth with all its power lives inside me." And again, a little later on, when Oedipus asks him if he thinks he can go on accusing him with impunity, Teiresias replies: "Indeed, if the truth has any power [*alētheias sthenos*, by the power of truth]." Teiresias thus places himself above the coercive and punitive power of the king. He *is* the truth. He is invested with a spiritual authority over which the king has no legitimate right to exercise his political power. This preeminence (which is in full harmony with what we know of the status of brahmans, druids, and flamines) is justified by Teiresias in a formula that clearly emphasizes the privilege of the sacerdotal function. To Oedipus he explains: "You are the king no doubt, but in one respect, at least, I am your equal: the right to reply. I claim that privilege too. I am not your slave. I serve Apollo."[6] Teiresias thus connects his legitimacy directly with Apollo, whose priest he is; his status frees him from all subjection to the monarch's power. As the servant of the god, he does not fall under the terrestrial jurisdiction of the Theban tyrant. In these remarks we can hear beyond question a precise and still quite audible echo of a very ancient division of sovereignties, the hierarchical difference between what can be designated without anachronism as spiritual authority and temporal authority. This conflict of sovereignties takes on critical significance in the confrontation between Oedipus and Teiresias. In spite of some flattering words of invocation to welcome the blind prophet, Oedipus does not respect the sooth-sayer's traditional preeminence. He soon seeks to force the old man's silence; he gets angry; he threatens; he wants to punish him. Teiresias is constantly led to remind Oedipus of the superior powers that he himself embodies.

Oedipus was able to conquer the Sphinx only because he was driven by a powerful intellectual presumptuousness, a confidence in himself and in man that excluded any subordination to the sacred traditions to which the soothsayer is heir. It was in opposition to Teiresias and all he represented that Oedipus conquered the Sphinx—and indeed that he eluded the initiatory phase of submission to the will of the gods and fidelity to the ancestors. Thus, the reciprocal animosity that separates the two mortals could not be more intense. If Sophocles chooses to construct the entire first episode (following the prologue) around the dissension between Oedipus and Teiresias, it is because the most deeply buried core of the drama is expressed here. The interpretation of the myth as a myth of telestic avoidance gives this dissension, which is more than a simple quarrel, its full value. Teiresias views Oedipus as a profaner and usurper who rules without having been qualified for sovereignty through a regular initiation, that is, without earning the endorsement of the gods and without paying ritual allegiance to the initiatory priesthood whose prerogative it was to consecrate him. Hence Teiresias's anger—the anger of a seer who knows what destiny awaits Oedipus, knows that he will be punished by Apollo himself. Oedipus is not just an ordinary tyrant. He is not one of those who conquered power by force. He won it through intelligence. He is thus in direct conflict with Teiresias, having perverted a first-function virtue. He is not only uninitiated by default, and charged with the sins appropriate to the warrior, but he claims to rival and surpass the soothsayer on his own ground, namely, knowledge of cryptophoric signs. He is not only usurping a royal function, he is also disqualifying priestly wisdom.

The confrontation with Teiresias thus brings to the surface, by contrast or antithesis, what is most striking in the Oedipus figure. The one serves Apollo, the other compares himself to Apollo. The one is blind, with a second sight that constitutes his strength. The other sees with the eyes of the flesh, and his strength is that of political power. The one owes his sovereignty to an uncontested first-function virtue. The other owes his, fragile and secretly ill-gotten, to what is (undoubtedly) a first-function crime. The one has undergone trials that made him an initiate, and he bears the mark of the sacrifice he has endured: the loss of sight. The other has dealt deviously with the Sphinx's trial, and boasts openly of his status as a noninitiate.

Readers have often been astonished by the lines in which the chorus attacks the excessive pride (*hubris*) that characterizes the tyrant. The features that define the excess, it has been said, appear to have nothing to do with Oedipus. A reading in the light of the telestic interpretation shows that this is not at all the case: Oedipus (apart from the question, which is not relevant here, of his intentions and his responsibility) is, by mythic structure, a hero who commits the gravest faults, and indeed precisely the one who commits the gravest possible fault in each register of the functional tripartition. For again, what greater sin of sacrilege (first function) could there be than profanation of the initiatory mystery? What greater sin of violence (second function) could there be than killing one's own father? And what greater sexual sin (third function) could there be than incest with one's own mother? To our great surprise, we find in Sophocles' text an evocation of the tyrant that corresponds rigorously to this triplicity of sins.

Let us reread the passage. The chorus first curses arrogance in a global way, placing stress, however, on rashness in the face of justice and on lack of respect toward sanctuaries: "But if any man comes striding, high and mighty, in all he says and does, no fear of justice, no reverence for the temples of the gods—let a rough doom tear him down." Immediately after this passage three lines stand out, each of which, upon close reading (and such a reading does not seem to have been done before) seems to correspond to the functional tripartition: "If he cannot reap his profits fairly, cannot restrain himself from outrage [*erxetai . . . asepton*]—mad, laying hands on the holy things untouchable [*athiktōn*]. . . ."[7] The tableau of the three functional sins is perfectly ordered here, beginning with the third and ending with the first: self-enriching fraud, a sexual ravisher's sin; impious action, a warrior's sin; the profanation of the sacred, a sacerdotal sin! These acts evoke, from the standpoint of the tripartition, the paradigmatic tyrant.

And Oedipus is that tyrant.

§ 6 The Wrath of Apollo

If Oedipus is the protagonist who marries his own mother instead of a young girl (in a failure of initiation), we can understand how at a precise moment in the development of the theatrical genre of tragedy he became its hero par excellence. For Oedipus, no true satyric moment is possible; his story lacks the final, joyous, Dionysiac phase corresponding to the young girl's emergence—if there is an equivalent to the marriage phase in the Oedipus plot, it lies in a catastrophic misunderstanding. From this point on in the history of tragedy, we may look for a correlation between the progressive disappearance of the archaic ritual link between tragedy and satyric drama and the promotion, with Sophocles, of the Oedipus figure as the embodiment of the tragic itself.

The role assigned to Oedipus corresponds at the same time to the growing importance of philosophic reflection, which tends to devalue and exclude as overly pathological the moment of Dionysiac madness (the moment of death and resurrection); as this reflection gathers momentum, the original meaning of tragedy tends to be forgotten, mistaken, or misunderstood.

We need to recall that philosophy, which implies purity and detachment, is placed under the patronage of Apollo. And in Sophocles' tragedy, it is Apollo who punishes Oedipus. Thus a question arises: To what extent can the interpretation of the Oedipus plot as a disturbance of initiation shed new light on the mythic and ritual connection between Apollo and Dionysus, and on their roles in Oedipus's destiny? In this troubled relation to the gods might we not get to the bottom of the curse that weighs upon Oedipus's existence?

We can make one key observation at the outset: Apollo and Dionysus, opposing divinities whose structuring role in the Hellenic imagination was demonstrated by Nietzsche, have particular functions in young men's initiation rites. They are associated as being the two major *kourotrophos* divinities of the telestic ceremony, the gods who preside over the rite of passage.[1]

Apollo's role as god of education, and more precisely as patron of young males reaching the state of manhood, is well attested: he and the daughters of Tethys "have youths in their keeping," Hesiod says of Apollo in "The Theogony." And Plutarch recalls that in Theseus's day, "it was . . . a custom . . . for youth who were coming of age [*metabainontas*] to go to Delphi and sacrifice some of their hair to the god." Jane Harrison emphasizes that the verb *metabainein* marks the rite of passage.[2] In his role as patron of the adolescent passage, Apollo is associated with Dionysus in a manner that is, moreover, still not well understood.

What has not been noted up to now (not even by Nietzsche, though he described with his celebrated acuity the opposition and complementarity between the two gods) is something that a telestic decoding brings to light: the fact that Apollo and Dionysus typify the two complementary aspects, active and passive, of every initiatory passage. Dionysus is the god who has been torn to pieces, dismembered, chopped up (by beings "born of the breed of Earth," like the Sphinx) and who, thanks to Zeus, has been brought back to life, resuscitated. He has thus undergone the central negative trial of all initiation scenarios, death followed by resurrection, a second birth after the torture of dismemberment. Apollo, on the other hand, is the god who has killed the (female) dragon; he has maintained his integrity, but he is obliged to purify himself after the killing by spending a prolonged period of time in the service of a king. Apollo thus embodies the active, positive aspect of the trial. He destroys the monster from afar, with an arrow shot from his silver bow, and he retains his full identity, his distance. Apollo is the god of healing and education. His trial does not deprive him of his head or his limbs, but gives him access to (his) center and (his) self: the Delphic navel.

Apollo and Dionysus thus typify, in contrasting and complementary figures, the two aspects that every initiatory trial combines in a segmentable oxymoron: kill / be killed—the victorious defeat, the losing victory. The neophyte has to die by the claws of the monster and he has to kill the monster. The distinction of two figures, Apollo and Dionysus, both patrons of male initiation, is made to order to render that contradiction thinkable.

Put in somewhat different terms, if the most powerful moment of the telestic trial is the severing of a bond, the sacrificial blow that cuts the cord attaching the life of the son to the obscure, negative, and monstrous maternal dimension (the dragon), then we can understand that this act may be refracted in the imaginary of dreams, rites, and especially myths in two apparently contradictory ways. The severed connection, the bloody cut, is a killing that is also the killing of the killer. It is killing by the son and killing of the son. From the active standpoint, it is the son who kills, who liberates himself. From the passive standpoint, this liberation is also experienced as supreme distress, absolute depression, a frightful annulling of every vital mainspring, an exhaustion of inner strengths: in a word, death. It is as if a living source of desire and élan dries up, leaving the neophyte like a torture victim drained of blood. Thus we have the Sphinx, who cuts off heads, ravishes the neophyte in a mortal embrace, but at the same time ensures the hero's survival, and must herself be killed.

The monster-mother is thus at once what is killed and what kills. Such a complex of meanings, attributes, and functions does not result from a lack of rigor or a historical succession of disparate significations and diverse extractions condensed incoherently over time into an all-purpose emblem. The monster-mother symbol is rather the fold in which is articulated, in a unique figure, an absolutely necessary interweaving of significations that must be taken together because they act together.

In this light, how is Oedipus's fault to be viewed? How is it inscribed within the bond (a bond that iconography repeatedly makes visible without supplying the key to its interpretation) between the Sphinx and the troop of Dionysian Satyrs?

Oedipus subverts the trial in a direction that ignores Dionysus and exasperates Apollo. His response, reduced to a single word that suffices to offend the Sphinx, implies an emotional disengagement, a distance with respect to the sacred that excludes all Dionysiac participation (through which the neophyte is moved, overwhelmed, gripped, possessed, carried away, but also dismembered like the god himself) and that rests upon an Apollonian pretension through which Oedipus exasperates the god by competing with him in the elucidation of the riddle. Oedipus purports to get through the trial on the strength of clarity and distance alone, without sacrifice. Oedipus is not killed and he does not kill. He purports to succeed without injury, without torture, without mutilation, through pure intelligence shorn of emotions, stripped of the mystery whose threshold the Sphinx is protecting. Oedipus thus purports to elude the Dionysiac ordeal and dismemberment by rivaling Apollo in the register that belongs to that god, the register of distance and clarifying light. Here we are approaching the profound rationality of the myth, its ethical and theological teaching.

If the structuralist filtering of the myth remains indispensable, it is because this process takes the myth's internal consistency seriously. Far from presenting itself as an almost random aggregate of varied and heterogeneous themes, as if it was the ill-elaborated product of disparate and superficial influences, the myth offers tightly knotted articulations in an astonishingly rigorous mechanism. This is why nonstructuralist attempts to account for the Oedipus myth, even if they draw upon materials worthy of interest, remain unsatisfying, for they continually underestimate its profound consistency, its internal logic and, in a broad sense, its rationality. The act of classifying and elaborating upon the various themes encountered in the myth does not permit us to grasp the myth's ordering principles and the extraordinary rigor of the displacements it effects. Only a systematic comparison of the myth with the regularity of the monomyth in its canonical formality allows us to reveal the compelling series of differential gaps that gives it its proper meaning.

But this operation, carried far enough, exceeds the structuralist undertaking in that it is not limited to a purely logical play of mythemes perceived as having only a differential and "positional" meaning, as Lévi-Strauss might say, but no intrinsic meaning. We move beyond structuralist play when we discover that the Oedipus plot is rigorously articulated as a failed initiation and is inscribed as an ordered anomaly within the trifunctional symbology; we begin to be able to take the myth's seriousness more fully into account, along with the ethical teaching it offers.

When we are dealing with the well-known swollen-footed pro-tagonist, it is all the more important to bring to light an archaic teaching of this sort because this process allows us to articulate the myth with the tragedy. A reader who has not perceived the internal logic of the Oedipus myth will not be able to discover the ra-tionality of Oedipean thought, starting with its Sophoclean expres-sion. If the Oedipus plot, in the economy that may be presumed to characterize it even before its theatrical expression, presents the differential meaning we have just discerned, Sophocles' tragedy unfolds that meaning implicitly, and gives Oedipus's destiny an ethical and theological rationality at least as powerful as those that the mythic plot brought to light.

From this point on, the controversial question of the "tragic flaw" can be raised in quite different terms and can be given a much more rigorous answer than an impressionistic, vaguely moralistic, vaguely humanistic reading could have imagined. We need not go into the details of this controversy, which is familiar enough in its broad outlines. At no point does Oedipus, the model of the Greek tragic hero, ever knowingly commit a fault, and yet he commits the greatest of crimes. Is he guilty, given that he is not responsible? At what level is the fault or flaw to be located? Is it not cruelty on the part of the gods to strike down someone who committed a crime without knowing what he was doing? What is the role of decision and what is the role of blind destiny in human life? When a person acts, is he or she really the agent of his or her acts? Is there not an obscure, irreducible dimension that transcends the individual? Questions about gods and humans proliferate—to such an extent that one is tempted to see the tragedy as an aporetic spectacle that is produced precisely in order to raise these questions all at once, in order to upset us, to shake us up and challenge our certitudes, but decidedly not in order to offer definitive answers to any of them.

Even if there is no doubt that the tragedy opens up new lines of questioning that the mythic narration does not incorporate (the individual as the source of his or her actions, the relation of human beings to their own acts, and so on), and even though the tragedy is undeniably contemporaneous with the formation of a new political, juridical, and philosophic subject that presupposes a still-unheard-of concept of individual responsibility,[3] the fact remains that the tragedy depends upon a preexisting narrative logic, a plot structure borrowed from a tradition; in a word, the tragedy is derived from—and derives its powerful inevitability from—what Aristotle calls a *mythos*. The logic of the myth guarantees the tragedy's rationality. The mythic core may have appeared to some readers as the irrational, obscure, unintelligible component of the tragedy, in contradiction with the more recent effort toward rationality that was contemporaneous with the dramatization of the myth. But such a reading ignores or underestimates the rationality proper to the myth itself, which is already invested with ethical and theological teaching. Thus, our tabular or differential analysis of the Oedipean plot quite clearly reveals the complex logic of its disruption. This analysis shows with precision the ordered and systematic anomaly that the myth constitutes. Without being able to speak of a "fault" or "flaw" in the modern sense, we can locate a sequence of deviations with respect to a norm or standard, a sequence that constitutes the lapse, the wandering of Oedipean heroism, the place where the hero goes astray. This ordered anomaly is the locus of the myth's teaching, not in the moralizing mode of a formulable precept, but in a much more powerful, although indirect, ethical form (it belongs to the domain of aspective rather than perspective, as we shall see further on), a form whose scope and registers are manifested in the Oedipean itineraries viewed as a whole.

Thus, if one cannot speak, in the modern moral sense, of any sort of responsibility on the part of the individual named Oedipus (to do so would be to suppose a subjective conception of "character" that is foreign to mythic narration), one can say that there is nothing gratuitous or vague about the myth, that it teaches something specific about the logic of human destinies, that it incorporates a lesson about the relation between mortals and gods that warrants an attentive hearing. Euripides himself, the most intellectualist of the Greek tragic authors, puts the following words in the mouth of Teiresias in *The Phoenician Women*, with regard to the unhappy son of Laïus and Jocasta: "The bloody ruin of his peering eyes is the gods' clever warning to Greece."[4] To be sure, it is Teiresias who is speaking. And if there is any position from which human destinies appear to offer a wealth of lessons, it is indeed that of the old sage. But what is the lesson or warning? It would be pointless if it was only a matter of instructing us in the dismaying absurdity of unpredictable destiny and the impenetrable cruelty of the gods. If there is a lesson, it is that a certain transcendent causality attaches acts to their effects, and that divine wrath is far from capricious and arbitrary, that on the contrary, it inscribes all things within an implacable rationality, a rigorous and irresistible justice.

Contrary to what most modern scholars, influenced by distorting and disparaging readings, may have thought, the Oedipus myth, as Hegel sensed, has its own strict rationality. This rationality is manifested as an equilibrium that is continually reestablished by the action of what takes the form of divine justice—an inexorable scale. In this sense, the myth's rationality consists in the never-arbitrary mechanism of specification through which the myth is completed in an epilogue that has the value of a theodicy: the hero's misfortune is proof that the gods exist. From this point of view, the step taken by structural anthropology toward the rehabilitation of the logic of myths would be insufficient if, in the last analysis, it merely discovered a simple, logical play, a pure com-

binatorial of the algebraic type. It is clear, at least in the cultural
sphere with which we are concerned here, that over and beyond
these formal transformations themselves there is a more powerful
reason that grounds them (a highly synthetic reason: it is always
simultaneously psychological, ethical, and theological) and without which they would remain completely gratuitous. Given the
central place myths occupy in symbolic and imaginal reproduction, and in the production of the real, it is quite out of the
question that they should present a formal gratuitousness of this
sort. All indications converge to show, on the contrary, that there
are no teachings more dense and powerful than those of myths,
whose transmission ensures the reproduction of a social bond from
one generation to the next.

Now, the essential fault, the one that leads to the tragic outcome,
is always an outrage against the gods. It is not the mere transgression of a civil law promulgated by human beings in a given country
at a given moment in a given language, but the violation of an
eternal law, a law that is identical in all times and places—the
unwritten divine law. If the courts and verdicts of mortals can
pursue, judge, and condemn someone who is guilty before the
written law, it is not men but gods who condemn the transgressor
of an unwritten law.[5] This means that such a transgressor will not
escape the execution of the sentence. At one point or another, after
a period of time that may be short or long, divine justice will
strike.[6] It is inexorable and inescapable.

This, then, is the mainspring of tragedy: the unfailing admin-
istration of divine justice. The tragic mechanism resides in a twofold condition: (a) the transcendental (as opposed to human and
secular) character of the fault; (b) the (unknowable) lapse of time
before divine justice is administered.

Paradoxically, the transcendental nature of the fault is what may
render it insignificant, or even nonexistent and invisible, to human
eyes. The lapse of time before divine justice strikes is what orches-
trates the properly tragic outcome, the misfortune that befalls the
hero when he does not expect it.

Tragedy thus makes the most of the apparent irrationality of human destiny (the blow of fate that strikes a supposedly innocent person), even as it suggests the perfect theological rationality underlying this destiny. To secular eyes, and according to human justice, the hero (Creon, Pentheus, Ajax) is not necessarily guilty. But he is profoundly so according to celestial justice. His transgression violates something more fundamental than the simple conventions of human legislation. Once the violation has occurred, his fall may be unexpected and may appear terrible, but it will be justified as a divine correction.

One of tragedy's most powerful messages is the recognition of a certain—partial—heterogeneity between divine law and human law. What is reprehensible in terms of human laws does not coincide exactly with what is reprehensible in terms of divine law. What appears to be an anodyne and inconsequential choice, an orientation of life that is humanly acceptable, may, on another stage, that of the gods, have the impact of a major flaw, and vice versa. Thus, the tragic representation is constructed so as to open the eyes of the shaken spectator to a hidden transcendental causality, a hieratic causality that rigorously moves destinies underneath their profane surface appearance of irrationality.

To speak of an "outrage against the gods" is too vague, however, and the expression skirts the subtlest and most profound aspects of myth and tragedy. The sacrilege committed by the hero is never unspecific. It is always a particular god who has been outraged by the hero's action or attitude; it is always that particular god who exercises his or her justice. For the Greek, there is no such thing as a general fault, with respect to the law of a single god or with respect to the undifferentiated body of gods. A specific, blameworthy action offends a specific god. It is thus possible to be guilty on more than one count, each particular violation punishable by the god in whose domain the violation falls. It is Athena who punishes Ajax for having believed that he could win in battle without her help. It is Dionysus who punishes Pentheus for having failed to recognize the sacred nature of intoxication. It is Aphrodite who is injured by the attitude of Hippolytus, who fails to recognize the power of love. In each instance, a faulty, one-sided approach offends a specific divinity, who reestablishes his or her power by what may appear, in human terms, to be a form of revenge, but which amounts to the reestablishment of equilibrium, the sometimes brutal and destructive return to a balance of passions that had been ignored.

In this retaliation of the offended god lies the rationality of the tragedy, and its most secret teaching. What god sends which delirium, and why? This is the question that is answered by the sedimented wisdom in the mythic—and later, the tragic—plot, the question that constitutes the plot as a conceivably unsurpassable form of knowledge.

What god sends which punishment, and why? We cannot claim to have understood the Oedipus plot without having made at least some progress toward answering that question. And we can only be astonished to discover that some of the best contemporary analysts of Greek tragedy have not spotted this fundamental mechanism. Instead, they have remained faithful to the superficial idea, advanced by many modern scholars, according to which divine wrath is totally arbitrary—thus rendering Greek myth meaningless and Greek tragedy absurd. Not to see that what lies behind Oedipus's misfortunes is Apollo's wrath—and not Athena's, or Aphrodite's, or Dionysus's—is to miss the deepest and most rigorous message this plot has to offer. The fact that it is Apollo and no other god who finally strikes Oedipus[7] has a precise meaning in the economy of the hero's fate: it means that his fault, his fundamental violation, the one that underlies and entails all the rest of his missteps, is of the Apollonian type. It is this god who is irritated by the behavior and outlook of the famous swollen-footed protagonist. If we recognize the principle of the rigorous rationality of divine wrath, such an indication holds the key to the most profound lesson concerning the Oedipus figure. And we shall perhaps suspect then, strangely, that patricide and incest—horrendous, frightful crimes, but not at all Apollonian—are only terrible misfortunes that themselves derive from a still more fundamental outrage in a more hidden or less noticed realm that falls under the sacred jurisdiction of the god of light.

It would be frivolous to suppose, here, that the psychoanalytic interpretation could arrive, from the outside, as it were, with all its concepts in hand, and proceed to determine the meaning of the myth. On the contrary: the concept of the Freudian unconscious is generated and situated by a more deeply buried mechanism that allows us, as we are beginning to suspect, to grasp the genealogy of the unconscious.

How does one injure a god? The pathology with which we are concerned has to be displaced and examined in depth by way of this archaic question. Two opposing attitudes bring the wrath of a god down upon a mortal: either neglect or rivalry. Someone who acts as if he is unaware of a particular god's specific power, someone who is unwilling to satisfy the existential demands arising from the god's sacred jurisdiction, will trigger the god's ire. Conversely, someone who, knowing the particular powers of a god, claims in his immense pride to be equal or even superior to that god will also fall victim to the god's terrible wrath. Examples of such acts of divine retribution are not hard to come by, and every example illustrates one aspect or the other of this retaliatory mechanism. Hippolytus, as we have seen, thinks he can ignore the power of the goddess of love; he is trampled under the feet of his own horses. Pentheus rejects all knowledge of the sacred powers of the god of the vineyard: he is devoured by his own mother. Conversely, Athena transforms the unfortunate Arachne into a spider after the mortal boasted that she could outdo the goddess herself in technical prowess. And Apollo, the musician-god, punishes Marsyas for claiming that his flute could make more beautiful music than Apollo's lyre. There is nothing arbitrary about these instances of divine wrath. Either a mortal believes he can ignore a fundamental dimension of existence (love, intoxication) and refuses to sacrifice to it (that is, to the god in whose jurisdiction it falls), or else he thinks, by a mad presumption, that he can measure up to the god himself or herself in an impious rivalry and go beyond the limits assigned to the human condition. In either case, the outcome is always a shattered equilibrium, always an exaggeration (either through insufficiency or through excess) that determines the god's wrathful retaliation. What is at stake is not an absolute fault committed under a unique law, but a certain one-sided orientation of life that threatens to destroy the balance of passions and that, in the terrifying and catastrophic form of divine anger, indeed reaches a point of irreversible rupture. It is thus incorrect to maintain that, for the Greeks, men are mere puppets in the cruel and omnipotent hands of the gods. This view is certainly not supported by the religious thinking of someone like Sophocles.[8] Dikē embodies a higher principle of correction: following the proper path of the sanctioning action of a god (Nemesis),[9] the goddess of justice reestablishes a general equilibrium that results from the transcendental coordination guaranteed by Zeus. And we hardly need insist on the tenor of the punishment itself, which does not have the quantitative indifference of a condemnation measured according to a single scale of values (a general equivalent), but always stands in a signifying relation to the fault committed. This signifying relation itself has a lesson to teach, of course. Each deficiency and each transgression entails its own special risk.

If Oedipus is punished by Apollo it is because he has outraged Apollo. It is necessary to look for his fundamental transgression in a realm of existence that falls within that god's jurisdiction. Now, our differential decoding of the plot corroborates this intuition. If Oedipus, through mythic construction, is the protagonist who believes he has succeeded in the trial of heroic initiation by the exercise of his intelligence alone, then the privileged quarrel with Apollo becomes obvious. Oedipus's crime (which is not reducible, moreover, to a single one of his acts, but which forms his most constitutive *ethos*) is his Apollonian conceit.

But who is Apollo? He is the god of light, of pure science, of theoretical knowledge. It is he who adjusts distances to things, who grants mortals the purity of vision requisite for knowledge. Science, no less than just action, requires purification. The cruder passions must be silenced, or sublimated, if pure contemplation is to be possible—calm contemplation, undertaken with clarity and detachment. Such a distanced vision, while it allows man to know the world's harmony, its beauty, and its sovereign order, carries with it the need for emotional disengagement and separation, perhaps the very separation that permits a clear distinction between the viewer and the visible realm, between sight and the thing seen. And that is why Apollo is perceived as a cold, always-distant god, the god of the horizon, the god of the far-reaching gaze (or arrow).[10]

Oedipus claims for himself the existential orientation that is typified by the luminous configuration of Apollo, but he goes too far, carries it to excess, in an exclusive inclination that becomes profanatory. What constitutes the Oedipean excess properly speaking is the unidimensionality of the Apollonian passion. "To shed full light": the young Oedipus's unique guiding motto is thus a maxim that exceeds a legitimate ambition for pure and detached knowledge and becomes a conquering presumption. "To shed full light" means not only to welcome the clear light one is given, the illumination offered by the god to a mortal who has proved capable of achieving a purified vision; it means taking the place of the god and causing this light to shine oneself, projecting it violently wherever there are shadows, in an indiscreet inquisition that leaves no room for mystery, no sheltered space for the sacred obscurities.

For there is more than one kind of light. There is the light one receives from a divine source, light that illuminates like the rays of the morning sun. This is a gift Apollo gives, the pure vision that inundates the world and the soul with the clear light of truth and beauty. But there is also the light that one professes to produce, project, or shed, all by oneself, in a violent usurpation, with the steely pride of an intellect that accepts only self-evidence and transparency, that denies or subordinates anything that is not exposed to view. And this is the Oedipean passion. It borrows its sacred resource from Apollo, claiming a more-than-human power for a mere mortal.

Understood in this way, Oedipus is both like and unlike Pentheus—the two figures stand in a chiasmatic relation. Whereas Pentheus attempts not to know Dionysus,[11] Oedipus wants to rival Apollo. Both heroes defy and challenge a god, but in opposite ways (one by neglect, the other by rivalry); however, since two contrasting divinities are involved, the tragic outcome has the same meaning in each case: it marks the extreme of intellectual conceit.

Pentheus wants to remain ignorant of Dionysiac delirium, wants to put his trust in stable reason alone; for his profanatory sobriety he incurs the punishment of the wrathful god of the vineyard. Similarly, Oedipus wants to base his victory and his power on the lights of rational, reflective intelligence alone; he draws down upon himself the judgment of Apollo, whom one cannot rival with impunity. Each protagonist refuses, in one way or another, the initiation that requires obscurity, crisis, madness, and the yielding up of the soul to the incomprehensible powers of a god.[12]

This arrogance is of course manifestly revealed in the confrontation with the Sphinx, the central episode condensing the initiatory moment in a superb ellipsis. It does not suffice to say that Oedipus traversed the initiatory trial imperfectly, that he cut short the confrontation with the monster, reducing it to its first moment while avoiding the trials of physical force and resistance to the monster's sexual seduction. Oedipus's role, rather, is to exercise his profanatory intellect in such a way as to dissolve the legitimacy of the initiation itself. He embodies enlightened intelligence, the strong mind, the freethinker who, through the light he purports to shed on all things, desacralizes the ritual of the solemn and anguishing trial and thus achieves a victory against initiation rather than within initiation. He desecrates the threshold, offends the Sphinx instead of penetrating toward the mystery she is defending. The conquering desire to shed full light, and to do this oneself, eludes any real confrontation with what can only remain obscure in the trial, and with what necessarily implies a transmission—that is, the reception of a wisdom that does not have its source in the neophyte hero himself.

Thus, those contemporary commentators who claim to find no feature in Oedipus that points to *hubris*, and who express astonishment at the famous passage in Sophocles where the chorus condemns "breakneck, ruinous pride,"[13] are missing what lies at the heart of the Oedipean plot: the Apollonian excess of a hero who solves the riddle of the Sphinx by the clear light of his intelligence alone, and then, in continued conformity with this stance, wants to shed full light on the king's murder by a methodical and rational investigation, but manages only to reveal himself in this light, in a self-knowledge that destroys him. Here, again, the precept "know thyself," an Apollonian precept, is turned back against the hero. All the features of the Oedipean deviation, including those that may also be legitimately perceived as conquests of thought opening up a new figure of knowledge, are Apollonian in their nature.

If this Oedipean excess can pass unnoticed in a contemporary reading, it is simply because infatuation with the intellect has become ingrained in us. We no longer even see it as a dangerous excess capable of clashing with the divine. We take it to be legitimate. However, our differential reading, like our taking account of the specific god who is angered, shows beyond any doubt that Oedipus's fault consists in a destructive hyperbole of the Apollonian orientation. Oedipus enrages Apollo by the rivalrous unidimensionality of his ambition.

The fact that Apollo is the god who punishes Oedipus confirms what the foregoing analyses have already indicated: Oedipus's sin, first and foremost, concerns knowledge. His other crimes may be more manifest, but they are only secondary, in this interpretation, with respect to the first sin. The visible crimes are only the consequence of the primary sin, if not in the sequencing of the plot, then at least in relation to an enveloping transverse or matricial causality. We have already identified two complementary ways of highlighting the mechanism of this causality. Initiation has the fundamental goal of shattering and transcending both the postulant's rivalry with a figure of the paternal type and his attachment to the world of the mother by providing symbolic access to the ancestors (the dead fathers). Only the heroic killing of a female monster (under orders from an authority) makes this outcome possible. This is the only way the bride can be won and wed. To avoid the dramatic and bloody passage by mere reflection, by the claims of pure knowledge (the answer to the Sphinx's riddle), is to fall short of this key step and to risk perpetrating the two crimes of patricide and incest. The initiatory failure is necessarily accompanied, in one form or another, by these two crimes, which are strictly speaking the negative inverse of two regular acts: obeying the dispatcher king and killing the female monster. In addition, we have seen how the tripartite symbology of initiation makes the meaning and implications of the Sphinx episode extraordinarily clear on the level of the structural mechanism. The unidimensionality of the trial (the fact that intelligence alone is brought into play, in the absence of the martial and sexual dimensions required in the standard monomyth) structurally calls for, and outlines the place of, two hyperbolic sins, a sin of violence and a sin of concupiscence—and this is manifestly what is signified when Oedipus beats old Laïus to death and when he marries Jocasta.

Pentheus and Oedipus, each in his own way, one visibly and the other in a way that goes unnoticed so long as the differential logic of the myth has not been reconstructed, both refuse to allow themselves to be seized by telestic madness. Each wants to escape being possessed by a god; each seeks to avoid the emotion that would take him outside himself, would create an inner schism, would overthrow his mastery, his identity, his autonomy.

That the avoidance of initiation should be at the heart of these two exemplary tragedies is in harmony with the deepest meaning of the tragic genre. If, through its origins, tragedy remains a ceremony in honor of Dionysus, it can still stage, for their value of theodicy and theophany, the dramas of those who thought they could avoid entering into the trial, thought they could avoid torture and ritual death, but who were in fact able only to postpone the moment of their ordeal without annulling its inescapable necessity.

The avoidance of initiation is a drama of deferral. What has not taken place according to the regular forms—because the power of the god has been ignored and the traditions mocked—makes a violent return into the reality of secular existence at an unexpected moment. This is the revenge of the sacred. Instead of a ritual death that ensures a new birth and the consecrated nuptial union, there is a mutilation leading to infirmity or actual death. Oedipus puts his eyes out himself. Pentheus is decapitated by his own mother. These acts are deferred and disordered substitutes for the initiatory severing. Both indicate that access to alterity, to transcendence, has not been achieved.

Thus, the dramas of Pentheus and Oedipus, if they allow the spectator to participate in the pitiable misfortune of a hero, are still not representations of the telestic sacrifice itself; on the contrary, they are representations of the catastrophe that avoidance of that sacrifice has brought about by its deferred effects. Hence the double and subtle possibility that tragedy offers: it can simultaneously have a sacrificial impact (the suffering of the hero) and have a valuable lesson to teach. Whereas Jason or Perseus have relatively little to offer in the way of tragic resource, owing to the excessive mythic regularity of their destiny, Pentheus and Oedipus, by their very misfortunes, demonstrate divine justice and the danger of avoiding the trial.

⁓

Reflective arrogance, an Apollonian fault, governs Oedipus's entire destiny. That is why, at a particular cultural moment, Oedipus can become a prototypical image of the philosopher, or rather of the philosophic risk.

Between Apollo and Greek wisdom there is close connivance. The desire for full visibility under the light from on high, the aspiration to reach an immutable plane beyond the vicissitudes of the world at hand, all this inspires the sage and remains, even after the latter has lost his sacerdotal aura, part of the heritage of the philosopher's sublime passion.

Let us not forget that Apollo has been honored as the patron of philosophers. Along with the Muses, he presides over their brotherhoods.[14] In the spirit of the tradition, to philosophize is to worship Apollo. For a long time, as we know, when a philosopher appeared marked with a celestial sign (Pythagoras, Plato), a legend persistently maintained that he was the son of that god.

If the philosopher places himself under the sacred patronage of the god of light, it is then certain that philosophic excess can count on meeting its point of catastrophic rupture in a divine sanction administered by that same god. A manifestly immoderate philosophic ambition will necessarily outrage Apollo and incur his retaliation.

The meaning that the Oedipus myth has for Sophocles thus

becomes clearer. In its mythic form, the Oedipus story no doubt already had the general meaning Sophocles was to see in it: cognitive arrogance, punished by Apollo, and at a deeper level, the initiation avoided through the protagonist's presumption of wisdom. The precision of the tradition in determining the domains belonging to each of the three functional levels, and the fact that the trial in which Oedipus triumphed concerns the first function (the riddle) alone, allow us to conclude that such a signification could have been fully in place prior to the tragic elaboration. But Sophocles reactualizes the plot in the light of a new reality that must have confirmed the plot's import from his viewpoint: the profanatory excesses of the nascent philosophic reflection. The philosopher does indeed perpetuate a first-function activity, but he perverts this activity by destroying the traditional, received wisdom, by shaking timeless beliefs in the place and role of the gods. Love of *theōria*, of distance, of disinterested knowledge, love of the lofty and prophetic approach to all things, seemed to have been unchallengeably situated under Apollo's sacred patronage; by an impious feat, this same love now appears to deny the very existence of the gods, or to lead insidiously and necessarily to such a denial. If reflective intelligence seemed to be a precious gift offered to someone capable of opening himself up to the divine light, it now becomes a destructive tool used without limits by the thinker so he can invent, all by himself, a view of things that no tradition guarantees, and that desecrates all traditions.

Initiation, whatever its form—and it may take forms very different from the one the myth condenses in its formidable ellipsis— is a situation of transmission par excellence; it is the contrary, the undoing, of autodidactic self-satisfaction. The initiation rite supposes the acceptance of a spiritual authority; it inserts the neophyte in a chain that marks the place of a master and the attachment to founding ancestors. The philosopher, in his most radical incarnation, no longer presents himself as an initiate, but on the contrary as someone who, by himself, by virtue of his own reflection, liberated from any heritage, can discover the truth. Through a rupture that is an unprecedented presumption, in opposition to the priest or anyone else invested with priestly wisdom, the philosopher is the noninitiate. Scandalously, this quality is not, in his own eyes, a privation; it signifies a liberation and a hope. It is through the autonomous activity of his own reason, it is by autoreflection, without the help of any god or master, that the philosopher in his most extreme form purports to gain access to truth.

Thus, we can see how the mythic persona of Oedipus was made to order, as it were, for typifying the philosopher's claim with unparalleled depth. Through the exercise of his intelligence alone, Oedipus seeks to thrust aside the Sphinx, who stands as a vigilant and terrible guardian on the initiatory threshold. Oedipus bypasses the enigma of initiation instead of overcoming the initiatory obstacle. Just like the radical philosopher, he perverts a first-function activity (reason, intelligence) by using it to disqualify all traditional wisdom. Just like the philosopher, Oedipus intends to set out to conquer truth all by himself and not under the authority of a master and a legitimizing inheritance.

It is thus no accident that Sophocles gave Oedipus the visage we know from his tragedy at a time when philosophic reflection had already profoundly shaken the pillars of ancestral beliefs, and in a culture where it continued to agitate them more passionately than ever. Xenophanes, Heraclitus, Parmenides, Anaxagoras, Empedocles, Protagoras, Democritus, and the others, breaking with the mythic explanations that legitimized the cults rendered to the gods, invented new systems for explaining the world. Whether, as "physicists," they were seeking the fundamental substance in air, water, or fire, or speculating about beings or atoms, about the mixture of elementary bodies, or about organizing intelligence, they opposed their own adventurous doctrines to the teachings of a priestly tradition and, more or less directly, they challenged the gods of their people.

That an individual may form his own conception of man, the gods, celestial and atmospheric phenomena, and so forth, is the constitutively individualistic starting point of philosophy. It is not in its explicit content, in the simple consideration of the space granted to a hypothetical "subject" in the modern sense, that we must expect to find the foundation of the individual by philosophy at its origins. We have to take into account the incredible proliferation of quite individual but coherent viewpoints toward the world. This proliferation attests to an unprecedented unlinking of knowledge from unreflective adherence to a tradition transmitted by the ancestors or by earlier masters. It is through this irruption of autonomous thought, this passion for knowing by oneself alone, that philosophy can be equated, in principle and through its structure, with the birth of the individual, the insurrection of the subject. Of Heraclitus it was said: "He was nobody's pupil, but he declared that he 'inquired of himself' and learned everything from himself."[15] The legend is significant. The same thing had already been alleged of Xenophanes. And its profound connection with the subjective position of a Socrates, and the development of all philosophy, could be demonstrated, even if Heraclitus's formulations, in their still-oracular style, have very little to do with the argumentative language of Socrates.

Learn everything by oneself. This autodidactic pretension may well be the essential and inaugural core of philosophic inquiry in its most extreme strain; and we could argue without difficulty that the philosophy of the Moderns, specifically that of a Descartes, is already, in its construction (and its posture), virtually summed up in that ambition. Following this line of reasoning, the Cartesian subject would mark only, as an aftereffect, the moment when the consequences of that imperative are made explicit and become capable of organizing all thought.

That is why philosophy, from its origins in Greek discourse, is doubly nonmythic. It is nonmythic in its concepts and its explanatory schemas, which presuppose a desacralization of the cosmos (even if certain affiliations between the abstract speculation of an Anaximander and a mythic tradition have been discovered[16]), but also and perhaps especially, over and beyond all conceptual features, it is nonmythic in the unprecedented posture of the thinker who, without guarantees or antecedents, proposes a new and coherent mode of explanation for things, one that embraces men and gods, stars, animals, and the earth. In this reckless explanatory investigation that seeks to find the reasons for things all by itself there is a profanatory dimension. Divinity itself, what is most sacred and most untouchable, does not escape this autodidact curiosity.

And in fact, even if we can affirm that there is a fundamental solidarity between the birth of the philosopher and the advent of the free citizen, even if there is a clear correlation between the formation of the democratic space authorizing each individual to express his or her own viewpoint and the origin of philosophy, the fact remains that a sometimes-violent contradiction has opposed the philosopher and public opinion. We know that Xenophanes of Colophon was driven out of his country; that Anaxagoras was accused of impiety because he had maintained that the sun is an incandescent mass, and that he was condemned to exile despite the support of Pericles; that Protagoras, also accused of impiety, was driven out of Athens because he had expressed doubt about the possibility of knowing whether the gods exist or not. These last two philosophers were contemporaries of Sophocles, as was also Diagoras "the atheist," accused somewhat later of denying the existence of the gods, of profaning and divulging the mysteries (the supreme impiety in Greece).[17]

The fact that these philosophers were condemned and violently excluded from the city-state for the sacrilege they had committed against the tradition gives them undeniable kinship with the figure of Oedipus. This kinship would seem quite remote and vague, however, if we had not come to a better appreciation of the successful strategies Sophocles deployed to bring about the junction between a preexisting mythic figure and the specific contemporary features of philosophy. Not that Sophocles' tragedy should be reduced to a mere reflection of the current Athenian situation; rather, in that situation we can see a fundamental conflict that, over and beyond the tensions and incidents of everyday politics, unsettled fundamental anthropological underpinnings.

In a study that resituates Sophocles' play in its own time, Bernard Knox properly insists on the polemical significance of *Oedipus the King* in Periclean Athens. Knox's analysis, at once philological and thematic, shows how the play can be read as a declaration of rejection of the new concepts of the fifth-century philosophers and sophists, as a reaffirmation of the religious views of a divinely ordered universe. Knox goes so far as to assert that "the intellectual progress of Oedipus and Jocasta in the play" (from a concerted but entirely formal reverence toward Teiresias to a total incredulity toward divine signs) "is a sort of symbolic history of fifth-century rationalism."[18] Oedipus is a figure of the new man who relies only on his own intelligence, who places man at the center; this new man is at once a tyrant and a democratic spirit.[19] His language, like his attitude toward the gods and toward existence, is that of the "enlightened," "humanistic" Athenian liberated from ancient beliefs. Oedipus seeks complete knowledge and enlightenment. In opposition to Teiresias and Jocasta, he wants to understand everything, he wants all the details, he wants to reconstitute events in an objective narrative, leaving no traces of obscurity. Knox shows the importance of the verb *zētein* (to undertake research, carry out an investigation) and its derivatives; their connotations are at once scientific (medicine, philosophy) and juridical (inquest). Words like *skopein* (contemplate, examine), *historein* (seek, investigate), and *tekmairesthai* (judge according to the evidence, infer) also seem specially chosen by Sophocles to evoke the style of discussion of the new *sophos*.[20]

In short, "the attitude and activity of Oedipus are images of the critical spirit and the great intellectual achievements of a generation of sophists, scientists, and philosophers."[21] According to this reading, then, Sophocles' intention would thus be clearly and directly polemical. He condemns everything Oedipus stands for (which we might call, borrowing Dodds's term, Athenian "Enlightenment") while reaffirming, through the tragedy, the profanatory sense of this attitude and its fatal outcome. Oedipus's catastrophic destiny typifies the divine threat that looms over the atheistic and irreverent Athenian spirit. The mechanism of the Oedipean tragedy can only take on its full meaning for a consciousness that is "reactionary" with respect to the claims of reason, the individual, man.

These analyses, which confirm our intuitions, need to be completed by a reflection on the tragic genre itself, situated at the turning point between two historical moments—a genre that attests, this time in its very form, to the clash between these two ethoses.[22] Does not Greek tragedy, in its essence and by its very construction, whether we are dealing with *Antigone* or *The Bacchae*, always have the same polemical underpinnings that make it a permanent lesson directed against rationalism and humanism: the unwritten law of the gods wins out over the presumption of men? But if this is the case, *Oedipus the King* is not the exemplary Greek tragedy by accident. It is the play whose plot without any doubt conforms most fully and exactly to this conflictual form. In no other tragedy (if our account of the underlying mythic and ritual mechanism is correct) does the philosophic spirit of free thought and profanation conflict so directly with the tradition of the fathers, with the methodical ramification of the consequences. What is revealed in *Oedipus* is perhaps the essence of the Greek tragic form, inasmuch as the play is constituted simultaneously as an exposition and a critique of the new reason.

We have already emphasized that philosophy, as it came into being in ancient Greece, found itself in an ambiguous position. In its ultimate goals, as in certain of its procedures, it resembled the initiations of the mystery religions, but it also participated in the controversies of the *agora*: it adopted the conventions of public discussion and presented itself as direct preparation for the exercise of political power.[23] Thus, philosophy was able to draw upon a past in which wisdom was still identified with the initiatory progression, but it was also prepared to transpose this traditional aspect completely, to the point of unrecognizability, in order to reach a conceptual rationalism that excluded the symbolist dimension. Discussion, argumentation, polemics among equals, the confrontation of individual viewpoints leading to the recognition of divergences, and, more importantly, to the possibility of an agreement [*homologia*], were to become the rule of the intellectual game as of the political game. Thus, in place of a mysterious wisdom that entails a long internal progression allowing aspirants to achieve, through an ordered series of trials, a vision of Truth inaccessible to ordinary mortals, and a vision itself presenting various degrees of symbolic expression and understanding, there appeared another form of wisdom, one exercised and dispensed in the public square, in the assembly and the marketplace, in lucid discussions among equal interlocutors, in free dialogue in which each participant in turn could contribute his point of view and defend it.

It is Socrates who best incarnates this democratic wisdom, Socrates of whom it was rightly said that he had not (unlike all those who sought wisdom) been initiated into the mysteries of Eleusis. Pythagoras, as we know, has maintained and even elaborated the close connection between philosophy and initiation. Socrates, on the contrary, by introducing a discussion of truth into the public square in the form of a dialogue among equal interlocutors, unravels this sacred connection, and thereby necessarily places truth on the side of the concept, rather than—to resort to overly modern language—on the side of the symbol. The immediate, negotiable transparency of the notion is substituted for the graduated and difficult trial of symbolist profundity. In political and social practice, the reciprocal and reversible relation between legitimately equal points of view replaces a nonreversible relation that implied an authority, a hierarchy, a multiplicity of levels. Truth is now nothing but a human point of view, and no longer a revelation or a vision that shakes and marks the person who experiences it ritually. A certain sacrificial notion of truth (through an initiation, an injury, or a violent impression that establishes a connection with the gods and the fathers) is undone.

But if Oedipus arose at this moment as "the ideal type of Athenian intelligence,"[24] then it can hardly be claimed that he was decoded as the exemplary figure of philosophy only late in the history of European thought, with Hegel, Nietzsche, and finally Heidegger. Already for Sophocles (and for reasons that the tradition in which he had been formed must have made thinkable), some aspects of the recent excesses of philosophy were embodied by the persona of King Oedipus.[25] The presumptions of philosophic reason, however unprecedented, were inscribed in a wandering, a straying from the traditional path, that tradition had already consigned to a plot, that of the hero who, appearances notwithstanding, manages to avoid the trials of the triple initiation and becomes king all the same, but whose secret usurpation is finally brought to light.

§ 7 From Aspective to Perspective

Oedipus is the dramatic type who exemplifies a new posture that philosophy takes on. Let us call it "anthropocentering" to avert the misunderstanding that the term "anthropocentrism" might entail. For it is no longer a question of unwittingly attributing human qualities to the world, of projecting onto being an array of motives, feelings, and intentions that belong to the human soul alone. Quite to the contrary, it is a matter of recognizing that such projections have already been made, and of withdrawing those investments that had charged the universe, unduly, with human *pathos*, in order to restore them to the self. "Anthropocentering" is thus the exact opposite of "anthropocentrism."

Xenophanes of Colophon offers the earliest evidence we have of this move when he recognizes that the gods (at least the gods as people imagine them to be) are only projections emanating from man. The gods merely borrow their features, naively, from their inventors. "The Ethiopians say of their gods that they are snub-nosed and black; the Thracians claim that they have blue eyes and red hair."[1] The withdrawal of projections leads to a recognition that the beings earlier viewed as supernatural are products of the human imagination. This philosophical revolution, which persists right up to Feuerbach and Nietzsche, is the revolution wrought by Oedipus. If his answer to the Sphinx's riddle proves fatal to the winged virgin (without bloodshed), it is because the answer "man" typifies the anthropocentering move whereby all gods, demons, or other monsters are recognized as mere products of the human imagination, related back to man, and thus disavowed as independent beings with powers of their own. Oedipus's incredulity is what kills the Sphinx. She does not have to be killed in bloody hand-to-hand combat, as Bellerophon kills the Chimaera or Perseus kills Medusa. Oedipus has only to withdraw his projective belief by reducing every enigma to man, by establishing man as the unique source and agent; this is all it takes to make the Sphinx vanish before his eyes. The simple hand gesture by which Oedipus points to himself (brings the question back to himself) brings about the monster's immediate disappearance.

And in this sense, it is true that intelligence can suppress the Sphinx single-handedly, contrary to what was postulated by the tripartite arrangement of the trials. This is at least what philosophy thinks, what Hegel thinks. Autoreflection, self-consciousness, sends the monster headlong into the abyss. Oedipus is not only a usurper, then, a presumptuous neophyte who eludes the telestic confrontation by reducing it inappropriately to a single trial, he is also the one who, by his reasoned incredulity, destroys the cryptophoric mode of symbolizing that is presupposed by any confrontation of the initiatory type. If supernatural beings are merely products of the human imagination, if the profundity of the sacred symbols is only an illusion, or is only the profundity of the unselfconscious human soul, then acknowledging the illusion renders initiation itself obsolete. Oedipus's self-centered response to the obscure question chanted by the riddlesinger not only constitutes success in the first of the three trials, it puts a stop to the confrontation by its profanatory disavowal. By the work of autoreflection, the autodidactic intelligence has unburdened itself of all naive belief in the very existence of the initiatory animal as an irreducible alterity that has to be confronted.

Thus, Oedipus can be taken as the emblem of the passage to a culture centered on man. He typifies the critical mutation achieved by the Greeks: the transition from myth to reason, the birth of the individual as an autonomous agent and juridical subject, the search for consensus, democratic debate as the basis of politics,[2] and so on. This historical innovation can be approached in any number of ways, whether one is attempting to understand it on an ideological or an institutional level. But it seems to me that on the level of the imagination the Oedipus figure is the most overdetermined of all the fictional representations of that mutation. As Hegel noted accurately, but without being able to explore all the relevant factors and implications, the Oedipus figure is, in a way, the richest evidence we have of the constitutive imaginal mechanism that undergirds this decisive transition.

Oedipus is emblematic of the movement by which the human subject, recognizing itself as the source and agent, withdraws what it had projected onto the external world, with the result that in a single two-sided operation of deprojection, the subject discovers the world as an object (rather than a sign) and situates himself as a subject. It would not be impossible to show that all the original features characteristic of the "Greek miracle," whether we are concerned with philosophy, politics, or aesthetic representation, refer in one way or another to that operation. The unique point of view of a subject (thinking, perceiving, or desiring) is taken into account, and whether we are dealing with Socratic dialogue, democratic debate, or even, more subtly, with foreshortening in painting or "optical correction" in architecture, the uniqueness of the viewpoint is what governs the approach. A driving tendency of European thought and of the formal mechanisms it has produced derives from this mutation.

On the philosophical level, Heidegger has amply demonstrated that a certain relation of man to being (even prior to the sharp modern opposition between subject and object) began to take shape with Greek philosophy, and that Protagoras, in making man the measure of all things (although not in precisely the same sense as the Moderns do), was already pointing to the new relation of man to being that grounds Western metaphysics. But the Heideggerian analysis, strictly limited to the domain of philosophical discourse, is unable to complete and corroborate its findings by examining what the signifying mechanisms put in place by the

Greeks reveal. These mechanisms supply not only an overall confirmation, but also a decisively more profound understanding of the
Hellenic anthropocentering move and of the difference between
this inaugural anthropocentering and the one that the thinking of a
Descartes reshapes and completes.

The case of pictorial representation, while it is doubtless not determining, is nevertheless curiously revealing insofar as this change
of optic is concerned. Greek painters were the first to draw a frontal
view (rather than a profile) of a human foot, or to draw a carriage
wheel seen from an angle as an oblong form. In this technique,
known as foreshortening, the painter's goal is no longer to present
the object in its canonical form, the way an anonymous imagination would represent it for all eternity. He takes into account the
angle from which the object is perceived by an individual viewer.
The form of the object varies according to the angle of vision.

The discovery of foreshortening in painting, which contrasts
with archaic Egyptian figuration of the "frontal" type, may appear
to be a modest innovation. However, it is contemporaneous with a
much more general revolution in representation. During the same
historical period, scenic theatrical mechanisms based on archaic
ceremonies honoring Dionysus were beginning to emerge. The
Greek city-states in which this new vision was elaborated had
political institutions in which a reckoning with differing viewpoints expressed by citizens of equal status and political representation of the democratic type were starting to develop. Foreshortening in painting, philosophy, theater, democracy, and also the
monetary system: there is a close and remarkable solidarity among
all these mechanisms of representation. They belong to one and the
same historical moment: the moment at which the perspective of
the subject begins to be instituted.

The difference between Greek perspective and the monocentered perspective of the Renaissance corresponds closely to the gap
that exists between the Greek beginnings of autocentered subjectivity and Descartes's thought, which finally attributed a founding
and constructive role to the thinking subject's certainty regarding
the self. Thus, all of Heidegger's analyses concerning the significa-

tion of the "subjectum" in these two philosophies find an exact correlative in terms of visual representation. The Greeks had already achieved foreshortening, which presupposes that an individual subject's viewpoint is taken into account, but they did not achieve the geometrical systematization of perspective that the Renaissance would elaborate on the basis of this single viewpoint.

Similarly, the principle of optical correction in Greek architecture has an import that surpasses simple techniques of building construction. What is at stake is the new status of the subject itself as the center of vision on the basis of which the building's form must be conceived. We know that the architecture of the Parthenon does not rigorously respect vertical and horizontal planes. If a tall building is constructed following perfectly horizontal and perfectly vertical lines, to an observer located outside the building it will appear to spread out toward the top and become narrower toward the bottom. In order to correct these optical illusions, the Greek architect undertook calculated deformations. Long horizontal elements like architraves, cornices, and stylobates have imperceptibly convex lines. They arch up and come down at midpoint in order to appear straight to the eye. The stylobate of the Parthenon has a slight convexity at its center. Similarly, the vertical shafts of the columns lean inward near the top in order to correct the optical illusion that would otherwise make them appear to tilt outward; moreover, a swelling (*entasis*) of the shaft corrects the optical illusion that makes a rectilinear contour seem to grow thinner. The architect thus applied a visual compensation using the viewer's eye as the starting point. He was not constructing a building in itself, offered to the unsituatable gaze of a god, but a building for humans who look at it. Oedipus's response and the optical correction of the Parthenon belong to the same moment in the history of the symbolic: the constitution of the perspective subject.

Greek man thus disengages himself from his fascination with the figure not by eliminating it but by inventing a new mechanism: he brings the subject into a position of mastery over the object by making appearances depend on the viewing subject's point of view. By thus producing appearances, by becoming the ingenious manufacturer of an optical illusion aimed at deceiving the eye (*tromper l'oeil*) (though no one was actually deceived except Zeuxis's birds), Greek man gains mastery over the perceptible. Images no longer impose themselves, no longer erect themselves as colossi; images are always constructed for someone.

No longer a mute, massive, and eternal presentation that ignores the observer's viewpoint, representation now includes in its formal constitution, as pre-vision, the specific site occupied by a viewer-subject. The object is painted for the subject in a painting that technically produces the object's optical appearance as that object presents itself, not in itself, or to imagination in general, but to the unique regard of some person precisely located in space. In this painting, the singular subject's awareness of being the focal point of a view of the world is part of the very mechanism by which the image is constituted. The technique of foreshortening attests, on the pictorial level, to the fact that a singular and accidental point of view vis-à-vis the object has been taken into account. What is represented is not the object in itself, as an invariant model, an absolute and endlessly repeatable form that no individual perception comes to distort and modulate; what is represented is the object relativized by the point of view constituted by the subject from the subject's own position in space.

Greek optical realism, which introduces foreshortening and other effects of spatial depth such as relief and shading, already constitutes a clear challenge to the prevailing solidarity between objectivity and subjectivity. It is just when the subject recognizes itself as source of a unique viewpoint that it can also situate a thing in its independent objectivity. Thus, imitative art, contrary to the symbolist and magical art of the Egyptians, corresponds to the type of objective truth that the effort of the Greek *epistēmē* attempts to identify, just as it corresponds to the ethical and political inclinations toward free individuality and the democratic inclination to confront individual viewpoints until agreement is reached.

While the Greeks did not go so far as to develop a systematic, mathematical construction of monocentered perspective (this was not achieved, as we know, until the Renaissance), they did develop a pictorial and sculptural vision based on optical realism that is the beginning of the perspectivist conception of the world. This is the sense in which we can speak of "perspective," even—already—in painting. Just as philosophy introduced a Greek rupture in the realm of thought, perspective constitutes the Greek rupture in the history of painting.

Several terms have been suggested to designate the "pre-Greek" mode of figuration common to all primitive peoples, whether in Mesopotamia, ancient China, pre-Columbian America, or Pharaonic Egypt. The expressions "frontality" (used by Julius Lange) or "based on frontal images" (Heinrich Schäfer) have been widely accepted for a long time. Scholars have also spoken of "ideoplastic" art (the Frankfurt school) or "ideogenic" art to emphasize that painters paint not what they see but what they think they see. As Gombrich says: "The Egyptians had based their art on knowledge. The Greeks began to use their eyes."[3] It is as though pre-Greek painting was always painting "from memory," based on a synthetic and simplified mental image left in the mind by objects of a given type (trees, birds, fish "in general"), while Greek drawing was done "from nature": the form of a particular tree is grasped from the point of view of the individual who is drawing. In this respect, the familiar comparisons of primitive representation with children's drawings are not illegitimate, except that it is important to stress the much more significantly constraining role of the canons established by tradition in primitive painting, especially Egyptian painting, which is the most highly developed and the best-studied case of this mode of figuration.

However, I have chosen to adopt a term proposed by Emma Brunner-Traut in her epilogue to the crucial work of Heinrich Schäfer, the term "aspective." In its very construction, this term succeeds in marking the clear opposition between the two modes of figuration, and beyond that, between two types of culture.[4] The difference between aspective and perspective in modes of figuration doubtless corresponds (if we set aside the stage of abstract art) to a rupture whose aesthetic and cultural significance has no equivalent in the history of representation.

In Egyptian painting, there are no effects of depth in the use of color or in the arrangement of lines. Everything appears flat, as if arrayed on a single plane. All the parts of the human or animal body are presented in frontal projection, either facing straight ahead or in profile, without any views from an angle. Feet are arranged in profile along a baseline. In the same image, several viewing angles may be combined with no concern for unity of viewpoint. A pool will be represented as a blue rectangle seen from above, while fish will be shown in profile, and trees shown as "cut down" along the sides of the rectangle. The general rule for each object is optimum visibility: the side of the object that allows for its easiest identification is the side represented. Hence the stereotypical nature of the forms: the same object is always represented in identical fashion, in a canonical presentation that seems to be independent of the viewer-subject's variable situation vis-à-vis the object. All this gives Egyptian painting its "fixed," "immobilized" character, that solemn and hieratic aspect that is so characteristic of this mode of representation. We might say that the Egyptians draw what "one" sees (or what "it" sees from the immutable standpoint of fantasy, or the gods), while the Greeks draw what an "I" sees. They have hit upon a mode of representation in the first-person singular.

It is significant that one cannot describe the innovation introduced by perspective without considering the new place man occupies in this mechanism. Construction in perspective places man at the center, as self-conscious point of view, as source, goal, and consequence. Whereas the Egyptian placed his object "straight ahead," as if the object existed independently, "a Greek places *himself* at the mid-point and assembles all the optical lines that start from the object in *his* eye, and so is acting anthropocentrically."[5] The description is valid for the mechanism of autocentering. But it would be better to speak, instead, of the optical lines that start from his eye to reach the object, for in Greek optics the luminous ray is thought to start from the eye and not the object.[6] Moreover, this notion only helps to emphasize the active and central role attributed to the point of view of the spectator, of man;

the strength of the fledgling mechanism of perspective itself may even lie behind this theory of eyes that emit optical rays, a theory that is accurate in terms of perspective construction of vision, though false as a physical theory of light.

This construction gives shape, in the realm of perception, to the operation whereby the subject identifies himself as the source and agent of vision while at the same time withdrawing the unconscious projections that had animated the world and given it magical density. No longer an obscure symbol overinvested with inexhaustible meanings, the perceptual landscape becomes a fact, an object. Thus, the passage from aspective to perspective in painting can become the index of a more general mutation that affects all institutions to such an extent that their characteristics can be usefully designated by these two terms in summary fashion.

To democracy, theater, philosophical dialogue, and foreshortening in painting, we need to add the Greek invention of money,[7] which is a particularly apt marker for the structural change we are examining. The Egyptians used counting money, an ideal standard that served as a unit of reference for the evaluation of merchandise that nevertheless continued to be exchanged in the marketplace under the apparent form of barter. The Greek innovation consisted in combining, through the state manufacture of coins, the ideal function of a standard and the everyday instrumental function of exchange within a single monetary unit. Greek money not only serves as a general measure of the value expressed in the body of a precious metal, it also comes down into the marketplace and takes part in the commercial transactions of traders. Each individual possesses a universal measure that is at the same time a means of carrying out exchanges. This system of circulating money, even in its probably "demagogic" origin (the decision of a "tyrant" seeking to satisfy the people at the expense of the aristocracy),[8] is perfectly congruent with what ultimately comes to constitute the institutional originality of the Greek world, whether we see it as the birth of democracy or the beginning of perspective.

The correlation between aspective and the Egyptians' ideal money is easy to grasp, as is the correlation between circulating money and perspective. Just as Egyptian painting is constituted as a series of views that always present the same side of an object according to a canonical form that has no place at all for the variable viewpoint of an individual spectator, so Egyptian money remains an ideal standard, an immutable evaluative archetype functioning in a place inaccessible to traders. On the other hand, just as perspective presupposes the use of a subject's individual and accidental viewpoint in the construction of an objective view, circulating money brings the immanence of the individual trading agent into coincidence with a universal standard.[9]

The transformation of the Greek myths into a tragic representation itself corresponds to the passage from aspective to perspective. The Oedipus myth is a story told in aspective. It presents the same "arrested," canonical, "remembered" character as the mode of painting that belongs to the same period in the history of figural representation. Moreover, it is the impersonal rigor of this anonymous production, at once memorable and timeless, that makes it the privileged object of structural analyses. The tragedy based on the Oedipus story draws upon mythic aspective while bringing it into a new regime of representation that tends to put its features in perspective. The tensions and contradictions of this transition are evident in the tragedy itself. That is why here, again, the form of tragic representation in general (as a transition from aspective to perspective on the narrative level) is so perfectly consonant with the Oedipus story in the singularity of its deepest meaning.

The Oedipus plot is the most overdetermined and the richest monument remaining to us that maintains traces of the imaginal conditions of the transition from a world dominated by aspective to a world dominated by perspective. The Oedipus story prefigures and exposes the passage from aspective to perspective. With Oedipus's response and his posture, the Sphinx vanishes, for this imaginary or symbolic being has truth only if the subject does not identify himself as the center of the visible, and if the unconscious external projection of an internal dimension of the human soul persists. The victory over the Sphinx is thus tantamount to the emergence of the perspective view of the world.

Yet in the same movement, the initiatory trial, which had been based on a ritual confrontation with the obscure projective images received from a timeless tradition, becomes (or seems to become) objectless, and it gives way to self-consciousness, to the immediate and specular transparency of a human subject's self-knowledge. For initiation, like Sphinxes, gods, and dreams, can exist only in aspective. Here we can grasp the power of the Oedipus myth: it is not enough to say that the mutation it exposes is anthropological, since in this mutation the very conditions of possibility of an anthropological view of the world are decided. The posture of Oedipus is the imaginal foundation for all anthropology.

A significant anecdote that might be compared, in a way, with Oedipus's solution, helps to show how Periclean Greece can be viewed as the time and place in which that possibility is realized. This is the anecdote Plutarch tells about Pericles' cloak. During a sudden eclipse of the sun that terrifies the helmsman of his ship, Pericles places his own cloak before the man's eyes, explaining that the cause of the eclipse is only an opaque body like his cloak, and nothing more. The Athenian leader thus frees the superstitious sailor from a sacred terror in the face of the sun's eclipse by giving him a lesson in perspective. Instead of perceiving the stars as divine signs, as celestial hieroglyphics whose meaning is subject to the interpretive wisdom of a seer, Pericles, who had spent time with Anaxagoras, sees only phenomena that obey the elementary laws of optics. It is through this new wisdom, which counters that of the priests and the soothsayers, that Pericles wins a victory over the sacred terror of darkness. And in this respect, his intellectual victory over the terrifying eclipse has the same meaning as Oedipus's triumph over the Sphinx. It is, in every sense of the word, a victory of perspective—or the rational viewpoint of man—over aspective. By situating himself as a viewpoint on the world, as the central and unique measure of all things, man simultaneously acquires the objective view that solves all riddles, calms all terrors, hurls all Sphinxes into the abyss. Such is the confidence that the moment of anthropocentering engenders and maintains. To stop seeing the world in aspective and start seeing it in perspective is to suppress all at once the enigmatic density of things that have been resonating with the language of the gods. The moon, sun, and stars are no longer mysterious signs overinvested with hidden meaning that have to be deciphered as presages; they are objects, physical phenomena. Man is no longer a fearful and expectant being torn between prayer and terror, always dependent on higher powers, his acts subject to ambiguous and changeable divine decrees that he tries to decode from signs that are always oblique. Freed from the help as well as the threats of divine powers, no longer learning from anyone but himself, no longer relying on anything but the evidence of his own reason, man governs himself alone, standing erect amid phenomena. The fact that Oedipus succeeds all by himself, and by pronouncing the word "man," condenses in a formidable mythic ideogram the entire philosophic ambition of a Protagoras: "Man is the measure of all things." That Sophocles should have perceived this new ambition as a real insurrection, full of greatness but also full of sacrilegious risk, is attested by the well-known chant of the chorus in *Antigone*: "Numberless wonders[,] terrible wonders walk the world but none the match for man. . . . And speech and thought, quick as the wind and the mood and mind for law that rules the city—all these he has taught himself." But is there not a danger that man, in the same autodidactic and autocritical move-ment, will "break the . . . laws," rising up in "some act of mad defiance"?[10]

Among the Greeks, unitary centering is produced above all as man's point of view. That is why, for them, the question whether the divine is one or many is neither essential nor foundational. It is not the monotheist inclination but the anthropological decision that brings men out of projective magic, frees them from the semantic attribution that overinvests the world with meaning. Dissolution of cryptophoric symbolism (symbolism that confronts the human being with an infinity of interpretations) and access to a world of facts that is no longer inhabited by obscure forces are not achieved by separation from a unique and unfigurable god but by the operation of anthropocentering and self-consciousness. It is perspective (in the broad sense, by no means restricted to pictorial technique) that brings about the disenchantment of the world. That is also why there is no need to destroy the idols, to refuse all figural constructs. The realistic optic, representation that follows the monocentered perspective, does not need to abolish images in order to undo projective illusions; it takes a different tack. By constructing illusion through technical means, by calculating the rational conditions of *trompe-l'oeil*, the Greeks disenchanted the world through re-presentation itself. This is why, again, the choice between monotheism and polytheism never appeared to the Greeks to be a crucial one. If they conceived of the divine in the singular, it was not because of a belief in a unique and exclusive God;[11] it was rather because, for them, the unitary centering did not start with God, it started with man. The injunction to "know thyself" is significant in this connection. The self is the reference point for the movement of demythologization. The fact that the decision in favor of self-knowledge transforms the relation to the divine and permits access to the One is a transcendental correlative rather than an inaugural imperative—to such an extent that even God will be conceived in the mode of absolute reflection: for Aristotle, God is "thought [that] thinks itself."[12]

~

Sophocles, with a profundity that is doubtless radical and unequaled, still sees the philosopher through the eyes of myth. A man of the old Greece, faithful to ancestral rites and beliefs, he recognizes, in the self-satisfaction of those contemporaries who put themselves forward as sages, an audacity that the story of Oedipus, with its fatal outcome, had already foreseen. While philosophers elaborate a new reasoning that attempts to divorce itself from mythic thinking—perhaps blinding themselves, in the process, to their own position in the play of ethical constraints that the myth incorporates into its plot—the dramatist uses the eyes of mythic wisdom to see the young figure of the philosopher in its emergence. In this respect, Sophocles' tragedy is rich in a kind of knowledge that has not exhausted its effects even today. The philosopher does not understand myths. He devalues their import; he fails to recognize their power and their logic; in his legitimate and heroic effort to detach himself from the old projective beliefs, he rejects in toto the ponderous accumulation of incoherent fables and the stubborn superstitions they nourish. But the dramatist, for his part, understands the philosopher's reasoning, makes room for it, situates it, even if he does so with such reticence and such partiality that he condemns it unreservedly to a fearful malediction.

But if Sophocles exemplifies the philosophical scene in the tragedy of the king of Thebes, what he produces is by no means an illustration or allegory. Having the key to this staging does not suffice for a complete decoding of an exemplary figure of the new *sophos* of the Athenian agora. The tragedy explores and unsettles the scene of philosophy, bringing to light what philosophy does not know about itself, what it cannot glimpse within the terms of its own language. Sophocles produces a critique in the strong sense, tracing the limits to which philosophy can only remain blind, disclosing the posture, unthought by philosophy itself, that institutes it. This tragic critique—unnoticed even by those who, like Hegel, recognized that Oedipus's intelligence inaugurated philosophical consciousness—is more powerful, in the long run, than the one Heidegger undertook in his meditation on "Being." What the Oedipus plot discloses is the protophilosophic posture that generates the conquering orientation of philosophy up to Descartes and Nietzsche. The enormous interest of this posture with respect to modern conceptualizations is that it does not suppress the imaginal preconditions of the philosopher's position. It reveals their forgotten footings, their irreducible fiber. It allows us to trace the frontiers of the philosophizing attitude—frontiers of which that attitude itself is unaware—so we can more readily cross them and emerge on either side of the enclosure where Heidegger's rumination confines and exhausts it. Let me make the point here and now, before returning to it in greater detail: what Western thought has had to acknowledge, since the Enlightenment, as another scene, foreign to the reflective subject, is precisely what the Oedipean posture—founding the subject as consciousness of self—excluded and denied. The gesture by which Oedipus situated himself so as to respond to the "riddling bitch," guardian of the initiatory threshold, and the belief that he could abolish her with the word "man" in a presumption of auto-initiation, are what institute, in a counter-effect, the difference between what will later be called consciousness and unconsciousness. Hegel glimpsed this but, for good reasons, was unable to see its implications.

Oedipus's posture is a perversion of the Apollonian principle that enjoins self-knowledge. It is as if the Sphinx's conqueror was committing himself to the path of the wrong self-knowledge, knowledge that wounds the divine instead of honoring it.

The myth of Narcissus gives an example of the way the Delphic injunction to "know thyself" can be misinterpreted. It is to Narcissus that Teiresias's prophetic statement applies: "When asked whether this child would live to reach well-ripened age, the seer replied: 'If he ne'er know himself.' "[13] We can readily see why Narcissus's self-knowledge is of the wrong sort: it derives from appearances, from a mirror image, from imaginary specularity, and it leads to the mortal love of his own face. Understood this way, the Delphic injunction would designate a hidden and invisible "one-self," rather than an apparent "myself." The Delphic instruction to "know thyself," a precept issuing from the center, the navel of the Earth, would concern the difficult access to a divine self within the soul, and not the specular view of one's mortal visage. But another possible perversion of Apollo's precept is more subtle and insidious, and destined to endure. This one lies not so much in the immediate fascination of one's own image, in the specular inclination of Narcissus, as in a speculative orientation that is more intellectual than aesthetic. This would be the perversion of Oedipus—and of philosophy. Thus the same Teiresias, the blind old priest of Apollo, Teiresias the initiate, warns against at least two misinterpretations of the Delphic pronouncement. Authentically Apollonian self-knowledge is neither Narcissus's version nor Oedipus's. It is not fascination with one's own image in the mirror. It is not abstract reflexivity, either, not consciousness of self by self that reduces the soul to its cogitating focalization and refers truth back to the "I," or to generic man. Egocentering of that sort, in which the inflation of the intellect and the self-importance of the ego are reinforced, leads to the negation of the gods and the denial of all teaching.

Such, however, is the *hubris* of Oedipus. For him, man's viewpoint is the unique center of perspective: the "I" that reflects consciousness of self, is the only source capable of shedding light and clarity on all things. From his answer to the Sphinx, which offends the obscurity of the sacred and denies the signs of the gods in making man the measure of all things, up to the inquiry designed to shed all possible light on the self, Oedipus is the one who inflects the injunction to "know thyself" toward total mastery of the ego, toward an autoreflective consciousness, without any transindividual alterity.

Sophocles' language is significant. The extraordinary lexical importance of first-person singular constructions in *Oedipus the King* has already been stressed.[14] In the first 150 lines of Oedipus's discourse, 14 lines end with some lexical form of the type "I" or "my," and 15 begin in the same way. There are also countless occurrences of the word "myself" (*egō*): "I must know my birth, no matter how common it may be—I must see my origins face-to-face"; or, later in the same tirade, "I, I count myself the son of Chance." This insistence on the self aptly underlines a decisive way of positioning oneself in being, of thinking with the self as starting point, as center of reference. "I, Oedipus": such is the hero's ontological posture, from the beginning of the play to the end. And this ego is an exceptional one, who assigns himself the task of shedding full light. Nothing is more telling than the way Oedipus formulates his decision to search for the person responsible for Laïus's death: "I'll bring it all to light myself!" (*egō phanō*).[15] The ambiguity of the Greek expression has been rightly remarked, for it can be read in two ways: I myself will shed light on the enigma (the mystery of the death of Laïus); but also: I will shed light on myself, I will discover myself, I will expose myself to the light.[16]

But even more than this, it is through the whole structure of the intrigue that constitutes him that Oedipus is defined according to a new mode, one that could provisionally be called "autological" (the meaning of this term will become clearer as we go along). Oedipus embodies an existence that defines itself self-referentially in an autoreflective, autoreferential, auto-ontological manner. According to a variant of the Oedipus myth, the protagonist's answer to the Sphinx's question was "myself," and this is an extremely interesting indication. On the celebrated Vatican plate that represents the riddle scene, we note Oedipus's hand turned toward himself as if he were designating himself by way of response. But even without resting our case on this mythic variant and on this small iconographic detail, we can demonstrate the amplitude of the autological mechanism through which Oedipus's fate is defined.

The connecting thread of the drama can be summarized in a few words in which the stress falls on a single feature: Oedipus, an autodidact who has become an autocrat through an autoreferential response, pursues an investigation that will become more and more autobiographical, in which he will discover that he himself is the guilty party, after which he will inflict self-punishment on himself. The entire plot of Oedipus's story is marked even in its details by this autological movement. Pursuing the argument, we can stress each of these movements in turn. Oedipus becomes the savior of Thebes by himself, without being helped by the gods or receiving instruction from any mortal. His response to the riddle (which, let us recall, causes the Sphinx to be hurled down from her stone in an act of self-murder—of suicide) was found by "simple reflection." The response is in itself, through its content, autoreflective: "myself" or "man." And the enigma, in its very formulation, concerns the counting of feet (*pous*), a word that is at the root of the name "Oedipus" itself (*Oidipous*, swollen foot) and the index of his identity. It is thus with a reference to himself, in an act of self-knowledge and self-identification, that Oedipus resolves (or believes he resolves) the riddle of the winged virgin. He becomes a "tyrant," that is, an autocrat without a royal heritage, a sovereign who has conquered power himself instead of receiving it as a legitimate heir. Then, in the face of a new riddle, the mystery of Laïus's death, he boasts that he can shed full light ("I'll bring it all to light myself"), and thus, without knowing it at first, he undertakes what will be only an investigation of himself—his birth, his origins, his true identity. The crime of incest that he discovers in this way is itself, in a sense, autological: he spawned lives, he says, "in the loins that spawned [his own] wretched life." With an untranslatable word Oedipus declares of himself that he is *homogenēs*: as used here, the Greek term denotes someone who has the same ancestry as oneself.[17] More tellingly still, we cannot fail to note that one of the Greek words signifying "incestuous" is *autogennētos*. Even if Sophocles does not use this term, it provides evidence that the notion of "self" and "oneself," even when parents are involved, is presented in the idea of incest, a sexual relation "among ourselves" and not with others. It is as if Oedipus's incest is the extreme point, pushed to an outer limit and a destructive consequence, of the autistic or autocratic (or in any event autologic) orientation of his destiny.

Oedipus, finally, judges himself, damns and condemns himself. Then he precipitates his autological destiny to a point of (punitive) self-mutilation by putting out his own eyes in order to unburden himself of sight. The term Sophocles uses to characterize this act is, once again, remarkable: *autocheir*, by his own hand, a term often used with the meaning "the one who kills himself."[18] Through a movement of implacable rigor and exemplary consistency, Oedipus's destiny is thus entirely placed under the sign "by oneself."

We cannot help but see here (still in mythic form) the emergence of a new subject: for the first time the singular individual—the autonomous subject. From the moment of his victory over the Sphinx without the help of the gods to the catastrophe in which he discovers himself to be deprived of, or abandoned by, the divine (in Sophocles' text, the term is *atheos*, "loathed by the gods,"[19] Oedipus' tragic trajectory is inscribed as a movement of autoreflection, of self-knowledge, of individuation, that coincides first of all with the conquest of power—including the extreme, exorbitant, unwitting power that consists in possessing his own mother by replacing his own father—up to the reversal that makes this process of autonomization and self-attachment an act of self-blinding. Oedipus traverses the entire circuit of acting "by oneself."

From the dramaturgical viewpoint, moreover, the autologic reversal is marked from the outset by the inaugural curse that Oedipus utters against whoever is responsible for the misfortunes that have befallen Thebes. The audience already knows that Oedipus himself is the responsible party—and that what is going on, even before the final self-punishment, is self-malediction. Sophocles' text as a whole thus concentrates the plot in such a way that the play completes the circle of the series of autisms, enclosing the blinded Oedipus within the tragic confines of absolute autonomy—which amounts to nothing less, for Sophocles, than Oedipus's "atheism."

Now, it is quite clear that what this tragedy, with its final reversal, exposes as the failure of acting "by oneself" constitutes a complete and developed expression of the futility of the attempt to avoid the initiatory passage, an attempt that characterizes, as we have seen, the internal structure of the Oedipus myth. Oedipus is an autodidact in a new sense, such a radical and subversive sense that he challenges the mechanisms of initiation, of transmission, and thus of symbolic reproduction. The rite of passage (royal investiture) is a sacred pedagogy that calls for the reception of a teaching. No neophyte is formed without a master whose word is respected, whose own received wisdom is recognized and venerated. Oedipus typifies the protagonist who stakes a claim to knowledge by reflection alone and without sacrifice, the one who intends to think for himself, and not to receive from someone else a tradition transmitted from generation to generation. He denies the knowledge of the fathers and wise men (the *patrios logos*) as well as the help of the gods. His refusal of all authority is expressed in the mythic ideogram of patricide. The way events are linked produces a whole chain of consequences: the father's murder violently inaugurates the Oedipean decision to be autonomous (defiance of all higher authority); the response to the Sphinx is the sacrilege that, as a result of the decision in favor of autonomy, brings about the triumph of pure knowledge and the power of the self; incest, finally, is the most reserved and most obscure but not the least necessary or the least radical consequence of the autologic orientation. There is an implacable autistic logic in the very narrative order of the crimes. The patricide, the response to the riddle, and the incest are successive crimes of violent autonomization. Oedipus deflects all the fertile moments in which an irreducible alterity ought to be recognized (the authority of a king, the strangeness of the sacred, the otherness of the feminine) by suppressing the encounter with alterity through an act of autological resolution in each case.

And what does the trial signify, at bottom, if not the moment when dependency on the secular family is broken by the son's death to childhood, but also when, after the torturous death, a new dependency is recognized, a deeper and more internalized dependency on the gods and the forefathers? The initiation is the moment of violent severance in which the subject frees himself from secular ties in order to submit to a sacred law, to become a member of a spiritual community, to inscribe himself within a symbolic rather than fleshly filiation that binds him to the line of dead ancestors and to divine transcendence. The subject thus acquires a new identity. Even in its most archaic forms, the trial, through varied but convergent symbolizations, reveals this essential structure. Rather than introducing the initiate to the absolute autonomy of reflective consciousness, the rite of passage, a puberty rite or a mysteric rite, moves the initiate from a primary and infantile heteronomy (dominated by the real mother and father) to a higher heteronomy that consists, after the monstricidal horror, in allegiance to the unwritten law of the gods and the dead fathers. In the heroic and royal myths, this new and superior heteronomy is embedded in plots less through the episode of the imposed trial than through the hero's recourse to gods and wise men during the difficult passage of the trials. The fact that the hero is often, like Oedipus, abandoned by his real parents is also the most adequate way of representing the situation that will confront him, the task that awaits him: he must distance himself, break away, and replace by a sacred affiliation the painfully broken bond with the parental filiation. The failure to make this replacement is the failure of initiation. Oedipus unwittingly rediscovers his own father and his own mother by a movement of return to the very moment when, according the logic of regular initiation (and the logic of the monomyth that embeds this movement within plots), he ought to have met a man who was not his own father and a woman who was not his own mother. This perverse return toward one's self and one's home is the very movement of avoided initiation that allows no superior heteronomy to be established. It results from an orientation in being that disallows the opening to the unknown through which the help of the gods and the mediation of the sages inaugurates a dependency upon unwritten laws. It is remarkable that the autological disruption that takes on extraordinary consistency in Sophocles' tragedy (from the automalediction that does not recognize itself as such to the intentional self-blinding) is already inscribed in the narrative texture of the myth through its ordered difference from the monomyth. With Sophocles it acquires new meaning: the philosopher, a deliberate noninitiate, encloses himself within the autological circle and is promised to disaster, to the tragic loss of god and light.

§ 8 Philosophy I

With respect to the autodidactic decision, the distinction, or the opposition, between the pre-Socratics and those who come after Socrates is secondary and derivative. Nietzsche indeed saw Socrates as an autodidact, but he exploited this feature for his own polemical denunciation of democratic man, overlooking the fact that among pre-Socratics such as Heraclitus or Xenophanes the autodidactic ambition had already been professed and valorized, and had become virtually legendary. Thus, the view according to which the origins of philosophy remain untouched by the autodidactic orientation cannot be sustained. If the autodidactic decision, in a strong and essential sense, is a major feature of the invention of philosophy, perhaps *the* major feature, this means that Descartes and Kant—who both, in one way or another, prescribed "thinking for oneself"—simply explore more deeply the implications of an imperative that was already at work at the outset, or that stands, at any rate, as the inaugural decision of the philosophizing activity, since it is the counterpart of the reflective ambition that constitutes such activity.

Even if the claim that all Western philosophies are equally Oedipean is false, philosophy remains oriented by the gap opened up with the gesture that Oedipus typifies; and its task, however variable, always takes this gesture into account, whether in extremist fashion (as with Descartes, Feuerbach, or Nietzsche), or (with

Plato, in the first instance) as an attempt to overcome the scandal that the gesture caused, an effort to quell the insurrection of the subject exemplified by Oedipus.

More than any other, the figure of Socrates is highly indicative of the autodidactic and individualist tendency of philosophical thought, and that is why this figure is often taken for an authentic beginning. Socrates is typically portrayed as the philosopher who received no teaching, the one who found truth in himself and by himself. A legend about Socrates' father offers an almost transparent indication that the attitude might be connected with a withdrawal of paternal authority.

Plutarch tells us that oracular instructions conveyed to Socrates' father "bade him let the child do whatever came into his mind, and not to do violence to his impulses or divert them, but allow them free play . . . surely implying by this that he had a better guide of life in himself [*en autōi*] than a thousand teachers and attendants."[1]

The real father's withdrawal, his retreat, his effacement, not to say his deficiency, thus permits access to an internal guide who is worth more than all the masters and teachers together. As a child, Socrates was left to his own devices. His father did not restrain him in any way, did not impose on him the yoke of any authority. The child was to find in himself, on his own, the guiding principle that would replace that external authority. The scene of the father's withdrawal, the scene of the son liberated from all external tutelage, thus is situated at the beginning of the formation of philosophical thought. The autonomy of the son gives birth to philosophy. If this new mode of thought is one of the major factors in the Greeks' break with the past, it is because it corresponds to an antipatriarchal agitation that can be detected in other characteristic features of Greek civilization, including the establishment of democracy.

If Socrates has none but an internal master, his teaching, in turn, proceeds from a position of nonmastery: the "empty" place that is his, and that constitutes the originality of his language. His way is to impose no preexisting knowledge, no dogma; to say that he knows nothing; to limit himself to urging his interlocutor to find the truth within himself. If Socrates was not formed by the dictatorship of the father, he was not destined to occupy the place of the patriarchal master or hierophant; rather, his is a paradoxical place, a nonplace, from which he will incite his interlocutor, by questioning rather than asserting, to think for himself, to discover truth within himself, apart from all imposed traditions and dogmas. What makes Socrates unique, what makes him the founder of philosophical interlocution, is this elision of the father that produces a new relation to discourse and to others and fosters the dialogical procedure for the search for truth.

Nothing is more telling, in this regard, than the famous dialogue in the *Meno* in which, although confronted with an interlocutor defined by a twofold empirical inferiority (he is a child of the servant class), Socrates still refuses to occupy the predictable place of father and master. Through his questioning, he succeeds in proving that every human being, whoever he may be, whatever his apparent inferiority, is capable of finding in himself the noblest and most difficult truths. In a paradox that embraces the full inaugural singularity of his position, Socrates is a professor of autodidacticism. He teaches only one thing, even to the servant child, and that is to get along without teachers—an approach that is not devoid of a striking subversive potential, even in the realm of politics.[2]

If one legend has it that Socrates' father imposed nothing on him because the child had an internal guide, Hegel recalls another legend that is no less significant.[3] In another remarkable exception to the Athenian rule, it is said that Socrates was never initiated into the Eleusian mysteries. Socrates, the wisest of the Greeks, is depicted as the only one who was not introduced to the mysteries, who did not receive their revelation.

All these features are completely consistent. Socrates found his principles of conduct and truth by himself and in himself. No father, no master, no hierophant taught him a thing. On this point at least, his resemblance to the Oedipus figure is peculiarly revealing.

Socrates, the noninitiate, introduces a new form of initiation, however: a form based on a relation of self to self, on one's own knowledge of oneself. It is certainly not a matter of reducing the "self" to an insulary ego. Socrates does find a guide within himself; however, he views this guide as a divine other, different from himself. The philosopher venerates his god, his "demon"—the personal and individualized messenger of a higher god, who for his part remains without relation to man.[4] The inner confrontation between Socrates and his own god is the basis for a new morality. If Socrates is accused of no longer believing in the gods of the city-state, it is because instead of worshipping the divinities the city has adopted, he puts his own "demon" first: a form of worship, as Apuleius astutely observed, "that is nothing but the initiation into the mysteries of philosophy."[5] The discipline of philosophy is born of an internalizing movement that makes auto-initiation possible, a movement summed up in the injunction to "know thyself." Philosophy is no longer an introduction, performed by a qualified priest, to the mysteries of an external and socialized god; it is the recognition of an internal, individuated god, a form of moral consciousness that is still personalized but that nevertheless places man in an ethical situation of autonomy rather than heteronomy. Socrates is the first individual. He is also, in another sense, the first free-thinker. He replaced the traditional hetero-initiation by philosophical auto-initiation.

In all these respects there is an affinity between Socrates and Oedipus. They are both situated at the moment of deprojection that brings back to the subject what had first been attributed to external reality or expected from the accomplishment of rites. The world is no longer invested with cryptophoric signs that attest to the multiple presence of gods: it is in man himself, and only in man, that the basis for all meanings can be found. Hegel masterfully highlighted this kinship between Socrates and Oedipus when he identified Oedipus's mythic response to the Sphinx with the imperative "know thyself" that inaugurates philosophy in its Socratic trajectory.

However, if Socrates presents a dangerous resemblance to the "wise man" who was able to solve the riddle on his own, Plato's philosophy, even as it puts Socrates in his well-known place, nevertheless provides a mechanism that offers protection against the Oedipean radicalism.

The Oedipean risk haunts Plato's thought like an unvoiced threat—to such an extent that the figure of the philosopher-king that Plato is seeking to define can be read as a methodical attempt to depict the true philosopher as the antithesis of the tyrant Oedipus. *Concerning a Non-Oedipean Figure of the Philosopher*: we might propose some such subtitle for the *Republic*, presenting this dialogue on justice as the answer that anticipated Hegel's bold move by some two thousand years. Hegel for his part does not hesitate—though perhaps without weighing all the consequences of his gesture—to portray the mythic Theban hero as the prototype of the philosopher.

What makes Plato's anti-Oedipean project so coherent is the fact that it is expressed within the very ideological framework that accounts for the symbolic mechanism of the Oedipus myth: the trifunctional hierarchy. There is complete homogeneity between the underlying conception of sovereignty in the Platonic project and the archaic imaginal figuration of sovereignty that produced the Greek monomyth and its Oedipean derivative. If the Oedipus myth can be understood in terms of irregular royal investiture and functional crimes tied to that irregularity, Plato uses the very same terms to define the bad king (the tyrant); in addition, he seeks to define the true king—the philosopher-king—in terms of regular royal investiture (in a transposed and renewed version).

Plato, as we hardly need to be reminded, is the one who most methodically set forth and studied the tripartite schema, spelling out its consequences in their multiplicity. Components of the body and the soul, virtues, pleasures, flaws, classes, social functions: everything is scientifically organized according to this ternary hierarchy. The city-state and the individual soul possess components that are equal in number and similar in function. Just as the city-state comprises three classes of men, those who assure the production and exchange of wealth, those who fight for the city's defense, and those who deliberate and govern, so the soul is made up of three elements. Each element is associated with a virtue: lust has the corresponding virtue of temperance; to anger corresponds the virtue of courage; and to intelligence, prudence. To these three virtues a fourth is added, involving the relationship among the three elements themselves—this is the virtue of justice, which ensures hierarchical harmony.

The difference between just and unjust political constitutions can be deduced with precision from the interplay of these three components and the relation of harmony or disharmony that prevails among them, and the same can be said of types of souls. If the best political and psychic constitution is monarchy, in which the hierarchy of the functions is perfectly regulated, the worst is tyranny, in which there is maximum deviance, the inferior parts taking the upper hand in the city-state and soul alike. Hence the position of the philosopher-king. The truly royal and philosophical soul is the one in which the most perfect justice reigns, the harmonious hierarchical composition of the three parts, with the rational element in charge. The philosopher-king alone is capable of ensuring that the same principle reigns in the city-state. Conversely, as we know, the tyrannical soul is the most disordered: murderous anger and unbridled lust get the better of right reason, and to the tyrannical soul corresponds the social constitution that is also the most deviant, worse even than the democratic constitution that opens the way—or rather, for Plato, the slippery slope—to tyranny.

Now, behind the Platonic notion of justice as the harmonious maintenance of hierarchic subordination, and behind the figure of the philosopher-king as the one who bears a complete image of this harmony in himself through the very constitution of his soul, it is not difficult to see the conceptual extension of the Indo-European principle of the monarch as a living synthesis of the three functions. Through an extremely fertile conceptual undertaking, Plato transposes the ancient and traditional principle of sovereignty onto the new figure of the philosopher. The difficult pedagogical path that leads to the formation of a philosophic soul is comparable to an initiation, and like an archaic initiation the new form has to recognize and move through the three stages so as to complete the process and harmonize it hierarchically. Plato's philosophy can thus be construed as a way of salvaging a timeless tradition on a new level after the disappearance of the social frameworks that had preserved that tradition—most notably the disappearance of priests and the initiated king.

Plato's contemporaries, moreover, undoubtedly still had a clear idea of what the synthesis of the three functions meant, even if Plato was the only one who put the notion to work philosophically. One incontestable indication of the king's simultaneously transverse and cumulative relation to the virtues arising from the three functional domains is provided by Xenophon in his elogium for Agesilas, king of Sparta. After praising in detail (but in an order that does not seem to correspond to a traditional intention) Agesilas's piety, loyalty, disinterestedness, temperance and continence, courage, patriotism, submission to the laws, urbanity, and simplicity, Xenophon is ready to present a kind of balance sheet of all the king's qualities, making him a veritable model of all the virtues, an exemplary sovereign.

At this point, Xenophon produces a formulation whose trifunctional value is immediately manifest: "The man who is foremost in endurance [*karteria*] when the hour comes for toil [*ponein*], in valour [*alkē*] when the contest calls for courage [*andreia*], in wisdom [*gnōmē*] when the need is for counsel [*boulēs*]—he is the man, I think, who may fairly be regarded as the perfect embodiment of goodness [*anēr agathos pantelos*]."[6] And such is Agesilas. Three domains of activity and three corresponding virtues are clearly identified and ordered in this remarkable formulation: work, which requires endurance; battle, which requires bravery; deliberation, which requires judgment, that is, intelligence. It would be hard to be more explicit and more concise. The perfectly accomplished man is the one who is capable of participating in each of these domains of activity and excelling in each. If such a man, in his own way, rises above the dominion of a single one of these hierarchically organized domains, it is not because he is, by his status, completely foreign to these domains, but because he is capable, through his exceptional virtue, of excelling in each realm of activity. Contrary to all those who are limited by their virtue and their function, the perfectly accomplished man is an integral, complete, whole man, since he belongs to each of the domains by a sort of addition and synthesis, and since he excels in each. In him are deployed all the resources of the soul and the full gamut of virtues. He will not be alienated by a tendency to favor one level over the others.

The formula Xenophon uses to designate such a man is remarkable. If to designate a virtuous man Plato readily and regularly uses the expression *agathos anēr*, which is generally translated as "good man," Xenophon's expression moves to the superlative level: *anēr agathos pantelos*, "peerless," or better yet, "a perfectly accomplished man." The word we are focusing on here is *pantelos*, constructed from *pan* (entirely, fully, in everything, completely) and *telos*, which indicates the idea of accomplishment, completion, realization, and whose root is found in a large number of composite terms used in the vocabulary of initiation. The noun *panteleia*, moreover, means "complete achievement," "perfect initiation."

Xenophon's expression is thus astonishingly suggestive and revealing. Not only does the exemplary king he is praising clearly achieve the synthesis of functions and the corresponding virtues in his own person, but Xenophon's choice of words here seems to incorporate a more or less direct allusion to initiatory investiture. The allusion could not be more explicit, moreover, without diminishing Agesilas's merit. The Spartan king Xenophon is honoring with his praises is presumed to have demonstrated these exceptional virtues in reality, and for the writer, who has been to Socrates' school, it is no longer a question of a simple investiture ritual that would risk offering only a purely symbolic value in his eyes. But it is indeed significant that what Xenophon requires of a king who warrants the status of ethical example corresponds to nothing less than a difficult and exceptional ideal bequeathed by an ancient tradition, the ideal of the reunion of the three functional qualities in one and the same person.

For Plato, the antithesis of the king who synthesizes and harmonizes the functional virtues in an ordered hierarchy is the tyrant. Far from repressing the ardent throngs of wild and terrible desires that, in royal natures, are kept in submission, weakened, or even extirpated thanks to the higher desires and with the help of reason (the divine element of the soul), the tyrant gives free rein to his most frenetic impulses, as he does to the numberless horde of passions governed by Eros. Far from subjecting his own desires to reason, the tyrant presses them into the service of his most illegitimate pleasures.

This impressive description, which gives Plato the opportunity to outline a theory of dreams (the tyrant attempts to live out in reality what others only dream of doing as they sleep, when their souls are agitated by unworthy desires), makes it possible to pinpoint what in Dumézilean terms could be called the tyrant's two functional crimes. For in his choleric irritability (a second-function passion), the tyrant will not hesitate to kill his own father, and in his unbridled erotic impulse (a third-function passion), he will do what others do only in their dreams (and even then, exceptionally): lie with his own mother.[7]

Plato's dual assertion,[8] extraordinary in its clarity, authorizes conclusions that we can now hardly avoid. The crimes of the paradigmatic tyrant are the crimes of Oedipus. Or, conversely, Oedipus's crimes are those of the paradigmatic tyrant: his crimes place "King" Oedipus (*Oidipous tyrannos*), with perfect symmetry, at the opposite pole from the philosopher-king Plato described. According to Plato, the philosopher is strictly anti-Oedipean, and this is so not by virtue of some simple ethical aversion, but, we might say—so rigorous is the trifunctional mechanism—by mythic construction. To the precise extent that the philosopher-king is constituted on the basis of the archaic figure of the consecrated king who accumulates and organizes the trifunctional virtues in a higher unity, this philosopher-king, a perfect initiate, has as his antithesis an exceptionally consistent figure of the uninitiated king who is logically destined to commit the three functional crimes. By attributing the crimes of patricide and incest to the paradigmatic tyrant, Plato confirms both the functional signification of these two crimes (which he situates perfectly within a tripartite topology of the passions of the soul) and the resolutely anti-Oedipean orientation of his entire philosophical enterprise.

Thus, Plato has not needed to circumvent, knowingly, the threat of a philosophic orientation that would be deployed according to the Oedipean logic in order to inscribe in his text, in a disjointed and laconic form (but one that can be reconstituted), the mythic figure of Oedipus. Owing to the very power of the symbological and ideological configuration in which his thought is inscribed and in which the myth of Oedipus is outlined, the paradigmatic tyrant that Plato describes has Oedipean features.

And yet there is a difference between Oedipus and Plato's tyrant. Oedipus's actions are involuntary. This distinction has a meaning that is internal to the Oedipean mechanism. For Oedipus, the exaltation of the rational element (thus, philosophic excess) is what leads to catastrophe. For the wicked tyrant, on the contrary, what overturns the hierarchy of desires and unleashes the furious and lustful beast is a complete and avowed absence of the rational element. The perverse tyrant exalts, disproportionately, to the point of patricide, his own impulses to anger and murder, and he excites his own erotic impulses, unhampered, to the point of realizing in a waking state what others only dream of in their sleep: union with his own mother. The perverse tyrant is thus an Oedipus, but a willful Oedipus. The Theban hero is an enlightened tyrant who commits the two extreme crimes unwittingly and unintentionally; the contrary figure of the perverse tyrant commits the same crimes with premeditation, on purpose, in full awareness of his acts, and his fate is that of a villain, not that of a tragic hero.

The lesson of the tragedy lies here. The enlightened tyrant, the one who places his full confidence in human reason, rejecting the tradition's superstitious fears as well as its obscure teachings about initiations and the gods, rejoins the perverse tyrant in a surprising twist. Externally, the two seem to be at opposite poles. The one places the prestige of intelligence at the highest point, the other wallows in the ignominy of the lowest pleasures. And yet, in a sudden reversal, the enlightened tyrant one day discovers that he has committed the same crimes as the perverse tyrant. The tragedy is this twist, which brings into convergence what had appeared to be opposites.

It is thus a play of oppositions among three poles and not just two that explains where Oedipus went astray. In one respect (the disordered tripartite hierarchy), the tyrant and Oedipus are on the same side. They are both opposed to the regular, just, king. In another respect (the privileged use of reason), the philosopher-king and Oedipus are on the same side, and they are both opposed to the typical tyrant, who in the interest of perverse and limitless sensual pleasure has allowed his unworthy passions of anger and lust to flourish. Oedipus's error is not the same thing as the tyrant's raging despotism. Both Oedipus and the philosopher-king have won their sovereignty through wisdom.

This dangerous similarity between the philosopher-king and Oedipus must have worried Plato. It must have been in order to lessen the risk that he anchored his arguments in tradition. Against a radical stance (whose effects do not become completely visible until Descartes), Plato's philosophy is then a compromise reaction, a grandiose attempt to moderate and measure the break with the past, to reinscribe its fruits, by a new twist, within the tradition that it rends and transcends. The youthful and democratic emergence of philosophic reason is at once recuperated and criticized by the Platonic wisdom.

One of Plato's dogmas lies at the heart of the philosophic distinction between Oedipus and the true royal sage. At the turning point in the *Republic*, or rather toward the end of this far-reaching discussion of justice, when it is time to reach conclusions as to the difference between the just man and the unjust man, time to spell out in no uncertain terms the risk to which the unjust man is subject, Plato resorts to an extraordinary image of the human soul. Its place leaves no room for doubt as to the profound instructional value Plato accords it. More than a theory, it borders on myth; it must be counted among the magnificent images Plato uses when he approaches ultimate horizons, when he wants to suggest a great truth and communicate its implications over and beyond discursive thought. And since what is involved is an image of the soul and its happy or unhappy destiny, we may suppose that Plato chose to speak to the soul in language that the soul itself could understand, language intended to initiate the soul to itself in a vision whose reverberations would be powerful enough to command the soul's assent, thus accomplishing the ethical goal.

What is this language of the soul that Plato calls on thought to form? Surprise: it will be an image resembling "one of those natures that the ancient fables tell of . . . as that of the Chimaera or Sylla or Cerberus, and the numerous other examples that are told of many forms grown together in one."[9] Now, Plato's Chimaera (just like the one Bellerophon encountered) has three parts. The first and largest is in itself a multiform and polycephalic beast whose heads are those of animals, docile and ferocious alike. The second has a simpler form, that of a lion. The third and last, smaller than the other two, has the form of a man. These three forms are joined in such a way as to make a single whole, and they are covered over on the outside by the form of a single being, a human form, so that in the eyes of someone who cannot see inside, and who perceives only the envelope, the whole appears to be a single being, man. This, then, is the Platonic image: within the apparent man (the only one visible to the uninitiated), there is an inner man, cast in the image of a monster—three more or less autonomous parts welded together to form a single entity (whose fabulous aspect is easier to imagine than it would be to mold in wax). With Plato, the triple monster has been internalized.

The polycephalic beast is the part of the soul that is the seat of sensual desires, multiple and unlimited: this is the concupiscent element. The lion is the irascible component, the fierce and audacious part that never ceases to aspire to domination and victory. The man signifies the wise and rational element of the soul, the one that derives pleasure only from knowledge of truth.

Plato's recourse to this terrifying image of the soul, quite different from the one he proposed in the *Phaedrus*, where a winged chariot sails through azure skies, sheds a most convincing light on what we have already suspected about the meaning of the Chimaera confronted by Bellerophon and the Sphinx confronted by Oedipus.

To be sure, the teranthropic being Plato described and methodically constituted in the image of the tripartite soul does not look exactly like the Chimaera, or the Sphinx, or Cerberus, or any other known monster of Greek mythology. But precise resemblance is not what counts. What is remarkable is that we discover in Plato, with all the clarity one could wish, the notion that in one single body a fabulous beast combines disparate forms, each of which, nevertheless, taken separately, has a quite specific meaning. What is more, Plato confirms beyond all expectation the principle according to which the monster is divided into three main parts that correspond precisely to the symbolics of the functional tripartition whose valences and correspondences he deploys so meticulously and completely in the *Republic*. What is unveiled here is the structural principle on the basis of which all of these imaginary beings are constructed. We cannot suppose that Plato would have simply amused himself by constructing a tripartite image resembling the Chimaera (or similar mythical creatures) unless he was preserving the memory of a more or less explicit teaching that credits them with triple significance. It seems perfectly understandable that he should have chosen not a monster actually known from myths but a comparable example, slightly redesigned. Plato's description is principial: it goes beyond reference to any particular myth, and he would certainly not have wanted his evocation reduced to any one particular myth, specific episodes and all.[10]

Plato's teaching, intended to define and shape the royal soul, extends the determination of royalty as a synthesis of the three functions in the strict sense. The soul of the philosopher-king is the soul that realizes in itself a harmonious and hierarchical equilibrium among the three heterogeneous elements that make it up: this achievement corresponds to the ritual power to combine and assemble the three functional levels, to unite them within the being of a single exceptional individual. For Plato, the rational element (the inner man) does not have to be capable of breaking the strength and boldness of the lion within the soul—that would be at once dangerous and impossible. But the reasonable element must be able to channel that resource of aggressiveness and anger in order to maintain its dominion over the soul's most obscure, most changeable, most voracious elements: the strange and disquieting polycephalic beast. A person who cannot depend upon the lion, a person who cannot count on having the lion on his side in the form of noble rage, a person who cannot bind the lion to the just cause of reason, is in danger of being overwhelmed by its powerful, undirected energies; worse still, such a person would be abruptly deprived of any ability to dominate the polycephalic beast, for in the absence of such a ferocious, ardent, vigilant guard, the creature is always ready to burst forth and invade the reasonable element. Unless it forms an alliance with the leonine element, the wise and properly human element is doubly threatened by the lower forces: it risks being crushed both by the disoriented power of the lion, transformed into lawless brutality, and by the now-unbridled and unguarded voraciousness of the polycephalic beast. In such a case, all the bestial elements, good or bad, are thus in league against the fragile rational element, which succumbs to their devouring and destructive passions.

Thus, the failed synthesis of the tyrannical soul is defined through opposition to the successful synthesis that realizes justice in the royal soul—and that makes justice possible, as a result, in social life. Plato resorts to monsters especially in order to underscore what terrible dangers threaten the perverted soul and what misfortunes await it. Here we can find an echo, weakened but still quite decipherable, of a veritable pedagogy of fear that initiation puts into practice.[11] To become a wise man, a philosopher or a king requires a fierce struggle against the bestial elements in his own soul, where greed, cruelty, the desire to dominate, and the unbridled desires of sensual jouissance are all rooted. These desires, in all their dangerous power, in all their disquieting depth, must therefore be portrayed in such a way as to become perceptible in their greatest disarray so that they will finally be resisted and turned into docile allies instead of destructive forces.

Now, with respect to Plato's triple-souled monster, what meaning can be attributed to Oedipus's response to the riddle posed by that triple-headed monster known as the Sphinx?

Oedipus's mistake is that he reduces the trial to the riddle, and thus humanizes the confrontation of mystery. The Sphinx's riddle belongs to the realms of intelligence and language, to the sagacity that is properly human. Its solution is always "man." On the contrary, the trial of combat (and that of sexuality) cannot be reduced to what is human; it is rooted in what is nonhuman within man, an alterity that reason can deal with but cannot fully comprehend.

Between the king, who according to tradition becomes an initiate through the synthesis of the three functions, and the monster, a paradoxical affinity comes to light, justifying their dramatic confrontation. Both are exceptional beings: they both achieve the union of three in one. The initiatory beast is a monstrous, terrifying, dangerous composite of the three powers, whereas the initiated king is a harmonious, pacific, and fertile symbol of these same powers. Their confrontation is a duel between one tripartite unity and another. The beast and the king are at once identical and different. The monstrous unity is the composite conflictual adversary offering the union of three in one as an obstacle and a problem—as obscurity. The king is the virtuous adversary: having first confronted this monstrous interaction as alterity and strangeness, he has succeeded in penetrating its obscurities and in appropriating its multiple and dangerous energies for his own accomplishment.

One of Plato's remarks allows us to grasp the paradoxical truth, along with the simultaneous profound falsity, of Oedipus's reply to the Sphinx. For this monster, whose form Plato constitutes as an amalgam of three figures, this fabulous being in three disparate parts, so difficult to combine and to harmonize, is indeed man, but only as external appearance. "Join the three in one, then, so as in some sort to grow together . . . then mould about them outside the likeness of one, that of the man, so that to anyone who is unable to look within but who can see only the external sheath it appears to be one living creature, the man."[12] For someone who sees only the external sheath, it would be quite difficult to guess the nature of the fabulous being that lurks within. And yet what appears from

the outside to be simply a human being can be perceived by someone who sees the inside (the soul) as an incredible, fantastic,
fabulous being, a conflictual and hierarchical combination of three
forms: a polycephalic beast, a lion, and again a man, in descending
order of size.

The fabulous tripartite being is thus an esoteric image of man
(his interior, his soul), just as the visible man is only an exoteric
form of the monster, a mere cover, a superficial envelope. The
response "man" can thus be interpreted as a profanatory neglect of
the two other components, the polycephalic beast and the irascible
lion. This very gap and the same unidimensionality turn up in the
mode of victory that characterizes Oedipus, a purely intellectual
victory, unlike Bellerophon's victory over the Chimaera.

Oedipus's "humanism" is, then, that illusion and that neglect: it
is the reduction of everything in man to man—the reduction of the
multiform monster of the soul to what is simply its noblest but
most fragile face, its human face, bearer and symbol of the superior
element of reason. If Oedipus had tried all the components of his
own soul, down to its voracious and polycephalic depths and its
leonine strengths, if he had been truly initiated, instead of knowing
only, by autoreflection (a speculative redoubling that leaves out his
constitutive inhumanity), he would have known that "man" is not
the last word in the solution to the riddle of man's soul. Far from
protecting him against the monstrous, Oedipus's humanist illusion
hurls him headlong into its depths.

Man and inner man (*ho entos anthrōpos*) are not the same. The
cryptic soul is not all human; it has dark, disturbing depths, unfathomable instinctual resources that elude humanity and plunge
into the dangerous darkness of animality. Reason, the privileged
attribute of inner man, is not a simple and readily available capacity
to know and understand. It is a force, an authority; it allows the
soul's animal components to be tamed. We can see what a mistake
it would be, from Plato's viewpoint, to confuse the inner (divine)
man with man as a whole, to overlook the essentially monstrous
structure of the soul and forget that the properly human part of the
soul is only one element in a larger composite; it is a mistake to

suppose that one can ignore that composite, neglect it, deny it, suppress its existence by means of thought.

What is attributed to the Theban hero as his "victory over the Sphinx" is precisely this anthropomorphization. Hegel does see this, but for him the victory has no dark side: it is the insurrection of man as the measure of all things; it is his aspiration to be fully and exclusively human (to have a proper nature, an essence, an identity that is completely subsumed by his humanity); and it is the end of terror in the face of powers that inhabit man and bind him to a more archaic order. Man being man and only man, in the innermost depths of his being, in the most invisible corners of his soul, he can no longer, in anguish and terror, encounter an other-than-himself within himself, he can no longer be invaded, seized, possessed by those disturbing and hostile forces that only images of beasts can evoke. In Oedipus's view, and Hegel's, man can break, once and for all, irreversibly, with those inferior and polymorphous realms, in all their discordant, enraged, or voracious harmony; man can install himself in the reason that is his proper nature, and there he can remain, self-sufficient. The victory of Hegel's Oedipus is a victory of unity (a single, unique reason in the unified mind of man) over the dangerous multiplicity of the passions, which are not confronted and consumed (in a fiery, bloody trial), but denied by an intellectual and self-reflective decree.

There are thus at least two ways of unbalancing the tripartite hierarchy of the soul: the one Plato describes with regard to the tyrant, and a rarer and more subtle one that, as it is embodied by Oedipus, is the extreme example of the philosophic risk.

Any isolation of the soul's philosophic element from its other two components (which are both, symbolically, of greater size) can only be dangerous. If the rational component is to cut itself off from its monstrous extension, the result will not be a radical liberation but the risk of an unmasterable insurrection. Once it loses its power over the leonine *pathos* that comprises aggressiveness, audacity, and the will to win, and once it loses its power as well over the unlimited sensual desires of its polycephalic *pathos*, the rational component can no longer keep what would otherwise be only fleeting dreams in nights of restless sleep from irrupting, in the form of perversions, into reality itself.

Oedipus brings about such a split. He relies on the victories won by pure reflection and on a clear consciousness of self. His failure to recognize the forces he should have controlled and integrated is thus allowed to burgeon. Instead of letting the wise element dominate the others, the irascible and the concupiscent elements, Oedipus detaches this reasonable element, gives it a kind of autonomy and independence (by self-reflection), to such an extent that the lion and the multiform beast find themselves unchained, released, liberated. Patricide and incest, even involuntarily committed, are the most searing and profound expression of that liberation, itself involuntary, unpremeditated, of two nonhuman elements. When Oedipus gets angry and kills Laïus, it is the lion element that is rebelling against the head. When Oedipus manages to share the queen's bed, it is the concupiscent element that is secretly satisfied. Each of Oedipus's involuntary crimes embodies a return of a part of the Sphinx, the return of an unconsumed and unconfronted element of the tripartite monster that represents the monstrosity of the soul itself in its cryptic profundity.

Thus, for Plato, to respond "man" to the Sphinx's riddle, in a radical gesture of anthropocentering that suppresses her monstrosity and makes man the measure of all things, is beyond question a heresy, an error, or an illusion. To harmonize the heterogeneous elements of the soul under the dominion of the human element, to succeed in realizing the hierarchical synthesis of the three functions expressed in those elements: this is the only objective that can be assigned to pedagogy, initiation, philosophy. One can go no further. Not only is the divine, and not man, the measure of all things, but man himself remains permeated by an irreducible alterity. Not everything in man is human. Humanism is a dangerous illusion that forgets that the rational part of the soul, the only human part, is constantly menaced by what is inhuman in the soul, the inferior but active components that threaten to take over as soon as the vigilance of reason falters. Thus, for Plato, no man will suppress the triple monster, for the soul itself is that triple monster. Plato thus warns conclusively against any Oedipean presumption.

Plato's implicit position taking governs a crucial problematic field, a distribution of divergences and antagonisms that resonate endlessly throughout the entire conflictual history of Western philosophy. A conflictual history: thus, a history that cannot be reduced to some homogeneous discourse that might have emerged at the outset and been pursued to the end. From the outset, with Plato at least, in opposition to the Oedipean orientation that marks philosophy's most extreme insistence and that Hegel first identified as philosophy incarnate, there stands an antihumanist warning that anticipates later oppositions. It is in this respect that, over and beyond Descartes, Hegel, and Nietzsche (to whom we shall return, emphasizing their Oedipean bias), the Freudian discovery was foreseen by the Platonic topology of the soul.

§ 9 Philosophy II

Even if an Oedipean presence takes shape only between the lines of Plato's discourse, he is linked to that discourse so intimately and by so many coherent threads that the unnamed Oedipus makes it possible to interpret later appearances of this figure quite conclusively. For Oedipus comes back: first with Descartes, who unwittingly but resolutely makes Oedipus's strategy his own and pursues it to the point of ontological purity; later with Hegel, who calls him by his name and makes him a shadowless, fully inaugural figure.

No philosopher allows us to appreciate the Oedipean strategy better than Descartes. In this sense, it is appropriate that Descartes's thought should be viewed as the starting point for the philosophy of the modern era. With Descartes, the very order of his method (his approach, the step-by-step advance he would like to make on secure ground), rigorously repeats the sequence of significant moments in Oedipus's story.

Let us look closely at the Cartesian gesture. It might be summed up in three movements. What is the role of the "I," the "I" that produces the *Discourse on Method*?

§ 1 It denies all masters, and asserts the superiority of the autodidactic position over any transmission of knowledge.

§ 2 It dissolves, suppresses, removes any indistinct and obscure thoughts by the acute form of self-consciousness we know as the cogito.

§ 3 As a consequence of the two preceding moves, it takes up a position as "master and possessor of nature"—or claims as much.

We need not insist: it is quite clear that beneath the intellectual rigor of Descartes's philosophemes we rediscover with astonishing precision the no less rigorous sequence of mythologemes that constitute the Oedipean posture. Of course, what is involved is not a simple transposition, but the persistence of a configuration, a decisively deepened understanding of a certain regime of subjectivity that was prefigured, whether Descartes knew it or not, by Oedipus's posture. Murder of the father, response to the Sphinx, possession of the mother: Descartes gives a perfected ontological dimension to the protophilosophical mechanism typified by the Oedipus myth. Each of these three great moments in the heroic Oedipean drama can be recognized in the three great moments of Descartes's undertaking.

The originality and subversive power of this undertaking have to be appreciated. Descartes is not a philosopher who frees himself from the tutelage of his masters and forefathers as soon as he makes their knowledge his own and becomes a master in turn. Nor is he a philosopher who has never learned from the masters. He is the one who methodically breaks the chain of transmission. He is not one of those disciples who, at the conclusion of a full cycle of teaching and initiation, becomes capable of assuming the role of master in his turn. Instead, he denounces all filiations. He breaks the chain. By an act of meditated rupture and of methodical repudiation, he purports to set himself up as a thinker with no master but himself. The thinker without a master as master thinker: the Cartesian revolution in a nutshell.

This is a way of saying that Descartes pushes the thought of the son to its metaphysical extreme, takes it further than anyone had ever taken it before. No longer the thought of a son who still defines himself relationally as son of a father, it is the thought of a son who has deliberately and consciously orphaned himself, disinherited himself, who has made himself the son of no one. Opposed to any genealogical position that attaches the individual to a line of succession (noble or initiatory) and that bases the existence of a subject only on its relation to an ancestral chain that it continues, the Cartesian gesture is the formidable claim of a subject who has broken away from his inheritance, proclaiming his absolute autonomy and basing his legitimacy on himself alone.

"I think, therefore I am": this act of ontological autofoundation comes on the heels of the disavowal of every teaching of the masters. The patricidal power stroke of the cogito acquires its coherence and its foundational value from the fact that it brings into coincidence an undeniable self-evidence and an assertion bearing upon the self.

The cogito is not merely a true proposition, like an arithmetical operation, it is a truth bearing upon the "I," and that needs no one but "I" to prove itself. It is a truth that brings the proof that *I* may be the source of unquestionable truths. The strategic function of the cogito is to show, by means of a striking and irrefutable example, that the disavowal of all inherited knowledge does not lead to the unfathomable abyss of doubt, but that it leads, quite to the contrary—after a brief period of anguish, fear of drowning—to gaining a foothold more solid than any the masters' knowledge has to offer. "*Cogito ergo sum*" has to be understood as a victory cry; the shout of the successful "patricide," the exultation of the son who now knows that he no longer depends upon ancestors or anyone else in order to stand on his own two feet. And to walk with assurance. Without limping.

Descartes's patricidal gesture is incommensurable, in its import and its radicality, with any individual killing of an individual father. Descartes is a principial and abstract Oedipus. He denies the ontological dimension of paternity. He attempts to establish truth in the absence of that dimension, taking on himself, as an "I," the function it purported to fulfill.

Descartes is a hero: we should not be astonished to find that word in Hegel, then in Valéry and Alain. Between the hero's combat and the formation of the ego there is complete congruence. Descartes is a hero because he mobilizes all the wellsprings of his being in order to constitute himself and take possession of himself. What the myth presents in the heroic adventure is represented and pursued by philosophy in the founding acts of subjectivity. What is more, by setting up the *ego cogitans* as the founding moment of truth, Descartes not only repeats an act of individuation that the heroic adventures prefigure in the language of myth, he pursues this figure to the point of unveiling what had been at work in the heroic imaginary, the effort that had led man to become a subject, and to discover himself as self-consciousness, and to rely on that certainty. In figural logic, the monster is the obligatory correlative of the hero. Descartes is a hero simply because he, too, has vanquished monstrosity, using the weapon of reason and self-consciousness. Descartes eliminates the profuse swarm of obscure and indistinct ideas. The cogito is the response to *that* Sphinx. She is undone by reflective self-evidence. After the blow struck by the cogito, she will cease to haunt thought.

The Oedipean strategy in philosophy thus appears in its simplicity and its ineluctable rigor nowhere better than in Descartes's gesture. He brings into the light of the concept the Oedipean definition of philosophy that had not been clearly disengaged before. With Descartes, the Oedipean strategy becomes methodical. There is no reason to be astonished, then, if we find—now brought to fruition—the mechanism that Greek thought had outlined but had not been able to systematize. Descartes's philosophy is the movement of deprojection fully accomplished: the subject, taken as point of departure, is radically opposed to the object; in short, a rational, monocentered perspective is achieved on an ontological level, a perspective that systematizes the acquisition of foreshortening through its apprehension of the unity of the center of vision.[1]

If Oedipus, answering "man" to the Sphinx's riddle, caused the monster to vanish by disclosing its projective character, Descartes opposes the existence of his "I" to the horde of obscure and indistinct ideas, putting forward this "I" as an unchallengeable basis for all certainty and the center of all its own representations. Descartes's gesture is no longer simply an anthropocentering move, as it was with the Greeks. It has become a systematized mechanism of pure egocentering. In this respect, he goes decisively further, plunges deeper than his predecessors. Descartes indeed goes beyond the anthropological outlook already acquired by the Ancients; he ventures further toward a principial egology—one that also augurs formidable aporias and major scissions.

Before its risks burst into view, however, Descartes's victory appears secure. Having removed from this thought everything obscure and indistinct so as to retain only clear evidence of demonstrative reason, having emptied the external world of all its shadows so as to reconstruct its transparent mechanism, having mathematized matter, Descartes can be imbued with limitless hope, can aspire to conquer a universe of intelligible matter, to pierce the secret of its intimate laws, to penetrate all its mysteries—in short, to make himself (this phrase bears a meaning that his reason can now no longer hear) "master and possessor of nature." The son, after setting aside the heritage of his forefathers, after decisively disavowing his patrimony and his tradition, has freed himself for an unprecedented conquest, an exorbitant dominion: possession of mother nature.

Descartes must indeed have lost the sense of enigmas and images, the metaphoric resonances that permeate the purest philosophic conceptuality in spite of everything, to dare to contemplate such a project.

~

Oedipus before the Sphinx . . .

In the confrontation between the obscure monster who poses riddles and the person who victoriously replies "man," we have the condensation of a decisive historical step, a threshold of thought, a turning point of the spirit.

Man is finally at the center.

That is why Hegel made this mythic episode the primitive scene of philosophy. Oedipus is the inventor of this new posture destined for a great future that singularizes the West. In Hegel's writing, the explicit reference to Oedipus is brief,[2] but its strategic importance is considerable: Oedipus is the one who ensures a passage, who makes history turn from one spiritual moment to another. With his response to the Sphinx, he engineers the overtaking, the replacement, the transition from the symbolist moment of subjectivity to the Greek—that is to say, the philosophic—moment.

The Sphinx, which Hegel considers as an Egyptian symbol, is a mixture of animality and humanity. By solving the riddle with the answer "man," Oedipus suppresses that mixture, dissolves the monstrosity. He makes man—who is now self-conscious—the answer that can be used against any obscurity.

For Hegel, Egypt is the land of symbols. There the human spirit is still prisoner of images that incarcerate meaning like a tomb that confines the soul. The symbolized is always subservient to the symbolizing object; it lacks the autonomy of an idea that is clear and transparent to itself. It is in this context and with reference to Egypt that Hegel speaks of "unconscious symbolism," or rather of an "unconscious symbolics" (*Die unbewusste Symbolik*). Everything is mystery and obscurity. Everything is an imbrication of underlying meanings, allusions, evocations. This unconscious symbolism both conceals and reveals. It always refers to something else. It is permeated by an irreducible alterity. Pyramid, colossus, Sphinx: "In Egypt, on the whole, almost every shape is a symbol and hieroglyph not signifying itself but hinting at another thing with which it has affinity and therefore relationship." Egyptian works of art are thus objective enigmas. Intuitions do not succeed in becoming thought, for the spirit does not yet know the clear and sharp language of "the spirit." Thus, "Egypt is the country of symbols, the country which sets itself the spiritual task of the self-deciphering of the spirit, without actually attaining to the decipherment."[3]

If Egyptian symbolism is enigmatic in itself, the Sphinx is the best symbol for this regime of the symbolic. A colossus with a human face and a lion's claws, it is a hieroglyph to the second power, the symbol of the cryptophoric profundity of the symbol. One has the impression that the spirit is trying to break free from obtuse brute force, but that it is not succeeding in its effort to conquer the freedom of the spiritual. With half its body still mired in the animal materiality from which it originated, the human spirit has not yet attained the self-awareness, the free and explicit interiority that would allow it to break the ties that attach it to what is not itself. The Sphinx bears witness to an aspiration to conscious spirituality, but in its mysterious and mute power the teramorphic colossus carved in stone remains welded, rooted, in the obscure unconsciousness of indecipherable materiality.

The Sphinx is thus, for Hegel, the symbol of symbolism, of that unconscious symbolism that is not an allegorical cloak, a disguise for a truth that could be stated and thought differently, but one that is an enigma in itself, a radical incongruence between the signifying materiality and the mind.

And this is where the Oedipean moment intervenes. For it is but a short step from the (male) Egyptian Sphinx to the (female) Greek Sphinx. All the more so in that Egypt is not first or solely the land described by geographers and historians; it is also the regime of a certain symbolic relation: the regime in which the spirit is still a slave to its own obscurity.

Now, Oedipus is the one who confronts this symbol of symbolism. He finds the riddle's answer in man—that is, he finds there the answer to every riddle, the response to the very principle of the enigmatic. The monstrosity of unconscious symbolism disappears. The animal figure is no longer merged, in a disturbing hybridization, with the human figure. Man can represent only himself, whether as body in a plastic form or as spirit in a self-reflective philosophy. Oedipus does not respond to just one particular riddle. He challenges and moves beyond the regime of unconscious symbolism by making man the source of all meaning. That is why Hegel purely and simply identifies Oedipus's response, "man" (the position of an essential anthropocentering before the alterity of the enigmatic), with the Apollonian and Socratic formula "know thyself." The light of consciousness, which is consciousness of self, obliterates all enigmatic alterity, suppressing the dimension of the unconscious.

A decisive moment: when "thought embraces itself" (and this is one of Hegel's definitions of philosophy),[4] it shatters the symbolist and mythic form that had dominated the free expression of the spirit. The symbol, unlike the concept, is an inadequate expression of thought. It attests to a lack of appropriation between an idea and a form that is supposed to signify it. It is only when the spirit has been able to liberate itself from the perceptible and reach a state in which it can be "for itself," can reflect itself, can attain subjectivity and interiority, that it divests itself of all symbolist expression. Thus, Oedipus, through his response, accomplishes not just *a* philosophical gesture but *the* philosophical gesture par excellence: the reflective movement of thought, the act of self-consciousness through which subjectivity knows itself. Oedipus's response to the Sphinx is the advent of philosophy, its beginning, its inauguration. Thought has finally approached itself. The deceptive Oriental unity of spirit and nature is shattered. Oedipus is the founder of philosophy: the prototypical philosopher. It is thus remarkable that Hegel should have discerned a turning point in historical life that is characterized at one and the same time as the exit from Egypt, the response of Oedipus, and the birth of Western philosophy—a philosophy itself originally determined as a humanism, a new posture based on anthropocentering. The present book in its entirety is a commentary on Hegel.[5]

If we juxtapose Plato's implicit disqualification of Oedipus with Hegel's extraordinary promotion of the same figure, the articulation between these two major philosophers takes on unexpected precision.

From Plato to Hegel: in a counteroffensive against the sacrilegious presumptions of a Protagoras or a Xenophanes, the former elaborates a philosophic strategy that can be represented as non-Oedipean, whereas the latter, after the insurrection of the modern subject unleashed by Descartes's cogito, on the contrary sees in an increasingly radical autoreflection and anthropocentering the principal axis of the history of the human spirit. Starting with Hegel, Oedipus becomes, retrospectively, an inaugural figure.

Hegel's conviction that the Sphinx was an Egyptian figure rather than Greek is not in conflict with the disclosure of an unnoticed articulation between the Platonic topology of the soul and Hegelian thought. The Hegelian exit from Egypt, via Oedipus's response to the Sphinx, is the break with a hierarchical, sacral world in which heteronomy reigns—a world in aspective, anterior to perspective. Plato was always convinced that in the Egyptians' world he had found the ideal separation of the social functions, the canonical hierarchy whose principle he was constantly defending. In the *Laws*, Plato explicitly valorized Egypt—immutable, hierarchical, and hieratic—against unstable and democratic Greece. A break in historical memory even allowed him to believe, it seems, that the principle of social tripartition was Egyptian in origin.

Plato and Hegel valorize the exit from that Egypt differently, but for both it is associated with an implicitly or explicitly Oedipean posture. Whether an Indo-European or an Egyptian structure is involved is not important in this regard: the Oedipean gesture of anthropocentering is what brings man out of a hierarchical regime and introduces him into a regime of democratic humanism, whether this is a matter for regret or rejoicing. The monstrous structure that expresses the spirit's alterity with respect to itself (and man's religious humility in the face of that cryptic alterity) will occupy the same position in both cases, although the will to dissolve this intimate alterity through reflective reason is judged differently.

Thus, Plato and Hegel are opposed on the same imaginary and conceptual terrain. The former maintains that the soul is a triune monster, an irreducible composite of heterogeneous beings that requires a principle of authority to stay in harmony, and the latter attributes to the rational and properly human element so exclusive a privilege that he can believe monstrosity has been left behind once and for all—in a historic rupture that has as its emblem the magnified victory of Oedipus.

The humanization of the soul in its entirety, which Plato would have viewed as a dangerous mistake, becomes a historic step that leaves the symbolic and unconscious depths behind. The human spirit conquers its autonomy in an act of reflexivity that leads to a new moment in history. Anthropocentering forever disqualifies the Egypt of the Sphinx.

~

Now, for Feuerbach, who takes up the same issue in turn, there is still, in Hegel, an unacceptable residue of transcendence. What is needed is a decisive operation that covers the entire set of theological outlooks and beliefs and completely absorbs that transcendence, reclaims for man all the images and representations of divinity that he has constructed. Feuerbach formulates the principle of this solution to every theological riddle with perfect clarity: "The new philosophy is the *complete* and *absolute dissolution of theology into anthropology.*"[6] All the attributes that dogma confers upon divinity are simply projections onto a separate, transcendent being of contents that originate in the human soul and that consciousness must now reappropriate for itself. Through religious belief, man separates himself from himself, divides himself, considers as other than himself what belongs to his own essence. He must bring back to himself what he has inappropriately transferred onto imaginary beings.

"The secret of *theology* is *anthropology.*"[7] Making this assertion as he confronts the mysteries of theology, Feuerbach repeats the word that Oedipus uttered before the mystery of the Sphinx. If he does not take Oedipus as the model for his undertaking, he does go back to Socrates. The precept "know thyself" imposes itself explicitly as the exergue of Feuerbach's entire philosophy, a philosophy he sees as developing all the consequences of that precept. Feuerbach relaunches and radicalizes the movement of deprojection that is initiated in Socratic thought; he carries it to the point of denying all divine alterity (which Socrates did not do) and thereafter to advocating man's reappropriation of those aspects of his own essence that he had alienated in the divine.

Feuerbach's operation of radical anthropocentering not only recalls Oedipus's position, but it is the clearest philosophic explanation for what had been offered only in figural form in the language of myth. Feuerbach's concepts may provide, after Hegel, the best philosophic interpretation of what is implied without being fully explained in the Oedipean mechanism.

What Oedipus discovers, in a prefiguration of the Feuerbachian gesture, is that the gods and their mysteries are simply products of the human spirit. Priests and believers let themselves be deluded into taking the reality of these monsters or gods seriously; they treat them as if they were real forces external to man and with which respectful and fearful relationships must be maintained. What Oedipus discovers is that behind the powerful representations that fill men with terror or hope there is no mystery other than man himself. Oedipus discovers that the sacred beings that man adores or fears as realities different from and foreign to himself are nothing but himself. Thus, to the question asked by the Sphinx—that is, to the interrogation articulated by the sacred symbols at the most solemn moment of the initiatory encounter—Oedipus, who has never received any instruction regarding these things, opposes a radical change of terrain, a reversal, that situates man rather than the divine as the ground and center. Oedipus brings back to its human source what had first, through a movement of forced misunderstanding, been transferred outside of humanity and given the form of a divine or demonic world. Henceforth, discovering the key to all symbol formation (projection, transference), he suppresses in a single blow all belief in, and all subordination to, symbolist profundity. He eliminates the hieratic beast.

Clearly, what Hegel explains in terms of spiritual liberation and reflexivity can be formulated in another register and another language: in terms of the withdrawal of projections. What is involved is the movement of disengaging from a naive and alienating attachment to symbols, or rather to imaginary beings that are only progressively recognized as perceptible symbols of inner realities. The Oedipean response marks the fertile moment of massive deprojection of the obscure contents that up to that point had been invested, transferred, projected onto the external world in the form of superhuman or subhuman beings. These contents are now assimilated to the ego of the conscious individual who appropriates them for himself as constitutive parts of himself. Whereas before he entered into relationships with these forces and these representations as if they were foreign and external beings endowed with their own lives, he now discovers that he is the unconscious producer of these forms, their active source, and that he can therefore bring to an end that division of himself from himself by reintegrating into his own transparent subjectivity what appeared to him to be an irreducible alterity charged with sacred enigmas.

Feuerbach's language and mode of thought are thus particularly adequate to describe the operation typified by Oedipus. Nevertheless, if Feuerbach's philosophy makes the demystifying and emancipatory mechanism of anthropocentering convincing (thus indirectly supplying a forceful amplification of the central episode, Oedipus before the Sphinx), he still does not reach (any more than Hegel did) the tragic core inherent in this movement and the irreducible obscurity that it maintains. The danger comes to a head with Nietzsche.

~

Nietzsche's thought is complex, fragmentary, and contradictory. We shall certainly not attempt to survey that labyrinth in a few pages. But in one of its aspects, perhaps the most insistent and certainly the most daring, it clearly extends the operation undertaken by Feuerbach. For Nietzsche, too, man is enjoined to reappropriate for himself what he had transferred outside himself, in the form of gods, God, and all the ideal otherworlds.

When Zarathustra comes down from his mountain, enriched by a long and profound meditation whose treasure he has decided to offer the people of the valley, it is to teach the human, all-too-human origin of all the magnificent fantasies that make up our sublime idea of the divine. Zarathustra is now disabused. He has ceased to be a visionary of the beyond:

> Thus I too once cast my delusion beyond man, like all the afterworldly. Beyond man indeed?
>
> Alas, my brothers, this god whom I created was man-made and madness, like all gods! Man he was, and only a poor specimen of man and ego: out of my own ashes and fire this ghost came to me, and verily, it did not come to me from beyond.

For it is the ego "that creates, that desires, that gives the measure and the value of things." The illusion of an alterity from which a message or a revelation would come must be abandoned. No! "The belly of being does not speak to humans at all, except as a human."[8]

Nietzsche, in the prophetic language of Zarathustra, thus renews the movement of anthropocentering, man's recuperation of the divine contents that had been transferred onto the Heavens, a movement that Feuerbach had cast as the principal operation of the philosophy of the future. Like Feuerbach, Nietzsche could have said that "the secret of theology is anthropology." But his tone would have been different—there would have been a note of bitterness and disillusionment that one does not find in Feuerbach. Theology is a human, all-too-human enterprise!

But this deep disillusionment also becomes the source of strength, a very great strength. Once the Beyond is demystified, once the gods are dead, man becomes the sole creator; it is man, enlarged beyond all measure, who determines the supreme values.

This new and different man, inflated with what the death of God causes to flow back into man himself, is the "superman." The movement is clear, ineluctable: "*Dead are all gods: now we will that overman live*—at some great midday let this be our ultimate will!—"[9] Freed from the hindrances that weakened him by attaching him to the Heavens and to all the illusory ideals that were based on that Beyond, the superman, in his now-unleashed will to power, sets himself an unprecedented goal, the supreme goal attainable here on Earth: the conquest of the Earth itself.

By that operation and that last promise, Nietzsche brings to light, in a much more fully developed way than Feuerbach, and in just as striking a way as Descartes, not to say more striking, the whole of the Oedipean strategy and destiny that had permeated the most audacious part of philosophy since its advent among the Greeks, as if he is taking them to an extreme point of visibility and exacerbation. For if we consider quite schematically the destinal logic that permeates all of Nietzsche's thought in its evident profusion and its irreducible fragmentation, we again encounter an inexorable linkage between three major phases that cannot fail to evoke the rigorous narrative and imaginal armature that undergirds the drama of Oedipus.

In the Oedipus figure, this armature is articulated in three acts that we can formulate here as abstractions: (1) Eviction of the Father; (2) Promotion of Man (and of the Ego); (3) Possession of the Mother. With Descartes, as we have seen, these three acts are readily recognizable, although in a specific ontological form that methodically stresses the place of the ego. It is striking that a similar movement, albeit through a different (though parallel) set of concepts, structures Nietzsche's thought: (1) Death of God; (2) Advent of the Superman; (3) Total domination of the Earth.

It is as if Nietzsche had taken to the extreme, on a conceptual level that is no longer that of the mythic image but that remains linked with it by close and necessary ties reflecting the lasting strength of a powerful structure, the originally Oedipean program of philosophy.

What was mythically prefigured in naively familial terms in Oedipus's strategy and his destiny here finds unexpected scope in modern conceptual language. This language of concepts at first appears to have nothing in common with the old mythologemes; nevertheless, it unquestionably retains a deep and compelling metaphoric bond with them. The persistence of this bond, which for example connects the notions of "Nature," "Matter," "Earth," with "the Mother," obliges us to take seriously not only the isolated metaphor but the entire mechanism. It is not just one notion or another that is conceptualized on the basis of a metaphoric archeology, but a system that has been established on the basis of a powerful mytho-logical constraint, which itself refers back to a deeply rooted anthropological framework.

Starting with Plato and the Christian thinkers he influenced, the supraperceptible world, the world of Ideas and Ideals, has been viewed as the true world, the only properly real world, whereas the world perceived by the senses is seen only as a "here below," changeable, apparent, and unreal. This idealism (which for the sake of simplicity we may take to have been the predominant tendency of philosophy up to the last century) has exhausted its power of mobilization and legitimation. After the age of idealism is finished (by Hegel's absolute metaphysics), the age that ensues is one of reversal—or rather reversals—of idealism. Feuerbach, Marx, Nietzsche: each in turn, adopting different though comparable strategies, accomplishes the maneuver whereby the Beyond (or the world of Ideas, source of all theological illusions) is emptied of meaning and plenitude to the benefit of the earthly "here below," which is restored to its founding truth under the name of "perceptible reality" (Feuerbach), "material base" (Marx), or Earth (Nietzsche).

That the death of God, atheism, should result in the advent of man is a decisive transition espoused by the young Marx in the following terms: "Atheism is a *negation of God,* and postulates the *existence of man* through this negation."[10] Nietzsche says the same thing when he exclaims: "Dead are all gods: now we will that overman live!" This exalting and audacious moment of the humanist insurrection reproduces and amplifies the act that Oedipus exemplifies. It repeats that act after the fact, bringing it to completion. And each time, this atheist insurrection of man leads to the same project: taking possession of the terrestrial sphere.

Marx conceives of the history of philosophy as a constant struggle between idealism and materialism, a struggle in which he sides with materialism against idealism (with the aim of reversing the relation of dominance), but a struggle whose terrain, stakes, and opposing principles cannot really be surpassed except in the allusive but undeveloped evocation of a certain "perfected naturalism" whose horizon remains to be examined. The return to matter and to the earthly "here below" becomes not only an appeal to reject postmortem compensations in favor of a struggle in this life, but it also takes the theoretical form of a representation of society and history starting from the objective conditions of the "material base" from which all ideals derive; ideals thus lose their eternal and unconditional aspect. For Nietzsche, "the sense of the Earth" is an appeal to renounce all nonterrestrial goals, and the superman who is born of this determined refusal to take fearful flight toward illusory ideals is called, under a newly emptied Heaven, to total dominion over the Earth.

It would not be difficult, then, to show what Marx's reversal and Nietzsche's have in common: a disqualification of the supraperceptible and of illusory other worlds, a reckoning with the struggle for power (of individuals and groups), considered as the revealed key to instituted reality, an appeal, finally, to a foundation opposed to the one the Platonic-Christian belief had proclaimed—matter in Marx's case, the Earth in Nietzsche's.

With these philosophies, the relation between man and nature reaches a critical point. Idealism, by making matter a less-being, an unreal shadow, indeed, by purely and simply denying its existence, affirmed the superiority of "the Spirit." But it was an intellected, speculative superiority. Idealism nurtured the principle of that devaluation and that negation through evasion, retreat, a mystic elevation above the quagmire of earthly things. The rehabilitation of the earthly by the great overthrowers of idealism signifies a simple inversion of this hegemony only in appearance. The need to criticize idealism arises because instead of dominating matter in reality and in practice, it denies matter. The point is thus not to reverse the relationship of dominance but to allow real dominion over the matter that idealism rendered unreal. By taking refuge too hastily in the Heavens, and by maintaining their murky, mystic whims, idealists win only an abstract victory, by default. After the simple break between man and nature, which is only an act of detachment, the overthrowers call for man to dominate in reality: to take possession. This can happen only if the true nature of the earthly things is taken into account.

The appeal to "Nature," to "Matter," and to "the Earth" is an appeal to conquer once and for all what still resists an idealism that is not "practical" enough (for Descartes), that is too "murky" (for Marx), or too "hallucinatory" (for Nietzsche). "Nature," "Matter," and "Earth" do not constitute a dimension to be respected like an enigma (whose mysteries will remain unfathomable and forever veiled); they constitute what reason attempts to master in its triumphant march toward objectivity and productive transformation.

Here is where the inauguration of the philosophical posture typified by Oedipus finds its most manifest accomplishment, and where taking this beginning into account allows us to clarify, more than any pure conceptuality, the stakes of this final reversal. If Oedipus exemplifies the protophilosophic posture more completely than any other figure or configuration, then it becomes clear that "the end of philosophy" (or what some, significantly if not legitimately, think they can predict as such) must be wrought by a conjuncture that brings to light the destinal accomplishment proper to the Oedipal configuration. The Oedipean philosophic program is accomplished better than ever before by the reversal of idealism.

When Hegel identified the foundational philosophic significance of the Oedipean posture, he took into account only a limited portion of that powerful configuration, the central sequence of absolute sagacity that corresponded to his own philosophy. But Hegel did not take into account the whole of the drama, the consequences of the response, the tragic element inherent in Oedipus's posture. It is as if the calling of later philosophies was only to pursue the unfolding of this logic, to complete the Oedipean configuration by pushing it to its extreme limits. The move to overthrow idealism and take possession of the Earth completes philosophy's Oedipean destiny.

Foreseen by Descartes to a limited extent, accomplished by Marx and by Nietzsche, the movement whereby human reason, having become instrumental, takes possession of "Nature/Matter/Earth" is a movement that unfolds, organizes, and amplifies what mythic language evoked with horror, in archaic personalized and sexualized terms, as "possession of one's own mother."

This, then, is the overturning of idealism: after all the regulating transcendencies have been discarded (death of God), and after man has taken power by means of his rational egocentered reason, man comes into his own total sovereignty, that sovereignty promising— at least as fantasy promises—complete mastery of "Nature," full possession of "Matter." The objectives that are pursued and accomplished here with astonishing rigor are indeed those of the Oedipean program. What the mythologemes articulated in their own language (a language whose enveloping power of symbolization it would be a mistake to disregard: "killing of the father," "response to the Sphinx," "incest with the mother") is amplified, structured, elaborated by the philosophemes, as a symphony at last brings into being the orchestral version of a slender melodic thread.

What we are seeing here is the deployment of a configuration that retains its imaginal resonance even in a purified and abstract philosophic form: this is attested by the fact that philosophic concepts—or rather, theological concepts (functioning as intermediaries)—have never broken with their metaphoric genealogy. Thus, in the wake of the modern configuration of the "overthrowing of idealism" there is a theology that could be evoked as follows: the Son has killed the Father; he has used his own Reason against all the Mysteries, and, having taken the Father's place, he is laying claim to mastery and to possession of Matter for his own enjoyment.

Quite clearly, with respect to this orientation of philosophy, the interpretation of Nietzsche's thought deserves to be considerably more nuanced. Nietzsche takes anthropocentering to such limits, to such an extreme, that he decomposes it and goes beyond it. In this connection, the abrupt resurgence of Dionysus in Nietzsche's work has to be understood as a decisive disruption of the moment of Oedipean mastery, a return at full strength of knowledge that Oedipus had avoided in order to reign—including, and perhaps especially, the initiatory wrenching in its most somber form. With Nietzsche, the Oedipean victory is at once carried to fruition, finished off, and fractured. This contradiction is what makes Nietzsche's thought so nearly unbearable and at the same time so compelling. His thought cannot be interpreted in a univocal fashion. It authorizes readings as dissimilar as those of Heidegger and that of Bataille. Nietzsche occupies a position of fracture or gap between the Oedipean assurance of total mastery of the Earth and the return of what this mastery has had to leave in the realm of the unknown in order to operate. That Dionysus should return with Nietzsche is a matter of implacable logic with respect to the Oedipean history of philosophy that we have traced. Nothing less than the entire history of philosophy since Socrates is called into question when Nietzsche explicitly proclaims himself to be one of Dionysus's "initiates." But then, in what sense (disorienting, unaccustomed, but nevertheless plausible) can the yielding to Dionysus be called a "will to power"? Here perhaps is where the greatest difficulty resides in Nietzsche's thought and experience.

Thus it is hardly astonishing that the Freudian discovery should have come about at a time when this powerful historical configuration was in the process of unfolding all its consequences and asserting itself in its full strength, even as it was showing signs of fracture. Hegel taught us that anthropocentering forever disqualifies the Egypt of the Sphinx. The Freudian discovery of the unconscious, like the Nietzschean disruption, is already outlined in that step, as a counterthrust and aftershock of that modern glorification of the Oedipean position. For Hegel, the passage from an unconscious symbolics (the Egyptians') to a conscious symbolics and to pure concept (the Greeks') leaves no residue. In conformity with the Hegelian notion of the history of the spirit, the new movement supplants the preceding one, takes over with no remainder. The stage of unconscious symbolics vanishes without leaving any traces except those that archaeologists can decipher on tombstones and papyrus. A moment of the spirit once existed; now the spirit has moved on. Only through the patient work of some Champollion can the mute, desanctified hieroglyphs of timeworn obelisks and columns be given voice.

For Freud, on the contrary, there is an irreducible residue. The unconscious symbolics, that archaic mode of speaking based on the affinity of images, their tropological power of evocation and correspondence, is never completely supplanted. If that symbolization has ceased to be collectively dominant, has stopped structuring the mode of communication of subjects in a society where conceptual thought reigns, it lingers in the subject's unconscious as the unrecognized counterpoint to the collective chorus that has submerged it; it persists as an effect of the split that it has instituted in the individual soul. The primary processes of psychic activity and dreams continue to operate according to the logic of the archaic writings. Egypt (figuration in aspective) did not fade away in the face of perspective without leaving any remainder. It has become internal and individual.

The order of historical succession that, for Hegel, articulates unconscious symbolics with what comes after and takes its place (conscious symbolics, then concepts), thus becomes for Freud a stratification of the psyche, the layering of a topology: unconscious, preconscious, conscious. Freud reinstitutes within the soul of the subject, as an articulation of agencies each of which has its own specific mode of symbolizing, what Hegel first conceived as consecutive moments in the history of the human spirit. It is as if the unconscious of the human subject has taken the place—which had become collectively vacant—of modes of symbolizing that had been historically surpassed, and has relocated that place in itself, on that "other stage" where, cut off from the clear light of consciousness, those symbolizations remain active.

In this, moreover, Freud rediscovers something of the Platonic topology of the soul, and the first Freudian topology could be systematically juxtaposed to Plato's more picturesque representation.

However, this Freudian restoration of the stratifications of the soul that Plato knew and that Hegel failed to recognize does not bring us back where we started. Freud undertook his analyses at a moment in the history of symbolics in which the concept and reflective consciousness prevail. Consciousness of self is the continuous suppression of the Sphinx. The unconscious is repeatedly constituted on the trace of that permanent suicide. Freud attempts to rediscover what the Oedipean cleavage, the anthropocentering and the egocentering, constantly force into the unconscious and never succeed in eliminating. Self-consciousness is the reiterated response to the symbolist enigma, which is cleared up and obliterated only to be reborn in obscurity, never resolved, always active. The interplay of the conscious and the unconscious is that continuous disappearance of the Sphinx, and her return, with the persistence of the twofold instinctual destiny that her unaccomplished murder promises and activates.

Here we touch on a point that reveals the encompassing power of the Oedipus figure in relation to all that psychoanalysis may attempt to articulate. Oedipus typifies the inauguration of a rift within the soul that produces the dimension of the unconscious. The encounter between psychoanalysis and the Oedipus myth is thus far more overdetermined than one might think. It is this very difference between the unconscious and consciousness, this cleft within the soul, that is Oedipean, that stems from the mechanism of psychic division instituted by the gesture of Oedipus.

It is not surprising that Freud discovers the unconscious and the two Oedipal drives at the same time. The modern subject's self-consciousness is constituted as "Oedipus's response," which leaves in obscurity, as a counterpart, the two never-extinguished drives that shape Oedipus's destiny. It is not only self-consciousness, reflective egocentering, that is Oedipean, as Hegel masterfully noted; it is also the unconscious and desiring counterpart that this response engenders, as Freud discovered. If consciousness is constituted in "response to the Sphinx," the unconscious is the obscure, pulsional side of that response: patricide, incest.

Freud thus takes the Oedipean configuration to an extreme, extending it far beyond the simple, heroic moment of anthropocentering Hegel saw in it. He extends it without surpassing it: Freud discovers that the unconscious, too, and not only consciousness, is implicit in the Oedipean mechanism. Certainly, Freud rediscovers within the individual soul what the Oedipean cleavage (self-consciousness) had vanquished and presumably suppressed; he finds once again the traces of an outdated but still-active mode of symbolizing that operates in the hieroglyphic and not the conceptual mode. But this topological discovery is necessarily coupled with a dynamic discovery. Oedipus's victory over the Sphinx, which was neither as complete nor as definitive as Hegel had believed, has a correlative anticipated by the myth itself. Freud restores to Oedipus's two crimes what Hegel had overlooked: their destinal necessity.

Freud thus undertakes an extensive clarification of the Oedipean logic that organizes the opposition between consciousness and the unconscious from both a topological and a dynamic viewpoint. To suppress the Sphinx is to free oneself from an agonizing link with a mysterious alterity; it means choosing not to recognize that cryptic monster—a precise image of the disturbing depths of the soul. That self-reflective suppression of the Sphinx institutes, as its counterpart, the site of the unconscious and the cleavage it maintains. It is as if what came to be described as "unconscious drives" had resulted from the absolute split brought about by Oedipus's response, a break between the "human" element of the soul and the two remaining elements. It is worth noting that the unconscious drives boil down to two: death-dealing aggressiveness and sexual libido. Thus, what Plato in his figurative language calls the "lion" and the "polycephalic beast" occupy the very site where the two fundamental drives of the Freudian unconscious are identified. The unconscious is Oedipean both in its structural institution (the cleavage between the "human" element and the two others) and in its pulsional content: a humanist failure to recognize the two tendencies, aggressive and sexual, that are the underlying factors in Oedipus's double crime. Once he has identified the unconscious, Freud cannot help but discover Oedipean desires.

Yet in doing so, he is only registering and exploring the historic mode of subjectivity instituted by the Greek anthropocentering move and then the Cartesian egocentering move. His analyses bear upon the effects of self-consciousness in their unconscious correlatives. In this sense, Freud does not step outside the Oedipean configuration; he simply discovers unsuspected ramifications within it, aftereffects and counterthrusts working on the subject.

This limitation has its own overwhelming historical necessity. It respects an anthropological constraint that is itself at the root of the anthropological vision of the world. Only the intimate relationship between the mythic singularity of Oedipus on the one hand and the emergence of humanism and the democratic subject on the other can account for it. It is the modern, Cartesian subject, and this subject alone, who is destined to be inscribed within the Oedipean drama and the cleavages it organizes—and thus, for example, to bypass the moment of the killing of the dark feminine.

These powerful constraints limit the scope of Freudian psychoanalysis, keep it from pinpointing the anthropological singularity of the West in which it is confined but which it does not conceptualize. Freud cannot see the monumental correlation that connects humanism, egocentering, democracy, the conscious/unconscious cleavage, and the avoidance of the radical and sacrificial monstricide for which he substitutes the twin drives of patricide and incest.

This limitation, as we saw at the outset, has at least one precise and readily identifiable repercussion for Freudian theory: the unjustified humanization of the incest taboo and the castration threat. Freud attributes the threat of castration to a father with a human face, whereas the most radical, unnameable threat comes from a "monster" who is female. Here the Oedipean character of psychoanalysis itself is revealed in contradiction with the mythic universality of the hero who must commit monstricide, must overcome the threat through sacrifice. Freud fails to situate the Oedipean singularity, fails to connect the myth of Oedipus with a monomyth of more deeply rooted universality. For the scene of the enraged father *is* the "exit from Egypt," the moment when what the monster was threatening to accomplish is imputed to the father. Freud starts with this moment of humanization in depicting the relation between consciousness and the unconscious, son and father, son and mother, and so on. But an anterior threat, a more fundamental, prehuman threat that is surmountable only by the bloody killing of the female monster, remains unknown to Freud. Hence his failure to recognize masculine desire in its most radical aspect— and also the nonmaternal feminine this desire liberates. These are the points where Lacan's suspicion, with which we began, slips in.

§ 10 Oedipus's Legacy

If Oedipus avoids the regular trial of initiation, is his destiny not shaped, even in its ultimate outcome, by the consequences of this gap? Don't his blindness, his wanderings far from his homeland, his extreme impoverishment, and finally his death at Colonus all share in the same necessity? The ultimate destinal constraint, still more hidden than the one that leads Oedipus to commit the two familial crimes, is no less powerful than the other; what it has to teach is forceful and fruitful in that it outlines a second Oedipean posture that is quite different from the first—at once its epilogue and an opening to the future.

The importance of properly understanding *Oedipus at Colonus* should not be underestimated. If philosophy, following its boldest line, is marked by the persistence of the Oedipean configuration, if this line also seems constantly to run into limits, which need to be conceived not necessarily as dead ends or exhaustions but as unsettling edges, as faults opened up by dangerous transgressions, as risks analogous to those that the tragedy explores, then it is of the greatest importance to understand how dramatological knowledge conceived of the Oedipean outcome, the stage beyond Oedipus's lapse into faltering sovereignty at Thebes. For what lies beyond certainly outlines, if only as a symbolic and aporetic sketch, the resolution of the disequilibrium that is inherent in his Theban posture. It is as if in the passage from *Oedipus the King* to *Oedipus at Colonus* was played out a solution that could prefigure the paths that the perspective subject ought to take, or will have to take, in order to move beyond the unidimensionality of his posture. Sophocles' dramaturgy anticipated a way of transcending the self-centered subject—or at least the alternative that, in an obligatory counterpoint, continually shapes, as a possible outcome, Oedipus's sovereignty and his fall.

It is a matter, then, of imagining two Oedipus figures: one at Thebes and one at Colonus, one young and the other old. It is between these two figures that philosophy's destiny is played out, between these two figures that the secret of moving beyond the Oedipean perspective lies. This movement does not entail discrediting that perspective (which will retain its impact as a bold stroke, its value as an intransigent appeal to freedom and autonomy), but opening up the possibility of thinking its other side, of delineating its risks and its unconscious presuppositions, of understanding how this point of view can become a vantage point for error.

What necessity links the one-sided victory of King Oedipus with his end at Colonus? The foregoing interpretation as a whole allows us to see the rigor of this bond in a new light. Oedipus thought he could avoid the initiatory ordeal: in fact, however, he only postponed it. Avoiding the ravages and suffering of the trial of investiture by means of an atheistic, autodidactic, and intellectual response, he believed he had freed himself from the obscure constraints, foreign to the clear light of human reason, that the initiatory encounter sets up. But his avoidance was only temporary. The succession of catastrophes and misfortunes he endured was the price he had to pay for his profanatory presumption. Instead of confronting just once, in regular, ritual form, the arduous and agonizing combat that would have torn him away from secular kinship and bound him to the gods, Oedipus is destined to live out, through a series of discoveries after the fact, the moment he evaded.

An initiation postponed, conducted after the fact, and thus under conditions different from those of the regular ritual confrontation: here is where the uniqueness of Oedipus's ultimate destiny lies. Hence the very powerful lesson of the drama at Colonus: what is presented there is an unprecedented, because delayed, form of telestic passage. The audacious innovation of Oedipus's first posture has repercussions that follow the hero all the way to the end, in a second and no less foundational innovation— indeed, in Sophocles' eyes, doubtless more foundational still. The singularity of this initiatory passage accomplished in extremis, the fruit of a whole life (and no longer belonging solely to the crisis of investiture or to the break at puberty) coinciding with death, is all the more edifying, as we shall see, in that it announces and pre-figures the modern ethical form, thought or unthought, that this passage has acquired. It is no longer a single event; it is a passage that is never completed, that must always be resumed and pro-longed. It is the threshold situation (the liminal moment) that pervades all of life, that becomes the lived condition of an entire existence. The human condition in its entirety as a liminal state: this is how we might sum up the new ethics that emerges with Oedipus.

What is striking about Oedipus's situation at Colonus is that it brings together all the characteristics of existential negativity. As an old man, Oedipus is a poignant figure of destitution, of the most total dispossession imaginable. Oedipus has nothing left. He has lost everything. He has lost his youth, his power, his fatherland, his eyes, his strength, his pride. Here he is, old, blind, exiled, vaga-bond, miserable, tired, dependent, impure, cursed by gods and men. Compared with the victory and sovereign power of King Oedipus, it is a situation of total reversal. Just as the young Oedipus had reached the pinnacle, Oedipus at Colonus has reached the nadir. He has touched bottom in terms of human misery.

Oedipus, once struck down by the god in a catastrophic reversal, approaches the horizon of an ultimate reversal that reestablishes him. Oedipus at Colonus is the moment of the ultimate uplifting of Oedipus. This recovery, needless to say, does not bring Oedipus back where he was. He does not gain access to secular heights. His is a sacred revival, accomplished on the threshold of death. The one who has suffered so much, who has become the most degraded, the most rejected of men, will also be a source of perpetual benediction for the people who welcome his tomb. Struck down when he was king, reaching the lowest depths of unhappiness, as death approaches and afterward, Oedipus is transfigured by Zeus into a saint.

An initiation avoided, an initiatory ritual finally accomplished, but on the threshold of death: this opposition accounts for the contrast between Oedipus the King and Oedipus at Colonus. Between the two figures, the young and the old, the king and the saint, there is a bond of rigorous necessity that becomes visible without remainder through the telestic interpretation of Oedipus's destiny.

The tragedy, this time, is slow, for everything has already been played out: access, in fulfillment of a prophecy, to the threshold of a holy and inviolable place by the most degraded of men who is also the most destitute; the anxious search for the right place to stand between the sacred limits; the patient acquisition of a detailed ritual of purification and expiation offered to the goddesses of this place—Oedipus's actions, when he arrives in the foreign city of Colonus, are inscribed in this way within a slow, precise, solemn, hieratic liturgy that leaves no room for whim or decision. This time Oedipus asks to be taught. In scrupulous obedience to the decrees of the gods, he accomplishes with humility the gestures that precipitate his fate. Everything is placed under divine jurisdiction, everything is ritualized, subject to the will of the Heavens. Oedipus is led, step by step. If *Oedipus the King* is a tragedy of profanation, *Oedipus at Colonus* is imbued from beginning to end with an intensely sacral atmosphere. And this sacredness has a dual aspect: not only is it opposed to the profane, but it is itself permeated by archaic ambivalence: the sacredness of impurity and transgression meets up with the sacredness of purification.[1] The man who is most degraded, and for that reason untouchable, enters the Eumenides' wood, a place that is pure, and therefore holy and inviolable—a solemn redoubling of the sacred that reactivates its originary power and prepares the ultimate reversal, the uplifting of Oedipus. The most rejected, the most excluded of men—this aged and polluted body of a criminal—becomes the miraculous source of blessings for Athens. Oedipus is transformed from an untouchable human wreck into a perpetual and inexhaustible treasure.

The well-known movement characteristic of every initiatory passage, a raising up after a lowering,[2] is at the center of the drama here. "The gods are about to raise you to your feet—till now they were bent on your destruction," Ismene says to her father. "Numberless agonies, blind and senseless, came his way in life—now let some power / some justice grant him glory!" the chorus chants. It is as if Oedipus knew and belatedly recognized this final moment of the trial in which the sacrifice of his being gives him access to a new identity. It is when Oedipus is no longer anything (when he is blind, miserable, exiled, old) that he becomes what he had never been able to be despite the power of his knowledge and his royalty. Hence his astonished exclamation: "So, when I am nothing—then am I a man [*anēr*]?"[3]

Here the old man Oedipus rediscovers the language of a secret wisdom. These are the very words an initiate might pronounce at the moment he is raised up, after the "death" (chaos, disorientation, ordeal) he has undergone. But here, in Oedipus's delayed itinerary, it is the approach of actual death that serves as a threshold, a line to be crossed. By virtue of his avoidance and delay, by virtue of his deferred passage, it is Oedipus's entire life that has been initiatory. The brutal sacrificial severing administered by the regular rite was unable to fulfill its function. Existence itself has become the trial, and death the supreme passage. With Oedipus, a different relation to the sacrifice and to the sacred is instituted: the relation of holiness.

But the most compelling aspect of Oedipus's death, in light of the logic of delayed initiation, is beyond all doubt the extraordinary finale: no less than the founding, by Oedipus, of a new ritual of initiation, the transmission, for the future succession of Athenian sovereigns, of a secret of which he is the origin. When Zeus's thunder announces to Oedipus that the hour of death has come, it is time for him to reveal to Theseus and Theseus alone the secret that holds inexhaustible benefits in store for Athens:

I will reveal it all to you, son of Aegeus,
the power that age cannot destroy,
the heritage stored up for you and Athens.
Soon, soon I will lead you on myself, no hand
to lead my way, to the place where I must die.
Never reveal the spot to mortal man,
not even the region, not where it lies hidden.
Then it will always form a defense for you,
a bulwark stronger than many shields,
stronger than the spear of massed allies.

But these are great mysteries . . .
words must never rouse them from their depths.
You will learn them all for yourself, once
you come to our destination, you alone.
I cannot utter them to your people here,
nor to my own children, love them as I do.
No, you alone must keep them safe forever,
and when you reach the end of your own life,
reveal them only to your eldest, dearest son,
and then let him reveal them to his heir
and so through the generations, on forever.[4]

Is this not the very language of initiatory instruction? Moreover, with this secret to be transmitted to the future kings of Athens who will reign after Theseus, Oedipus becomes the founder of a symbolic lineage, a lineage that will not pass from father to son but from sovereign to sovereign. By this originary act, Oedipus himself becomes the founder of an authentic ritual of royal initiation. Thus, in what is a paradox only on the surface, the person who avoided regular royal initiation and belatedly experienced the agonizing trials that his profanatory avoidance entailed reintroduces himself here into the chain of symbolic transmission of knowledge by becoming an initiator. Only now is his destiny fulfilled.

There could hardly be a better corroboration than Oedipus's end for the telestic interpretation that our study has developed. His final words attest to the fact that the question of initiation, of transmission, is truly at the heart of the Oedipean drama. If the old

Oedipus finds reconciliation and achieves fulfillment only in this death, where he is at once the initiate in the supreme passage and the founder of a new initiatory line, it is indeed because the breach opened by the subversion of the passage, the investiture, was the most searing wound of the destiny of the king of Thebes, the major fold in his destinal logic.

Sophocles placed the play as a whole under the sign of an interdiction (against entering into the sacred wood) and of the "mysteries," in the original sense of the word, which referred to the "mutism" of the *mystē*, guardian of the secret. In contrast with the profanation that dominates *Oedipus the King, Oedipus at Colonus* is placed under the sign of the inviolable. The chorus's allusion to the "Great Goddesses [who] tend the awesome rites offering life to mortals after death, their lips sealed by the golden key of silence pressed upon them by the priests" has the same value of counterweight in *Oedipus at Colonus* as the chorus's evocation of the *hubris* that characterizes the tyrant in *Oedipus the King*. The entire dramaturgy of the second Oedipus is organized around a scrupulous identification of frontiers and a respect for limits,[5] just as the first Oedipus was played out in their transgression: limits that are not to be overstepped, for they mark the inviolable interdiction, or else limits to be crossed ritually, and thus a sacred threshold where a passage is accomplished. In this sense, the significance of the rite of passage, its import as liminal situation, are marked and remarked in this drama from beginning to end. From the standpoint of plot, very little happens, for the action in its entirety amounts to a passage, the identification and crossing of a threshold. Oedipus seeks his site, he tries to find his place with respect to the constraints of the sacred—to cross over, but not to overstep. It is a question of steps (*pas*)—as the riddle of the Sphinx, too, was a question about passages, and steps. But this time the old Oedipus knows that he must pass on, pass away (*trépasser*), accept the negative (the crossing out [*le "pas"*]). Thus, having missed the opportunity for crossing offered by the confrontation with the Sphinx, Oedipus is left with death alone as a limit, an unavoidable passage.

Initiation may be eluded, but not death: such is the lesson of Oedipus at Colonus.

It is thus as if the negative phase of initiation (passivity, destitution, torture, loss of identity) that Oedipus missed in his Theban victory is experienced belatedly. Once he has arrived at Colonus, Oedipus brings together all the characteristics of the postulant in the liminal situation—except that he is a belated initiate. For him, the true passage will be actual death, and a kind of investiture into a posthumous sacred royalty. What the initiate must endure according to the consecrated rites, Oedipus, who missed out on that regular symbolic access, is condemned to undergo belatedly and in a mode that actually accomplishes what he was unable to ritualize. Thus, it is no longer a phase of symbolic death that Oedipus traverses: real death, passing away (*le trépas*), becomes the true passage. If, for the adolescent postulant, to be initiated is to die symbolically, for Oedipus, to die in reality is to reach the initiatory moment at last, to reach the end point of a life that has constantly deferred that step by failing to recognize the sacred. Oedipus has been initiated through life experience; the long sufferings of his existence have taught him the strength of the sacred, the power of the god, the truth of signs. If in the beginning he refused the teaching of the sages and the help of the gods by a presumption of rational reason, if in a word he refused all heteronomy, he has been able to rediscover, after the fact, by himself and in another mode, the dimension of truth contained in the fathers' knowledge. Here is where we find the uniqueness and the novelty of Oedipus's position at Colonus. He has not completely repudiated the autological posture that accounted for his ephemeral greatness. He continues, at bottom, to be moved by the same drive he started with; but when that drive is pushed far enough, after his lifelong journey through tragic experience, the will to know on one's own converges with the truth that had at first been set aside. The aged Oedipus thus experiences simultaneous failure and fulfillment of auto-initiation in the Eumenides' wood. It is as if he was rejoining Teiresias, as if he had become identical to that seer (old, blind, guided by his daughter, protected by Apollo, bearer of Apollo's presages)—but a Teiresias who had been King Oedipus before becoming the wise old man, thus personifying an unprecedented moment in the history of knowledge. This is the sense in which Oedipus, once he has reached Colonus, is the bearer of a secret.

If Oedipus complies scrupulously with the ritual of purification, he nevertheless takes a kind of initiative toward the end. Summoned by the god, it is Oedipus who, though blind, guides his daughters; it is he who orders the rite to be followed before his disappearance. Now directed by Hermes and the goddess from below, Oedipus can lead the sighted. The messenger who later relates his gestures watches in wonderment as Oedipus places himself in a spot whose precision can only correspond to a sacred intention. He reaches the threshold of a steep ledge, stands upright on one of the many paths leading away from that point, finally stopping short at an equal distance from four objects: the krater upon which the oath of Theseus and Peirithoüs is inscribed, the rock of Thoricus, a hollow pear tree, and a marble tomb. Oedipus, the blind man who has placed himself, with the gods' guidance, at an equal distance from four sacred objects, thus finds himself standing at the center of a cross. Here, in this center, he reveals to Theseus the ultimate secret for Theseus to transmit in turn; here he disappears immediately afterward, before the terrified eyes of the sovereign of Athens, in a mysterious rapture that is, according to the messenger, a genuine miracle (*thaumastos*).

What is the significance of this center, which is also a threshold, and this cross? Whether these indications, obscure for us, were intelligible to Sophocles' contemporaries or whether they were already enigmatic is something we do not know. Beyond the powerful symbolism that is attached, no doubt universally, to the cross (reconciliation of opposites) and to the center (place of passage among different levels: Heaven, Earth, the subterranean world) it does not seem out of the question that Sophocles might be alluding to a ritual paradigm involving sacred royalty. After all, we are dealing with the death of Oedipus, and Oedipus does reveal a secret to be transmitted to every new king before the death of the old one. In effect, the old Oedipus makes a place for himself in the lineage of Athenian kings, since at the moment of his own death he transmits the secret that Theseus is to transmit in turn, just before he dies, to his successor.

Belatedly, at the moment of his death and not at the triumphant beginning of his reign, Oedipus is impelled to take up the rite he had avoided, but in an unprecedented and solitary form; he is to rework what had remained open, incomplete. Oedipus's final moments have to be conceived as his accession to a new posture, another way of being that transcends the perspective of the young Oedipus without going back to an earlier state. The old Oedipus rediscovers his authority, his independence: he finds his way alone, despite his blindness. But this rediscovered autonomy with respect to those who are leading him rests upon a higher dependency, a new heteronomy. It is easy to imagine that the secret of the old Oedipus, the one he transmits to Theseus, is the secret of this still-unprecedented moment: the posture of the subject who has surmounted both the aspective in which Teiresias still remained confined and the perspective of the young Oedipus. This is the secret of Oedipus at Colonus, a third figure of subjectivity.

Oedipus the king had lost the center. He had not reached the hearth. With death he finds a site. After Oedipus's disappearance, when Antigone is overcome with the desire to see her father's tomb, to transgress the interdiction that guarantees the secrecy of the place, she exclaims to Ismene: "I'm mad with longing . . . To see that last home in the earth . . . Father's!" The word she uses is *hestia*, signifying foyer, hearth, but also altar, dwelling-place of the god, temple, tomb. This plurality of related meanings takes on striking relief in Oedipus's case. It is only on the threshold of death that he finds a center. His subverted initiation had given him only a deceptive appearance of home. He has never gained access to Hestia,[6] divinity of the hearth (*hestia*). It is only on the occasion of the supreme passage, when "the lightless depths of Earth [burst] open in kindness to receive him," only with his final resting-place, that he finds that center, that place.[7] He finds it on foreign soil. And its site must remain secret. A triple requirement (death, foreign soil, secrecy) finally opens up the autological circle in which Oedipus had been confined. If he had been unable to open himself to mystery, to enigma, to unnameable alterity, he has now crossed the threshold, he has passed over to the other side of death; his tomb lies within the sacred circle of a foreign land, and its place will remain a mystery—except to the initiate.

A locus of distance, alterity, unsituatability: such is the hearth where Antigone seeks her father. The body has vanished; the tomb has no topology.

Oedipus's persistent, unyielding animosity toward his sons has seemed to many readers to contradict the movement of reconciliation that subtends the drama's finale. This sustained anger, this fury that does not diminish even with the approach of death, has seemed to mar the paradoxical saintliness that the old Oedipus attains. Yet this animosity has a very clear and coherent meaning in the reading we are proposing. Oedipus, who has suffered from having reduced all kinship to real kinship (he eludes the initiatory severing only to encounter his own father and his own mother), at last distinguishes, during his ultimate passage, between filiation by blood and a higher filiation. It is Theseus, the foreign king, and not his own children, who will receive his inheritance, the blessing of his tomb for Athens. Having been unable to situate himself in a symbolic sonship at the moment of his royal passage, he finally, after the self-sacrifice of his vision and after long and arduous ordeals, gains access to symbolic paternity. He has not been the fulfilled initiate (according to the regular tradition): he will be the initiator of a new tradition, which itself presupposes a moment of rejection of all tradition.

The powerful signification of Sophocles' diptych (Oedipus at Thebes, Oedipus at Colonus) now appears in its full amplitude. Only the interpretation of the drama as eluded initiation can offer a comprehensive overview of the Sophoclean mechanism. The meaning of Oedipus's death in the sacred Eumenides' wood is inseparable from the meaning of his initial transgression.

The cause of Oedipus's tragedy is that he broke the chain of transmission. He can reconcile himself with the gods only by becoming a source of revelation himself in the ultimate sacrificial moment of death. This is his act of reparation. He who had gained power by an act of usurpation (with respect to unwritten laws, even if for Creon and the Thebans he had earned his legitimacy by an exploit) now becomes the spiritual founder of the sovereign line of Athens. After the sacrificial offering of his eyes, and at the very instant of his agony, the moment of supreme passage, the former and fallen "*tyrannos*" is transfigured into the protector of the city, into a mystical benefactor of the future succession of sovereigns. In this new initiatory chain, Oedipus's death is the founding moment.

Thus, Oedipus has paid: and yet his reparation is not a simple annulment that would bring us full circle. He has restored—but differently, through the charisma of his own tomb—the very initiatory dimension that he had mocked, ignored, and desecrated by his intellectualist avoidance of the trial that had the Sphinx as its threshold and that could only have patricide and incest as its tragic correlative. He thus institutes, but differently, at the end of his existence, what he had eluded as a young man by a dissimulated usurpation: a transmission.

One of Sophocles' strokes of genius was to have made Oedipus the founder of a new tradition, the point of departure for an initiatory lineage of which Theseus, the legendary founder of Athens, is the first depository. Thus, despite his own hostility and fear toward the new philosophic reason, which was destructive of the sacred enigmas and which made man and not the divine the measure of all things, Sophocles finally rehabilitates Oedipus. In the end, it is not Teiresias, the priest of Apollo, who holds and transmits the secret of the future; it is Oedipus, the only one who has gone through both the triumphant experience of philosophic reason and the blinding test of its limits. The treasure of Athens resides in that twofold experience.

Oedipus is the figure of the freethinker who has taken on the unprecedented risk of affirming the supreme dignity of human reason, with the presumptuousness that such an affirmation entails. He is ultimately crushed by what surpasses man. He undergoes the tragic experience of the limits of perspective. Nevertheless, he is reconciled with himself and with the gods. And his experience becomes the token of the future of a people—a people who welcome this wanderer who is not only a foreigner to the city but the most degraded, the most abject of beings. Thus, Oedipus is not only the one whose autodidact intelligence was able to respond to the Sphinx, he is also the one who becomes, for the future, the point of origin of a new position. Oedipus's first knowledge is contained in his response to the Sphinx, "man." But he has a second and ultimate knowledge: the knowledge he reveals to Theseus before he dies in the Eumenides' wood, in a sacred place that is to remain unknown. This knowledge is destined for the future, it is forward-looking. While we do not know the words in which Oedipus formulated it, we do know that it is a new position. We do not know Oedipus's secret, and yet it is this unknown knowledge that henceforth governs the destiny of Athens.

In Oedipus a passage is accomplished: with his response to the Sphinx he brings to an end the cruel ancient initiation rites of which the winged virgin stood as both guardian and entrance. But before his death, with a new secret he establishes a new transmission. If Oedipus is the source of a new revelation, it is because in him are conjoined the knowledge of the young philosopher and the wisdom of the old sage. The old Oedipus by rights cumulates the young autological knowledge of the philosopher and, by the experience of blindness, the hierophanic knowledge of Teiresias. Surpassing both the aspective of the old sage and the perspective of the philosopher who responds "man" to the enigma, the old Oedipus is at the origin of another knowledge. We shall use the term "transpective" to designate this new orientation in being that is personified by the complete figure of Oedipus.

～

The limits of the first operation can be anticipated in a few words: to suppress the Sphinx with the reflective and anthropocentered response is not to destroy her forever, it is to internalize her. Deprojection does not destroy the affects and images that have been projected; it brings them back within the soul, where they remain unrecognized. Oedipus's posture creates the site of the

unconscious. The unconscious is that part of the soul that continues to live, to feel and perceive, in aspective, but in a culture
massively dominated by the subject's constitution in perspective. In
Plato's work, this dimension is already being prepared.

After Oedipus's victory, after the successful insurrection of the
subject in the mode of egocentering and self-consciousness, a new
rupture thus comes into play: the encounter with the internalized
Sphinx. How can this new figure of subjectivity be designated? For
it is not the archaic presentation in aspective of projections emerg-
ing from a subject that does not identify itself as a source and agent;
and it is already no longer the triumphant presumptuousness of a
perspectivist self-consciousness that lays claim to transparency and
to autoreflective certainty.

We have called this figure transpective. It presupposes the successful constitution of the egocentered subject; but this subject
now—again—recognizes as irreducible, and first of all in anguish,
the dimension of aspective, which has been internalized and situated as the "unconscious." Through the Sphinx, the relation to the
strangeness of the monstrous and enigmatic is still experienced in
the form of alterity. Fear had an object, and that object had the
status of an other-than-oneself. The fear of the Sphinx was still a
fear of "someone." Once that being is suppressed, the confrontation with the unknown takes place in a different mode. The now-
faceless internal alterity is confronted not in fear but in anguish.

The myth of Oedipus, in its aftereffects, thus also has the
following meaning: with the Sphinx's suicide, with the precipita-
tion into the abyss of that symbol of symbolism, the heroic age of
fear comes to an end, and the rationalist era of anguish begins. No
longer a recollection of a primordial event maximally charged with
meanings from time immemorial, no longer an imaginable and
dramatic confrontation with a being engendered and sent forth by
the gods, the encounter will be only an absurd affect that grips man
as he confronts the unknown. Anguish is the *pathos* of a culture
without *pathos*.

The withdrawal of projections, the reappropriation by self-
consciousness of the contents that had been externalized and that

had enchanted the world, underlies the emergence of the unconscious. This is why it is only after the complete traversal of the
Oedipean or Cartesian epoch that a subject can recognize the
cleavage of the unconscious and be introduced, as in an initiation,
to his own unconscious. But by the same token, the Oedipean
conquest that postulates the internalization and individuation of
any imaginary is preserved and prolonged in that recognition. If
aspective is accepted as irreducible (dreams, fantasies, and the
"gods" can present themselves in no other mode), it is an aspective
internalized and individuated through the acquisition of the Oedipean egocentering. It is situated in relation to self-consciousness
instead of being integrally reappropriated by self-consciousness—
for such a reappropriation remains impossible. The subject has to
recognize that there is something other within himself. This is the
posture of transpective.

The old Oedipus should have been the first to know that the unconscious exists, that the gods are internal. We might easily imagine that this was his secret message to Theseus and all his Athenian posterity. Oedipus at Thebes exemplifies the disproportionate
strengthening of the ego that affirms its power and its mastery only
by competing with the father-king, by suppressing him, and by
eluding the encounter with what, for the masculine subject, is
entirely other: the feminine, the divine, death. But this perspective
ego, which has foreclosed all transcendent alterity, has to admit
defeat, has to die (through the self-sacrifice of sight) in order to be
reborn to a greater consciousness while integrating the darkness of
inner vision (Oedipus at Colonus). It is a drama of individuation.
First fortifying his ego by a hyperbolic orientation, he becomes
isolated, excluded, dispossessed, an exile, a loner. He then experiences the ordeal of individuation and a deeper internalization that
integrates obscurity and death. The grandeur (the ego autonomous
and victorious) and the misery (dispossession, solitude) of individuation: this opposition sums up Oedipus's itinerary.

In fact, this position of transpective that is now our own, this
position that recognizes the unconscious (as internalized aspective)
in its irreducible relation to consciousness (as perspective) has been

acquired only much more recently. It could not become our own model of subjectivity until the tyrannical posture of Oedipus had been reenacted and elaborated in decisively modern terms (from Descartes to Nietzsche), until the site of the unconscious, as the ineradicable counterpart of the claims of the ego and the consciousness of self, had been recognized, first philosophically and then technically (with Freud).

What is more, it is only at the moment when all theology becomes psychology, at the moment when all tragedy (existential or staged) can be clearly interpreted as a mechanism rigorously describable in terms of human passions, that the site of the unconscious is constituted. So long as *pathos* and its extreme devices (madness, perversion, and all the deviations of tragedy) are still experienced and conceptualized in terms of sacred communication with the gods (sacrifice, vengeance, expiation, prayer, and so forth), the site of the unconscious is not posited. Only when all theological externalizations are abandoned does the archaic transcendency of the gods become that other modern form of transcendency: the internal and internalized rift that is the unconscious.

Tragedy can thus be seen as an essential moment for reconstructing the genealogy of the unconscious. Greek dramaturgy is the fertile, contradictory, ambiguous moment when a critical transition is played out, the passage, from an old, mythic polytheology that spontaneously externalizes the multiple passions of the soul (and their regulation) by way of the asserted transcendency of the gods, to a secular psychology that exclaims suspiciously, like that Ancient cited by Hegel: " 'From out of thy passions, oh, man,' exclaimed an ancient, 'thou has derived the materials for thy gods!' "[8] Once that exclamation is uttered, the gods are finished as living and transcendent forces that carry out their actions from the heights of the Heavens or the depths of the Earth. Once that exclamation is uttered, all the desires, forces, and capabilities that animated Olympus, all its storms, its chants, and its ruses, are now situated within the human soul, constituting its deep and characteristic treasure. Once that exclamation is uttered, the site of the unconscious is marked. The cleavage between the ego and the other stage is now placed within the individual and no longer in a divine transcendence. For the recognition that Eros is not an external god but a *pathos*, that Ares is not an external god but a *pathos*, does not suffice to suppress the passion of love or aggressive energies. It is only the relation to this *pathos* that has changed, the lived experience of its depth, the mode of communication with it. *Pathos* outlives the death of the gods. But its position, its site, the relation experienced with it, are no longer the same. Perhaps the soul's communication with its own pathological powers becomes more difficult, more devious, more indirect, paradoxically, when the gods are dead? The unconscious will become that place that can come into being only for post-traditional man, in whom *pathos* (secularized, individualized, internalized) outlives the death of the gods—and then of God.

Not that ancient tragedy was able to liquidate the sacred transcendency of the gods once and for all in order to replace it with the secular and individualized cleavage of the unconscious. Far from it. And Plutarch, belatedly, will still condemn as impious the movement (explicit in someone like Chrysippus) that consists in reducing each of the gods to a personification of our faculties, our virtues, our passions; for Plutarch this movement can only lead to an abyss of atheism. "If it is impious to identify the gods with our passions, it is equally so, on the other hand, to consider our passions as gods."[9] On the other hand, according to the same Plutarch it is right to say that a given tendency (for example the tendency of the human soul to be courageous and energetic, or the tendency that impels us to love) depends upon a specific god (Ares, Eros). However, if tragedy does not effectively and completely liquidate the theological projection to the sole benefit of secular and individualized psychological interiorization, structurally and constitutively it certainly marks the moment of passage, of oscillation and contradiction. It is here that the myth of Oedipus, in a way that Hegel both glimpsed and glossed over, has to be the object of special attention. In the process to which we are referring, the Oedipus story is not just one myth among others. It is a myth of passage—of historical passage. If Greek tragedy, considered in general, occupies the transitional position we have claimed for it, it is noteworthy that the tragedy of Oedipus specifically occupies an exceptional position as the turning point, as the precipitant, within that transition. For the tragedy of Oedipus is precisely, structurally if not explicitly, the tragedy of the deprojection of the gods.

Hegel indeed saw that deprojection, at least in his own way and in his own language. But he failed to see that the same deprojection is the movement that also, necessarily, constitutes the site of the unconscious. If Hegel was unable to see this, it was not because he lacked the notion of the unconscious. Not only did he have access to that notion, but he even quite specifically depicted Oedipus's response to the Sphinx as the moment of passage from unconscious to conscious symbolism. Hegel was led astray by his own view of history as a sublation that combines surpassing and suppression. Hegel believed that self-consciousness, pure reflexivity of self to self, could supplant the transcendency of the gods with no remainder, and that the passage from unconscious symbolism (Egypt) to conscious symbolism (Greece) could be a historical achievement of the spirit, a revolution that leaves no residue, abolishing the dimension of the unconscious once and for all, rather than, on the contrary, defining its site for the first time. Hegel could not see that consciousness itself, that transparency of the self-aware spirit, is what establishes, simultaneously with itself, the dimension of the unconscious. In this respect, Hegel was as blind as Oedipus. They both failed to recognize the fate, the catastrophic outcome, the ultimate retaliation of the injured god, the Sphinx's revenge. Hegel did not see that Oedipus's response, while it suppresses the (projected) Sphinx, inaugurates by that very token the age of the inner Sphinx.

But if the tragedy of Oedipus established the site of the unconscious, then the connection between the unconscious and Oedipus is far more constitutive and radical than Freud was able to perceive. The unconscious itself is, *by disposition*, Oedipean. The site of the unconscious can come into being only for the subject who constitutes himself in the posture of Oedipus. That is why Freud can discover only the unconscious and the "Oedipus complex." Subjects for whom there is an unconscious, in the modern sense, are, and can only be, post-traditional subjects who constitute themselves within a mechanism in which the "I" occupies the tyrannical place. The Freudian construction suggests that the two Oedipean fantasies are discovered in the unconscious, whereas it is the mechanism of subjectivity whereby the unconscious/conscious cleavage is constituted that is Oedipean in its very principle, because it is shaped by a desire for absolute autonomy. A subjectivity formed in the Oedipean mode and the unconscious are one and the same historical mechanism of subjectivity.

Conclusion

It is now apparent why the discovery of the Oedipus complex and the discovery of the unconscious had to have been simultaneous. The conscious/unconscious cleavage is Oedipean. And this cleavage constitutes the very mechanism of castration avoidance (the initiatory sacrifice), for it blocks the apprehension of the enigmatic depths (cryptophoric symbolism, aspective) that opened onto the other side and the abyss and called for matricide. It is this fundamentally Oedipean cleavage between conscious and unconscious that Freud identifies and that every analysand confronts. Each one, in a particular, personal, biographical way, has had to produce that cleavage in order to gain access to the mode of subjectivity that characterizes Cartesian societies. Each one has had to respond individually to the Sphinx through the insurrection of an autocentered "I" that has suppressed her dangerous dimension and provided access to perspectivist truth. But this discovery is not enough. Freudian psychoanalysis lacks the articulated conception of what may signify a surpassing of the Oedipus complex, with the ethical consequences that these stakes entail. Only an accurate recognition of the truth dramatized by the monomyth and of the interpretive power of the telestic intrication can determine what lies beyond Oedipus.

But if the monomyth expresses masculine desire more fundamentally in the way it structures the story of Jason or Perseus than does the aberration of the Oedipus plot, the fact remains that access to desire according to the monomyth remains problematic for modern man. The permanent break with tradition, a type of knowledge and vision structured by the Oedipean avoidance that has become an active mode of historicity, the cleavage between consciousness and the unconscious that reinforces that avoidance and that blocks the authentic liberating matricide, all these characteristics of the modern subject transform the Oedipean disruption into a new filiarchal normativity, a veritable tradition of the anti-traditional. The modern form of the Oedipean disruption makes the desire at work in the monomyth inaccessible, or at least makes it difficult to translate that desire into socially acceptable forms. The madness of Oedipus has become Western reason.

And we could argue, after all, that the philosophies of reversal achieve a successful, because sublimated, transposition of the Oedipean drives: patricide becomes the stubborn rejection of ancestral authorities, and incest a conquest and unlimited enjoyment of the Earth. Where is the tragedy?

Modern man, the man of democratic and individualist societies, in fact only transcends the aporias of the Oedipean ego through the itinerary of Oedipus himself, through the position achieved at Colonus. There is no way he can be, naively, the monomythic hero. He can only suffer deferred initiation. The monomyth and the matricidal sacrifice are fully experienced only in aspective. And modern man is constituted as an active, thinking, socialized subject only in perspective. If Oedipus rediscovers at Colonus the truth of what he had first avoided at Thebes, he cannot begin the passage all over again; he can only invent a new mode of being on the basis of his discovery. Oedipus will never again be Jason or Perseus. He will never return from his heroic voyage with the Golden Fleece or Medusa's head. At most, he will forge a secret message that he will confide, before dying, to Theseus, for transmission to his successors.

Never again will modern man cross the threshold in a decisive, bloody trial that severs the entanglements of the snake-mother by order of a dispatcher-authority and with the help of gods and wise men. Modern man's destiny will be one of prolonged liminality, experienced in an uncompletable, open, undecidable process of auto-initiation. Modern filiarchal subjectivity is one of liminality that has become an endless process rather than a passage. All of existence has become the critical threshold. The unfulfillment, the openness of the heroic trajectory unsettles and unseats patriarchal stability. Where the mythicoritual initiate attained a telos that made him, according to the play of meaning that the old Greek word associated with the idea of "being initiated," a "completed," "accomplished," "mature," fully "ripened" being, this outcome is no longer favored by the filiarchal structure of subjectivity. The modern subject remains a neophyte until death, for he always defers the trial by deploying the creative virtuosities of reflective intelligence, by repeating the detour of autodidactic responses that cause the Sphinxes of symbolism to fade away and that keep consciousness cut off from the unconscious. The will of the modern subject is to be liberated from any *telos*.

Teiresias, in Euripides' *Bacchae*, leads Cadmus by the hand toward the sacred ceremonies in honor of Dionysus and says to him: "We do not trifle with divinity. No, we are the heirs of customs and traditions hallowed by age and handed down to us by our fathers. No quibbling logic can topple *them*, whatever subtleties this clever age invents."[1] An exemplary hierophantic discourse. It is only in periods of irrefutable inheritance that the figure of the initiate acquires its full weight, only in times when the truth taught by a master who himself had it from a master in an uninterrupted chain, a master who maintains its purity and infallibility, has more dignity than new truths. Teiresias still typifies that wisdom in the tragedy of Oedipus, as he does in the tragedy of Pentheus. But when the truth of the son takes on more weight, in structural terms, than the truth of the father (a situation summed up by the notion of "historical progress"), the figure of the initiate (and even any idea of teaching) is emptied of substance, and the *mystē* becomes a mystifier.

Between history and Oedipus there is a close connection. Ideally, in a society "without history," a society based principally on repetitive transmission of an intact tradition from one generation to another, a figure like Oedipus cannot take on an essential meaning. It is only an aberration. But as soon as the received wisdom of the ancestors ceases to be an infallible guide directing the thought and actions of the living, every individual, however involuntarily, ends up desecrating the discredited teaching left by the great departed; everyone is condemned to Oedipean audacity and disarray. Thus, every culture that experiences history as a second nature, every society that breaks away from repetition and experiences something on the order of "progression," "development," or permanent "innovation," is Oedipean; it is torn in its innermost being, in its destiny and in its spirit, by the tragic nature of Oedipus.

In this respect, for us, the myth of Oedipus is not a fiction. It is the mechanism of significations in which we are effectively caught up as subjects belonging to an "open" or "detraditionalized" or "autotelestic" society. It preserves the most deeply rooted core, the most substantive matrix that orders our horizons of meaning. It problematizes, or rather it "imaginalizes," the aporias of humanism and individualism. As soon as autoproduction determines the constitution of the subject, Oedipus—at Thebes and at Colonus—is our destiny.

Western civilization is not patriarchal in the sense in which certain societies have been or still are patriarchal.[2] It is pervaded by the abstraction of the Father. Its anomaly and its originality, ever since the "Greek miracle," have continued to lie in the filiarchal impulses that perturb it. The liberation of the son with respect to the fathers, the movement in which the individual as such is torn away from the imperatives of the ancestors, such is the driving impulse that defines Western civilization as history. Patriarchy and matriarchy have in common the reign of tradition, respect for the past, imitation of ancestors, truth based on authority. The thought of the son springs from a break in symbolic reproduction, from a disavowal of kinship. All pre-Greek societies are based on the idea of a metasocial norm originating elsewhere, transcendent. Action and thought are governed by sacred prescriptions that originate with the gods and are transmitted by the ancestors. This "universal" schema is undone by the Greek innovation. It is man who creates his own laws in a scandal of autonomy and humanism that at once opens up the possibility of an auto-institution of the social in an absolutely sovereign community (*autonomous, autodikos, autotēlēs*)[3] and also allows the emergence of the individual. The Oedipus plot, in its very archaism, reveals something of the imaginal background of that irruption of free thought and autotelestic motion. If the Oedipus plot, at a certain moment of Greek culture, could acquire such resonance, could hold onto such a position by its power of philosophic ramification, it is because this plot condenses the rupture that will never cease to mark Western destiny. That it should be a myth of initiation eluded by reflective intelligence sums up, in the density of the symbolic presuppositions that this motif entails, the principal stakes of the rupture. The emergence of the individual comes about as a filiarchal revolution.

To be completely autonomous is, in the language of myth, to take the place of one's father. The democratic subject, as a subject constantly moved by the will to autonomy, is thus confronted with this difficulty. In his own way, Plato had seen that the democratic son who lays claim to equality with his father turns into a tyrannical son who suppresses his father in order to take his place, in the Oedipal sense among others. The place of psychoanalysis is assigned by its function within a democratic sociosymbolic regime: it takes over the shadows, the unconscious symbolic counterpart that the democratic subject's will to autonomy cannot fail to create: the subject's Oedipean conflict.

The Oedipean structure of *pathos* and knowledge is thus the distinctive feature of the post-traditional world in which the dramaturgy of transmission has entirely disappeared as an established social practice and in which the passage through castration (separation, severing) remains free, individual, self-generated, and in a sense deferred, permanent, indefinite. The historical world would thus be not so much a world in which the process of initiation has disappeared as a world in which no one is ever done with it—a world of the son, who structurally, fundamentally, cannot stabilize himself in the knowing posture of the father: a world of prolonged liminality. In short, a world of (permanent, provisional, repeated) auto-institution, thus of history. It is the position of the initiator (and not the necessarily "mystifying" and "empty" place of the initiate) that informs the constitutive imaginary.

There is no question, then, of blindly asserting the truth conveyed by the myth, of countering all the radical attempts at autonomy, all the forms of autocentered subjectivity, with the timeless curse promised by the story of Oedipus. Such is not my intention. I do not mean to wrest Oedipus away from the heroic positivity that Hegel granted him. Not only does that heroism seem to inaugurate an exit that marks a break and a point of no return with respect to the sociosymbolic regimes of the past, but what is more, Oedipus remains for us a constantly necessary moment, a risk, a permanent opening, a posture always to be readopted. However, any passage from heteronomy to autonomy, any will to free oneself from what is transmitted, is burdened with a tragic risk. Negatively, and moreover in an aporetic and undeterminable way, one always encounters a problem of limits. The tragedy of Oedipus indicates, in this sense, the folds of the symbolic that shape every passage from heteronomy to autonomy. The Oedipean tragic, however complex and novel its modern conceptual or existential transpositions may be, is the permanent counterpart of the democratic subject in that this subject is, more than any other, solicited by the will to autonomy. This subject is thus constantly fashioned and inhabited by a rift; he will always stand between Oedipus's victory at Thebes and his final stopping point at Colonus.

To think through the relationship that necessarily unites the young Oedipus and the old, the "scientist" and the "saint," is to restore to philosophy the alterity that it has sometimes been accused of ignoring. Between the lines of the Sophoclean interpretation this reproach can already be heard. Oedipus at Colonus breaks off the autological trajectory of Oedipus at Thebes. To provide an adequate account of the destiny that unites the two Oedipus figures is to exit from autoreflective unidimensionality while nevertheless keeping intact the insurrectional Oedipean subject's powers of innovation, of insolence and desacralization, without which the senile and servile fascination with the timeless threatens to become paralyzing and free thought risks annihilation. Nothing less than the democratic and individualist wager is at stake here. We cannot choose between two Oedipus figures, the philosopher-king of Thebes and the dispossessed saint of Colonus. While the narrative logic of theater can produce these two positions only in succession, we must think them through together, as the tension that constitutes the Occidental subject in its tragic dimension.

Notes

Notes

Introduction

1. Marie Delcourt, *Oedipe ou la légende du conquérant* (Liège: Droz, 1944); Jean-Pierre Vernant and Pierre Vidal-Naquet, *Tragedy and Myth in Ancient Greece*, trans. Janet Lloyd (Brighton, Sussex: Harvester Press, 1981), and *Mythe et tragédie en Grèce ancienne*, vol. 2 (Paris: La Découverte, 1986).

2. Driek Van der Sterren, *Oedipe: une étude psychanalytique d'après les pièces de Sophocle* (Paris: Presses Universitaires de France, 1976); Didier Anzieu, *Psychanalyse et culture grecque* (Paris: Belles Lettres, 1980); André Green, *Un Oeil en trop: le complexe d'Oedipe dans la tragédie* (Paris: Minuit, 1969). See also Conrad Stein, *La Mort d'Oedipe* (Paris: Denoël-Gonthier, 1980).

Chapter 1

1. Attempts to discover a prototype myth of the male hero on the basis of a comparison of a large number of myths began well before the appearance of an explicitly structuralist methodology. The most important attempts are the following:

Johann Georg von Hahn, *Sagwissenshaftliche Studien* (Jena: F. Mauke, 1876. Hahn's schema is reproduced in John Colin Dunlop, *History of Prose Fiction* (1814; reprint, New York: Burt Franklin, 1970).

Alfred Trübner Nutt, "The Aryan Expulsion-and-Return Formula in the Folk and Hero Tales of the Celts," in *The Folklore Record* 4 (1881): 1–14.

Otto Rank, *The Myth of the Birth of the Hero: A Psychological Interpretation of Mythology* (1909), trans. F. Robbins and Smith Ely Jeliffe (New York: R. Brunner, 1952; reprint, New York: Johnson Reprint Corp., 1970). The French translation, *Le Mythe de la naissance du héros*, (Paris: Payot, 1983) includes an interesting introduction by Elliot Klein.

Vladimir Propp, *Morphology of the Folktale*, trans. Laurence Scott (1928, Austin: University of Texas Press, 1968).

Baron Raglan, Fritz Roy Richard Somerset, *The Hero: A Study in Tradition, Myth, and Drama* (London: Methuen, 1936).

Joseph Campbell, *The Hero with a Thousand Faces* (Princeton, N.J.: Princeton University Press, 1949). Campbell uses the term "monomyth," which he borrows from Joyce.

Joseph Eddy Fontenrose, *Python: A Study of Delphic Myth and Its Origins* (1959, Berkeley: University of California Press, 1980); Fontenrose attempts to tabulate the themes of the myth of battle.

2. Sophocles, *Ajax*, in *Tragedies*, trans. F. Storr, 2 vols. (Cambridge, Mass.: Harvard University Press, Loeb Classical Library, 1967), 2: 65, lines 773–74.

3. Sophocles, *Oedipus the King*, in *The Three Theban Plays: Antigone, Oedipus the King, Oedipus at Colonus*, ed. Bernard Knox, trans. Robert Fagles (New York: Viking Penguin, 1984), line 453.

4. Marcel Détienne and Jean-Pierre Vernant, *Les Ruses de l'intelligence, la Métis des Grecs* (Paris: Flammarion, 1974), p. 50.

5. *Oedipus the King*, lines 569–71, 453.

6. Ibid., lines 46, 48–49, 445–53.

7. For a critique of certain aspects of the notion of structure in Lévi-Strauss, see for example Victor W. Turner, *Dramas, Fields, and Metaphors: Symbolic Action in Human Society* (Ithaca, N.Y.: Cornell University Press, 1974), pp. 236–37. It has also been pointed out that the atemporal permutation of "mythemes" cannot account for the hero's unidimensional destiny, or for the necessary order of events such as it is prescribed, in contrast, in Propp. See Albert Cook, "Lévi-Strauss and Myth: A Review of *Mythologies*," *Modern Language Notes* 91 (1976): 1099–1116.

8. Claude Lévi-Strauss, "From Mythical Possibility to Social Existence," in *The View from Afar*, trans. Joachim Neugroschel and Phoebe Hess (New York: Basic Books, 1985), p. 172.

9. Ibid., p. 173.

10. Claude Lévi-Strauss, "Cosmopolitanism and Schizophrenia," in *The View from Afar*, p. 184.

11. Ibid., p. 179. Examples of this knowledge concerning madness can be found in Claude Lévi-Strauss, *From Honey to Ashes*, trans. John Weightman and Doreen Weightman (New York: Harper and Row, 1973), pp. 179–80, and in idem, *The Origin of Table Manners*, trans. John Weightman and Doreen Weightman (New York: Harper and Row, 1978), pp. 114–22.

Chapter 2

1. I am thinking in particular here of Pierre Solié's important recent work on the Great Goddess and her lover sons. Solié's research brings to light a configuration different from that of the Oedipal son. See *La Femme essentielle: mythanalyse de la Grande Mère et de ses Fils-amants* (Paris: Seghers-Laffont, 1980).

2. Jacques Lacan, "Le mythe individuel du névrosé," reprinted in *Ornicar?* 17–18 (1979): 289–307.

3. Alain Juranville, *Lacan et la philosophie* (Paris: Presses Universitaires de France, 1984), pp. 162–63 and pp. 194–214.

4. See Jean-Joseph Goux, "Moïse, Freud: la prescription iconoclaste," in *Les Iconoclastes* (Paris: Seuil, 1978), pp. 9–29.

5. See Marie Delcourt, *Oedipe ou la légende du conquérant* (Liège: Droz, 1944). We must also recall that in Late Greek one popular word to designate a prostitute was "sphinx."

Chapter 3

1. Among the many studies devoted to the anthropology of initiations I shall cite the following: Arnold Van Gennep, *Les Rites de passage: étude systématique des rites* (Paris: E. Nourry, 1909); Jean Cazeneuve, *Les Rites et la condition humaine* (Paris: Presses Universitaires de France, 1958); Mircea Eliade, *Initiations, rites, sociétés secrètes: Naissances mystiques, Essai sur quelques types d'initiation* (Paris: Gallimard, 1959); Victor W. Turner, *The Ritual Process: Structure and Anti-Structure* (Ithaca, N.Y.: Cornell University Press, 1969); idem, *Dramas, Fields, and Metaphors: Symbolic Action in Human Society* (Ithaca, N.Y.: Cornell University Press, 1974); Serge Moscovici, *La Société contre nature* (Paris: Union Générale d'Editions, 1972); Pierre Solié, *Médecines initiaques* (Paris: Epi, 1976).

2. Vladimir Propp, *Les Racines historiques du conte merveilleux* (1946, Paris: Gallimard, 1983), p. 315.

3. Propp, *Racines historiques*, p. 319. This version is also mentioned by Robert Graves, *The Greek Myths* (Baltimore, Md.: Penguin, 1957), narrative 137.

4. Turner, *Dramas, Fields, and Metaphors*, pp. 253–60.

5. See the work of Jane Ellen Harrison, *Prologomena to the Study of Greek Religion* (New York: Meridian, 1903), pp. 478–594, and *Themis: A Study of the Social Origins of Greek Religion* (1911); reprint, Cleveland: World, 1962), pp. 13–25. Let us recall that J.-F. Lafitau was the first, in 1724, to compare Greek initiations with the more archaic initiations of American Indians. (See Pierre Vidal-Naquet, "Recipes for Greek Adolescence," in *The Black Hunter: Forms of Thought and Forms of Society in the Greek World*, trans. Andrew Szegedy-Maszak [Baltimore: Johns Hopkins University Press, 1986], pp. 129–56.)

6. Aeschylus, *The Seven Against Thebes*, trans. Christopher M. Dawson (Englewood Cliffs, N.J.: Prentice Hall), 1970.

7. Eliade, p. 62.

8. Euripides, *The Phoenician Women*, trans. Elizabeth Wyckoff in *Euripides V* (Chicago: University of Chicago Press, 1959), lines 805–807, 1019–41.

9. Ibid., lines 1026, 820; idem, *The Bacchae Euripides V*, trans. William Arrowsmith (Chicago: University of Chicago Press, 1959), lines 520–27.

10. According to Saint Epiphanius: see *The Panarion of Epiphanius of Salamis*, Book 1, sec. 1–46, trans. Frank Williams (Leiden: E. J. Brill, 1987), pp. 20, 221.

11. On the distinction between the Egyptian and Greek sphinxes, and the interplay of influences between them, see Wilhelm Heinrich Roscher, *Ausfürliches Lexikon der Griechischen und Römischen Mythologie* (Leipzig: B. G. Teubner, 1884–1937; reprint, New York: Georg Olms Verlag, 1977–78). See also Nikolaos M. Verdelis, "L'Apparition du Sphinx dans l'art grec," *Bulletin de correspondance hellénique* 75 (1951): 1–37.

12. The reference to "the line of Kadmos" is from Sophocles, *Oedipus Rex*, in *The Oedipus Cycle*, trans. Dudley Fitts and Robert Fitzgerald (New York: Harcourt, Brace & World, 1949), lines 1–2. Subsequent citations are from Sophocles, *Oedipus the King*, in *The Three Theban Plays: Antigone, Oedipus the King, Oedipus at Colonus*, ed. Bernard Knox, trans. Robert Fagles (New York: Viking Penguin, 1984), lines 36, 44–46.

13. Gilbert Murray, "Excursus on the Ritual Forms Preserved in Greek Tragedy," in Harrison, *Themis*, pp. 341–63. For later developments, see Harold Caparne Baldry, *The Greek Tragic Theater* (New York: Norton, 1972).

14. Murray, p. 349.

15. Harrison, *Prologomena*, p. 211.

16. Reproduced in John Boardman, *Athenian Red Figure Vases, The Archaic Period* (New York, Oxford University Press, 1975), fig. 169 (Paris, Louvre CA 1947).

17. Harrison, *Prologomena*, pp. 173, 278, 279.

18. Bowl from the fifth century, Vatican Museum.

19. See the quite extensive iconographic collection on Oedipus and the Sphinx assembled by Ulrich Haussmann in "Oidipus und die Sphinx," *Jahrbuch der Staatlichen Kunstsammlungen in Baden-Württemberg* (Munich: Deutscher Kunstverlag, 1972), pp. 7–36. The representation mentioned is found on p. 29.

20. M. Renard, "Sphinx ravisseuses et 'têtes coupées,'" *Latomus* 9 (1950): 299–310.

21. Marie Delcourt *Oedipe ou la légende du conquérant* (Liège: Droz, 1944), p. 54. The adage plays on the homophony between *teleutan* and *teleistai*.

22. Red figure vase from 470 B.C. by the painter Syleus, Boston Museum; reproduced in Emily Vermeule, *Aspects of Death in Early Greek Art and Poetry* (Berkeley: University of California Press, 1979), p. 171, fig. 22.

23. Vase from 530 B.C., Stuttgart Landesmuseum; reproduced in Haussmann, p. 23.

24. This association is indicated by Louis Gernet in "Quelques Rapports entre la pénalité et la religion dans la Grèce ancienne," in *Droit et institutions en Grèce antique* (Paris: Flammarion, 1982), pp. 170–71.

25. Vermeule, p. 9.

26. Pierre Vidal-Naquet, "The Black Hunter and the Origin of the Athenian *Ephebia*," *The Black Hunter*, pp. 106–28.

Chapter 4

1. Ludwig Laistner, *Das Rätsel der Sphinx* (1889); cited by Marie Delcourt, *Oedipe ou la légende du conquérant* (Liege: Droz, 1944), pp. 109–10; on the three trials, see p. 128.

2. Here I must refer the reader to the numerous important studies Georges Dumézil devoted to the functional tripartition in Indo-European ideology (myth, epic, rites, theologies, law, and so forth). Dumézil's most synthetic work is *L'Idéologie tripartite des Indo-européens* (Brussels: Latomus, 1958).

3. Dumézil, *Mythe et épopée*, 3 vols. (Paris: Gallimard, 1973), 2:358. This notion has been developed and enriched by Daniel Dubuisson, "Le Roi indo-européen et la synthèse des trois fonctions," *Annales E.S.C.* 1 (1978): 21–34.

4. Dumézil, *Horace et les Curiaces* (Paris: Gallimard, 1942). See especially p. 50, concerning the "exploit," and "Epopée, mythes et rites: le combat contre l'adversaire triple," p. 126. See also *The Destiny of the Warrior*, trans. Alf Hiltebeitel (Chicago: University of Chicago Press, 1970).

5. See in this connection Dominique Briquel, "Initiations grecques et idéologie indo-européenne," *Annales E.S.C.* 3 (1982): 454–64. We may note the extraordinary resistance of this tripartite structure of initiation, since it is found again in the Arthurian legends. To gain access to the sacred, Arthur has to face three trials: the clairvoyant use of riches, the forcible removal of the sword, and the wise reply. See Joël Grisward, "Uter Pendragon, Artur et l'idéologie royale des Indo-européens," *Europe* 654 (Oct. 1983): 111–20.

6. In the initiation myth of Cúchulainn, Dumézil analyses the trial of "women's nudity." See *Horace et les Curiaces*, p. 35.

7. Hesiodus, "The Theogeny," in *The Homeric Hymns and Homerica*, trans. Hugh G. Evelyn-White (Cambridge, Mass.: Harvard University Press, Loeb Classical Library, 1974), p. 103.

8. Louis Gernet, "The Mythic Idea of Value in Greece," in *The Anthropology of Ancient Greece*, trans. John Hamilton and Blaise Nagy (Baltimore, Md.: Johns Hopkins University Press), 1981.

9. Dumézil, *Horace et les Curiaces*, p. 45.

10. Modern readers tend to appreciate myths as a wild preserve of unruly fantasies that appeal to the taste for ambiguity and the thirst for irrationality, whereas, to the contrary, for countless generations who have transmitted their timeless "truths," myths have been a resource for ordering, an immense effort of symbolic organization in the face of the dangerous exuberance of the imaginary. The tripartite composition of the Sphinx does not make it an allegorical construction. To be sure, the code of the functional division that makes it possible to give a precise meaning to the parts that constitute it and to discover their symbolic necessity seems to deprive this amalgam of something of its oneiric quality. Far from being an uncontrolled production of a spontaneous imagination, the figure of the Sphinx is rigorously inscribed within a complex ideological order. However, the tripartition itself is shaped and

modeled by a requirement that is situated below this level of ordering. The Sphinx has to be a monster, and it has to be a female monster. This kernel of the imaginary, required by the telestic narration, is the starting point to which the other features can be added. "Vanquish the female monster": there is the irreducible mythologeme which has provided a base of support for the more highly developed ideology of the graduated triplicity of the trials. But this plurality in turn has a more general kernel of meaning: it signifies that all the strengths, all the virtues, the totality of the powers available to human beings will have to be mobilized by the protagonist who intends to vanquish the monster. The confrontation is not partial; it engages the hero heart and soul, as it puts at risk his very life.

11. Apollonios Rhodius, *The Argonautica*, trans. R. C. Seaton (Cambridge, Mass.: Harvard University Press, Loeb Classical Library, 1967), bks. 3, 4.

12. Ibid., bk. 3, p. 229.

13. Dumézil, (*Mythe et épopée*, 1: 446–47) discusses a text by Herodotus and one by Quintus-Curtius on the Scythians that unquestionably bring into play as talisman of the third function "a yoke of oxen and a plow," alongside the axe (or spear, or arrow) and the bowl, talismans of the second and first functions respectively. Benveniste pointed out that in the language of the Scythians as in that of the Avesta, a single word must have designated the set "yoke and plow."

14. Among the Celts, for example. See Dumézil, *Mythe et épopée*, 1: 615.

15. Gernet, "The Mythic Idea of Value," pp. 73–111, sec. 4, "The Golden Fleece."

16. Apollonius Rhodius, *Argonautica*, bk. 4, p. 307.

17. Cf. Daniel Dubuisson, "L'Equipement de l'inauguration royale dans l'Inde védique et en Irlande," *Revue de l'histoire des religions* 2 (1978): 153–64, and the complementary discussion by Dominique Briquel, "Sur l'Equipement royal indo-européen, données latines et grecques," *Revue de l'histoire des religions* 200 (Jan.–Mar. 1983): 67–74.

18. Gernet, *The Anthropology of Ancient Greece*, p. 97.

19. Briquel, "Sur l'Equipement royal indo-européen."

20. Friedrich Nietzsche, *The Birth of Tragedy*, in *The Birth of Tragedy and The Genealogy of Morals*, trans. Francis Golffing (Garden City, N.Y.: Doubleday, 1956) sec. 9, p. 61.

21. Ibid.

22. Sophocles, *Oedipus the King*, in *The Three Theban Plays: Antigone*,

Oedipus the King, Oedipus at Colonus, ed. Bernard Knox, trans. Robert
Fagles (New York: Viking Penguin, 1984), lines 963, 972–77.
23. Euripides, *Phoenician Women,* trans. Peter Burian and Brian Swann
(New York: Oxford University Press, 1981), lines 1896–97, p. 83. Let us
add that the enigma posed by the Sphinx ("What walks on four legs in
the morning, two legs at noon and three legs in the evening?") probably
had in turn, originally, a specific initiatory meaning in relation to the
functional tripartition. In fact, what Dominique Briquel has shown
about the example of the riddle of the legend of Glaucos ("What does the
tricolored cow of the king's herd—the colors are white, red, and black—
look like?") could also be shown to be true of the (tripartite) enigma of
the Sphinx. Once again we have three states of the human being (in
relation to the functional tripartition) that constitute the meaning of the
enigma. On the interpretation of the riddle of Glaucos, see Briquel,
"Initiations grecques et idéologie indo-européenne," 454–64.
24. Dumézil, *Mythe et épopée,* 2; a summary of Heracles' three sins is
found on p. 18, and the theme is developed in chapter 6. On the warrior's
three sins, see also *The Destiny of the Warrior.*
25. Dumézil, *L'Oubli de l'homme et l'honneur des dieux* (Paris: Gallimard, 1985), "Le Triple Péché de Laomedon," p. 31.
26. That is also why Oedipus's faults have a structural or generative
order, as it were, that does not coincide with their sequential order.
According to the tripartite hierarchy, the first fault would consist in his
stance before the Sphinx. Next would come the patricide, and finally the
incest. However, in the order of the narrative, the patricide comes first.
King Laïus has to have been killed for his replacement by a hero capable
of eliminating the Sphinx to be conceivable. Moreover, the killing of the
king enters into the narrative logic of the regular myth since it is the
negative version of the trial imposed by a king. Thus, the need to
maintain the appearance of the regular heroic myth requires a modifica-
tion in the hierarchical succession of faults.

Chapter 5

1. See Bernard Sergent, "La Mythologie grecque," in *Magazine lit-
téraire: Georges Dumézil* (April 1986): 49; and, more extensively, "Les
Trois Fonctions des Indo-Européens dans la Grèce ancienne: bilan critique," *Annales E.S.C.* 6 (1979): 1155–86.

2. Richard Bodéüs, "Société athénienne, sagesse grecque et idéal indo-européen," *L'Antiquité classique* 41 (1972): 455–86.

3. Raymond de Saussure, *Le Miracle grec: étude psychanalytique sur la civilisation hellénique* (Paris: Denoël, 1939). In "L'Image du père dans la pensée grecque," Hans Georg Gadamer evokes "a crisis in the image of the father" in the era of Greek sophistics, and an "unsettling of paternal authority" in fifth-century B.C. Athens, but he does not bring out the connection, which in our view is fundamental, between this crisis and the specificity of the Greek mutation. See *L'Image du père dans le mythe et dans l'histoire*, ed. H. Tellenbach (Paris: Presses Universitaires de France, 1983), pp. 129–44.

4. In Euripides' *The Bacchae*, Cadmus says to Teiresias, "Expound to me, Teiresias, / For in such matters you are wise [initiated]." *Euripides V*, trans. William Arrowsmith (Chicago: University of Chicago Press, 1959) lines 185–86.

5. Sophocles, *Oedipus the King*, in *The Three Theban Plays: Antigone, Oedipus the King, Oedipus at Colonus*, ed. Bernard Knox, trans. Robert Fagles (New York, Viking Penguin, 1984), lines 323–25, 340–45, 376, 406, 450.

6. Ibid., lines 404–5, 421, 464–67.

7. Ibid., lines 972–76, 978–80.

Chapter 6

1. Jane Ellen Harrison, *Themis: A Study of the Social Origins of Greek Religion* (1911; reprint, London: Merlin, 1963), p. 440. On the *Kourotrophos* divinities, see Henri Jeanmaire, *Couroi et Courètes: essai sur l'éducation spartiate et sur les rites d'adolescence dans l'antiquité hellénique* (Lille: Bibliothèque universitaire, 1939).

2. Hesiodus, "The Theogeny," in *The Homeric Hymns and Homerica*, trans. Hugh G. Evelyn-White (Cambridge, Mass.: Harvard University Press, Loeb Classical Library, 1974), p. 105; Plutarch, "Theseus," in *Plutarch's Lives*, 11 vols., trans. Bernadotte Perrin (Cambridge, Mass.: Harvard University Press, Loeb Classical Library), 1914B 1: 11; Harrison, *Themis*, p. 441.

3. Jean-Pierre Vernant and Pierre Vidal-Naquet, *Tragedy and Myth in Ancient Greece*, trans. Janet Lloyd (Brighton, Sussex: Harvester Press, 1981).

4. Euripides, *The Phoenician Women*, trans. Elizabeth Wyckoff, in *Euripides V* (Chicago: University of Chicago Press, 1959), lines 870–71.

5. Xenophon, reporting the words of Socrates, in *Memorabilia*, trans. E. C. Marchant, in *Memorabilia, Oeconomius, Symposium and Apology* (Cambridge, Mass.: Harvard University Press, Loeb Classical Library, 1968), 4.4.19–24, pp. 321–23.

6. Plutarch, "On the Delays of the Divine Vengeance," trans. Phillip H. De Lacy and Benedict Einarson, in *Plutarch's Moralia*, 16 vols. (Cambridge, Mass.: Harvard University Press, Loeb Classical Library, 1984), 7: 180–299. See also Jacqueline de Romilly, *Le Temps dans la Tragédie grecque* (Paris: Vrin, 1971).

7. Chorus: "Dreadful, what you've done . . . how could you bear it, gouging out your eyes? What superhuman power drove you on? Oedipus: "Apollo, friends, Apollo." Sophocles, *Oedipus the King*, in *Three Theban Plays*, ed. Bernard Knox, trans. Robert Fagles (New York: Viking Penguin, 1984), lines 1464–67.

8. On this point I adhere to the interpretation offered by H. D. F. Kitto, *Sophocles, Dramatist and Philosopher* (London: Oxford University Press, 1958).

9. On Dikē and Nemesis, see Jean Coman, *L'Idée de Némésis chez Eschyle* (Paris: Alcan, 1935).

10. Walter Otto, *Les Dieux de la Grèce: la figure du divin au miroir de l'esprit grec*, trans. Cl.-N. Grimbert and A. Morgant (Paris: Payot, 1981).

11. Charles Segal, *Dionysiac Poetics and Euripides' Bacchae* (Princeton, N.J.: Princeton University Press, 1982).

12. In the *Phaedrus*, Plato established a distinction between ordinary insanity and "divine madness." Here he distinguishes among four types of divine madness: the prophetic madness whose patron is Apollo; the telestic or ritual madness whose patron is Dionysus; the poetic madness inspired by the muses; the erotic madness inspired by Aphrodite and Eros. See Eric Robert Dodds, *The Greeks and the Irrational* (Berkeley: University of California Press, 1968).

13. Among others, see Suzanne Saïd, *La Faute tragique* (Paris: Maspero, 1978).

14. Pierre Boyancé, *Le Culte des Muses chez les philosophes grecs* (Paris: E. de Boccard, 1937).

15. Diogenes Laertius, *Lives of Eminent Philosophers*, trans. R. D. Hicks, 2 vols. (Cambridge, Mass.: Harvard University Press, Loeb Classical Library, 1970–72), 2: 9.5., p. 413.

16. Jean-Pierre Vernant, *Mythe et pensée chez les Grecs* (Paris: Maspero, 1969).

17. See Paul Decharme, *La Critique des traditions religieuses chez les Grecs des origines au temps de Plutarque* (Paris: A. Picardet et fils, 1904), and Eudore Derenne, *Les Procès d'impiété intentés aux philosophes à Athènes au Ve et VIe siècles av. J.-C.* (Paris: Champion, 1930).

18. Bernard M. W. Knox, *Oedipus at Thebes: Sophocles' Tragic Hero and His Time* (New Haven: Yale University Press, 1957), pp. 47–48.

19. Ibid., pp. 25, 60.

20. Ibid., p. 120.

21. Ibid., p. 117.

22. Jean-Pierre Vernant and Pierre Vidal-Naquet, *Tragedy and Myth in Ancient Greece*, trans. Janet Lloyd (Brighton, Sussex: Harvester Press, 1981).

23. Jean-Pierre Vernant, *The Origins of Greek Thought* (Ithaca, N.Y.: Cornell University Press, 1982).

24. Bernard M. W. Knox, *The Heroic Temper: Studies in Sophoclean Tragedy* (Berkeley: University of California Press, 1964), p. 143.

25. It is to the extent that Oedipus became an explicit figure of the philosopher fairly recently (with Hegel), at the point when philosophy seemed to have reached its apogee and to be showing signs of decline, that Oedipus can be said to be "the last philosopher," to use an expression that Nietzsche also applied to himself. (See Philippe Lacoue-Labarthe, "Le Dernier Philosophe," in *L'Imitation des Modernes* (Paris: Galilée, 1986), pp. 203–23. However, my reading of Sophocles shows that Oedipus is already undoubtedly a typification of the "first philosopher" for the Greek dramatist. My analysis will also show that the Oedipean constitution of philosophy is much more profoundly inscribed in the philosophy of the Moderns, from Descartes to Nietzsche, than the explicit references to Oedipus (in Hegel or Nietzsche) may suggest.

Chapter 7

1. Xenophanes of Colophon, Fragment 16, in *Les Présocratiques*, ed. Jean-Paul Dumont (Paris: Gallimard, 1988), p. 118.

2. See Moses I. Finley, *Democracy Ancient and Modern* (New Brunswick, N.J.: Rutgers University Press, 1972); Jean-Pierre Vernant, *Mythe et pensée chez les Grecs* (Paris, Maspero, 1969); idem, *Les Origines de la pensée grecque* (Presses Universitaires de France, 1962), and Cornélius Cas-

toriadis, "La Polis grecque et la création de la démocratie," *Le Débat* 38 (Jan.–Mar. 1986): 126–44.

3. Julius Henrik Lange, *Darstellung des Menschen in der ältren grieschischen Kunst* (Strasbourg: Heitz, 1899); Heinrich Schäfer, *Principles of Egyptian Art* (Oxford: Clarendon Press, 1974); Ernst Hans Gombrich, *The Story of Art* (London: Phaidon, 1966), p. 52.

4. Emma Brunner-Traut, "Aspective," epilogue to Schäfer, *Principles of Egyptian Art*, pp. 421–46.

5. Ibid., p. 425.

6. Cf. Gérard Simon, *Le Regard, l'être et l'apparence dans l'optique de l'Antiquité* (Paris: Seuil, 1987).

7. See Edouard Will, "De l'aspect éthique de l'origine grecque de la monnaie," *Revue historique* 212 (1954): 209–31; Jean-Pierre Vernant, *Les Origines de la pensée grecque* (Paris: Presses Universitaires de France, 1962), and *Mythe et pensée chez les Grecs* (Paris: Maspero, 1965).

8. See Edouard Will, "Réflexions et hypothèses sur les origines du monnayage," *Revue numismatique* 17 (1955): 5–23.

9. Jean-Joseph Goux, *Les Monnayeurs du language* (Paris: Galilée, 1984), and "Catégories de l'échange: Idéalité, symbolicité, réalité," in *Encyclopédie philosophique* (Paris: Presses Universitaires de France, 1989), 1: 227–33.

10. Sophocles, *Antigone*, in *The Three Theban Plays: Antigone, Oedipus the King, Oedipus at Colonus*, ed. Bernard Knox, trans. Robert Fagles (New York: Viking Penguin, 1984), lines 376–77, 395–97, 423–24.

11. Gilbert François, *Le Polythéisme et l'emploi au singulier des mots Theos et Daimon dans la littérature grecque d'Homère à Platon* (Paris: Belles Lettres, 1957).

12. Aristotle, *The Metaphysics*, trans. Hugo Tredennick (Cambridge, Mass.: Harvard University Press, Loeb Classical Library, 1969), 9.7.7, p. 149.

13. Ovid, *Metamorphoses*, trans. Frank Justus Miller, 2 vols. (Cambridge, Mass.: Harvard University Press, Loeb Classical Library, 1984), 1: 149.

14. Bernard M. W. Knox, *Oedipus at Thebes: Sophocles' Tragic Hero and His Time* (New Haven: Yale University Press, 1957), p. 21.

15. Sophocles, *Oedipus the King*, in *The Three Theban Plays: Antigone, Oedipus the King, Oedipus at Colonus*, ed. Bernard Knox, trans. Robert Fagles (New York: Viking Penguin, 1984), lines 1184–85, 1188, 150.

16. Jean-Pierre Vernant and Pierre Vidal-Naquet, *Tragedy and Myth in*

Ancient Greece, trans. Janet Lloyd (Brighton, Sussex: Harvester Press, 1981), pp. 91–92.

17. Sophocles, *Oedipus the King*, lines 1494–95, 1496. On *homogenēs*, see the note by Paul Mazon in *Sophocle*, vol. 2, ed. Alphonse Dain, trans. Paul Mazon (Paris: Belles Lettres, 1958), p. 122.

18. Sophocles, *Oedipus the King*, line 1469; John Crosset, "The Oedipus Rex," in *Oedipus Rex: A Mirror for Greek Drama*, ed. Albert S. Cook (Prospect Heights, Ill.: Waveland Press, 1963), p. 150.

19. Sophocles, *Oedipus the King*, line 1493.

Chapter 8

1. Plutarch, "On the Sign of Socrates," 589e, in *Plutarch's Moralia*, trans. Phillip H. De Lacy and Benedict Einarson, 16 vols. (Cambridge, Mass.: Harvard University Press, Loeb Classical Library, 1984), 7: 459.

2. Socrates says of the child: "Then he will come to have knowledge without having been taught by anyone, but only having been asked questions, and having recovered this knowledge from himself." Plato, *Meno/Plato*, trans. R. W. Sharples (Chicago: Bolchazy-Carducci, 1985), 85d, p. 79.

3. Georg Wilhelm Friedrich Hegel, *Lectures on the History of Philosophy*, 3 vols., trans. Elizabeth S. Haldane and Frances H. Simson (London: K. Paul, Trench, Trübner & Co., 1892–96), 1: 79.

4. Lucius Madaurensis Apuleus, "De deo Socratis," *Opuscules philosophiques . . . et fragments* (Paris: Belles Lettres, 1973), 5.132.

5. Ibid., 22.171.

6. Xenophon, "Agesilaus," trans. E. C. Marchant, in *Xenophon*, 7 vols. (Cambridge, Mass.: Harvard University Press, Loeb Classical Library, 1925), vol. 7, *Scripta Minora*, p. 125.

7. Plato, *The Republic*, trans. Paul Shorey, 2 vols. (Cambridge, Mass.: Harvard University Press, Loeb Classical Library, 1969–70), 569b, 571c (2: 333, 337).

8. The mention in the *Republic* of the dream of incest and patricide that makes Plato a precursor of Freud has been underlined by Sarah Kofman in her article "Miroir et mirages oniriques, Platon précurseur de Freud," *La Part de l'oeil*, 4 (1988): 126–35; reprinted in *Séductions* (Paris: Galilée, 1990), pp. 61–86.

9. Plato, *The Republic*, 588c (2: 399–400).

10. Thus, if the Sphinx cannot be identified point for point with the

fabulous being Plato describes, it is nevertheless clear by their functional composition that they belong to the same family; they even have a leonine element in common. However, the Sphinx's most human element, the woman's head, is manifestly the erotically seductive part, whereas the eagle wings appear to symbolize what is most divine in the soul, the element that escapes the earth's pull and is poised toward the heavens. If we now say that the neophyte, encountering the female monster, meets an image of the soul, a terrifying image of his own soul whose mystery comes forth to confront him, we are proposing nothing that cannot be deduced from what Plato says.

11. Victor W. Turner, *Dramas, Fields, and Metaphors: Symbolic Action in Human Society* (Ithaca, N.Y.: Cornell University Press, 1974), p. 253.

12. Plato, *The Republic*, 588d (2: 401).

Chapter 9

1. On the theme of "one alone" [*un seul*] in the *Discourse on Method* and the perspective schema that it implies, see Jean-Joseph Goux, "Descartes et la perspective," *L'Esprit créateur* 25 (Spring 1985): 10–20.

2. Georg Wilhelm Friedrich Hegel, *Aesthetics: Lectures on Fine Art*, 2 vols., trans. T. M. Knox (Oxford: Clarendon Press, 1975). The allusion to Oedipus appears at the end of the chapter entitled "Unconscious Symbolism" (1: 360–61): "The works of Egyptian art in their mysterious symbolism are therefore riddles; the objective riddle *par excellence*. As a symbol for this proper meaning of the Egyptian spirit we may mention the Sphinx. It is, as it were, the symbol of the symbolic itself. In innumerable quantities, set up in rows in hundreds, there are sphinx shapes in Egypt, constructed out of the hardest stone, polished, covered with hieroglyphics, and [one] near Cairo is of such colossal size that the lion's claws alone amount to a man's height. Some of them are recumbent animal bodies out of which as an upper part, the human body struggles, here and there again there is a ram's head, but elsewhere most commonly a female head. Out of the dull strength and power of the animal the human spirit tries to push itself forward, without coming to a perfect portrayal of its own freedom and animated shape, because it must still remain confused and associated with what is other than itself. This pressure for self-conscious spirituality which does not apprehend itself from its own resources in the one reality adequate to itself but only contemplates itself in what is related to it and brings itself into conscious-

ness in precisely what is strange to it, is the symbolic as such which at this peak becomes a riddle.

"It is in this sense that the Sphinx in the Greek myth, which we ourselves may interpret again symbolically, appears as a monster asking a riddle. The Sphinx propounded the well-known conundrum: What is it that in the morning goes on four legs, at mid-day on two, and in the evening on three? Oedipus found the simple answer: a man, and he tumbled the Sphinx from the rock. The explanation of the symbol lies in the absolute meaning, in the spirit, just as the famous Greek inscription calls to man: Know thyself. The light of consciousness is the clarity which makes its concrete content shine clearly through the shape belonging and appropriate to itself, and in its [objective] existence reveals itself alone."

3. Ibid., 1: 323, 357–58, 354.

4. Georg Wilhelm Friedrich Hegel, *Lectures on the History of Philosophy*, 3 vols., trans. Elizabeth S. Haldane and Frances H. Simson (London: K. Paul, Trench, Trübner & Co., 1892–1896), 1: 76.

5. On the relation between Egypt and Greece for Hegel, a relation typified by the opposition between Osiris and Oedipus, see the complementary observations in my article "The Phallus: Masculine Identity and 'The Exchange of Women,'" *Differences* (Spring 1992): 41–75. Oedipus appears quite clearly as the philosophical dispensation of the initiatory castration undergone by Osiris.

6. Ludwig Feuerbach, "Principles of the Philosophy of the Future," in *The Fiery Brook: Selected Writings of Ludwig Feuerbach*, trans. Zawar Hanfi (Garden City, N.Y.: Doubleday, 1972), sec. 55, p. 241.

7. Ludwig Feuerbach, "Preliminary Theses on the Reform of Philosophy," in *The Fiery Brook*, p. 153.

8. Friedrich Nietzsche, *Thus Spake Zarathustra*, trans. Walter Kaufmann (Harmondsworth: Penguin, 1978), pp. 31–32.

9. Martin Heidegger, *Nietzsche*, trans. Joan Stambaugh, David Farrell Krell, and Frank A. Capuzzi, 4 vols. (San Francisco: Harper and Row, 1987), vol. 4, *The Will to Power as Knowledge and as Metaphysics*, p. 227.

10. Karl Marx, *Economic and Political Manuscripts of 1844* (Moscow: Progress Publishers, 1959), p. 144.

Chapter 10

1. See Roger Caillois's careful analysis of the ambivalence of the sacred in *L'Homme et le sacré* (Paris: Gallimard, 1988).

2. Regarding this movement, see for example Victor Turner, *The Ritual Process: Structure and Anti-Structure* (Ithaca, N.Y.: Cornell University Press, 1969), especially chapter 5, "Humility and Hierarchy: The Liminality of Status Elevation and Reversal."

3. Sophocles, *Oedipus at Colonus*, in *The Three Theban Plays: Antigone, Oedipus the King, Oedipus at Colonus*, ed. Bernard Knox, trans. Robert Fagles (New York: Viking Penguin, 1984), lines 431–32, 1775–78, 430–31.

4. Ibid., lines 1717–37.

5. Ibid., lines 1199–1202. On this point and several others, see the analysis by Charles Segal, *Tragedy and Civilization: An Interpretation of Sophocles* (Cambridge, Mass.: Harvard University Press, 1982), chapter 11, "Oedipus at Colonus: The End of a Vision."

6. Sophocles, *Oedipus at Colonus*, lines 1947–48. If Oedipus never managed to gain access to Hestia, philosophical thought is founded initially, in an entirely congruent manner, upon the forgetting of Hestia. It is only in the critical movement of "metaphysics" that Hestia is rediscovered anew. I have tried to show that the insistent question of Being for Heidegger is governed by the Hestia/Vesta configuration that refers to the dimensions of "habitus," "hearth," "Earth," "preserve," and so forth, and finally to the very etymology of the word "being." See "Vesta, or the Place of Being," *Representations* 1, no. 1 (Feb. 1983): 91–107, and "L'Oubli de Hestia," *Langages* 85 (March 1987): 55–61. Let us add, in this connection, that Heidegger's vestalic orientation is quite different from, and even at the opposite pole from, Nietzsche's Dionysiac impulse. But the two approaches share a readiness to venture beyond the Oedipean configuration in philosophy.

7. Sophocles, *Oedipus at Colonus*, lines 1886–87.

8. Georg Wilhelm Friedrich, *Hegel's Lectures on the History of Philosophy*, trans. E. S. Haldane and Frances H. Simson, 3 vols. (New York: Humanities Press, 1974), 1: 154.

9. Plutarch, "The Dialogue on Love," trans. Edwin L. Minar, Jr., F. H. Sandbach, and W. C. Helmbold, in *Plutarch's Moralia*, 16 vols. (Cambridge, Mass.: Harvard University Press, Loeb Classical Library, 1972, 9: 355.

Conclusion

1. Euripides, *The Bacchae*, trans. William Arrowsmith, in *Euripides V* (Chicago: University of Chicago Press, 1959), lines 200–204.

2. This differential evaluation is lacking in my earlier work (see *Symbolic Economies: After Marx and Freud,* trans. Jennifer Curtiss Gage (Ithaca, N.Y.: Cornell University Press, 1990), which identified the structural domination Money-Father-Phallus-Logos. The father, in this chain of measure using the "general equivalent," is already quite different from the archaic persona of the despotic patriarch; he occupies an abstract regulatory position homologous to the position of "intermediary" and "judge" that Aristotle attributes to money.

3. Cornélius Castoriadis has convincingly demonstrated the singularity of the Greek innovation, while stressing these terms borrowed from Thucydides. See "The Greek Polis and the Creation of Democracy," *Graduate Faculty Philosophy Journal* (New York: New School for Social Research, Fall 1983), 9: 79–115.

MERIDIAN

Crossing Aesthetics

Jean-Luc Nancy, *The Experience of Freedom*

Jean-Joseph Goux, *Oedipus, Philosopher*

Haun Saussy, *The Problem of a Chinese Aesthetic*

Jean-Luc Nancy, *The Birth to Presence*

Library of Congress
Cataloging-in-Publication Data

Goux, Jean-Joseph, 1943–
[Oedipe philosophe. English]
Oedipus, philosopher / Jean-Joseph Goux ;
translated by Catherine Porter.
p.   cm. — (Meridian: crossing aesthetics)
Includes bibliographical references.
ISBN 0-8047-2169-6 (alk. paper) —
ISBN 0-8047-2171-8 (pbk. : alk. paper)
1. Oedipus complex.   2. Psychoanalysis and
philosophy.   I. Title.   II. Series:
Meridian (Stanford, Calif.)
BF175.5.O33G6813   1993
292.1'3—dc20
92-40387
CIP

❧ This book is printed on acid-free paper.
It was typeset in Adobe Garamond and
Lithos by Keystone Typesetting, Inc.